M. MᶜKEOWN .

Sociology, phenomenology
and Marxian analysis

International Library of Sociology

Founded by Karl Mannheim
Editor: John Rex, University of Warwick

Arbor Scientiae
Arbor Vitae

A catalogue of the books available in the **International Library of Sociology** and other series of Social Science books published by Routledge & Kegan Paul will be found at the end of this volume.

Sociology, phenomenology and Marxian analysis

A critical discussion of the theory and practice of a science of society

Barry Smart
Department of Sociological Studies
University of Sheffield

Routledge & Kegan Paul
London, Henley and Boston

For C.C.S.

First published in 1976
by Routledge & Kegan Paul Ltd
39 Store Street,
WC1E 7DD,
Broadway House,
Newtown Road,
Henley-on-Thames,
Oxon RG9 1EN and
9 Park Street,
Boston, Mass. 02108, USA
Set in Monotype Times by
Kelly, Selwyn & Co., Melksham, Wiltshire
and printed in Great Britain by
Unwin Brothers Limited
The Gresham Press, Old Woking, Surrey

ISBN 0 7100 8372 6 (c)
ISBN 0 7100 8373 4 (p)

Contents

Acknowledgments

I should like to thank Tony Giddens and Mark Mitchell for their critical comments on the first draft of my manuscript. They are of course in no way responsible for any 'errors' and 'limitations' which may follow. I am also very grateful to Carol Smart for much help and support and to Ian Taylor for encouraging me to publish. In addition I received invaluable assistance from Rene Shaw, Thelma Kassell, Margaret Sayles and Margaret Scarr, each of whom worked on the typing of the manuscript.

The author and publisher would like to thank the following for permission to reproduce copyright material: Northwestern University Press for extracts from *The Function of the Sciences and the Meaning of Man* by E. Paci and *The Crisis of European Sciences and Transcendental Phenomenology* by E. Husserl; Heinemann Educational Books and Basic Books Inc. for extracts from *The Coming Crisis of Western Sociology*, by Alvin W. Gouldner, © 1970 by Alvin W. Gouldner, Basic Books Inc., Publishers, New York.

It goes without saying that this analysis is not enough and that it is but the first moment in an effort at synthetic reconstruction.

Sartre, *Search for a Method*, p. 27

Sociological writing itself is ineluctably part of the psycho historical process, engaged as it is in persuasive redefinitions of action that alter the action.

Rieff, *The Triumph of the Therapeutic*, pp. 22–3

The science of man itself is critique and must remain so.

Habermas, *Knowledge and Human Interests*, p. 62

Introduction

The institutionalization of sociology has not been accompanied by the emergence of a consensus within the discipline. Over the most basic of questions the sociological community does not seem to have reached any degree of substantial agreement. Debates and differences still arise over the nature, methods and purposes of the discipline and disagreements over the character of the subject matter, as well as the appropriateness of adopted methodological procedures, remain important sources of controversy. The increasing awareness of, and attention given to, this absence of a consensus within the sociological community has led to the evaluation of sociology as a pseudo-science, as a science in a pre-paradigm stage of development (a state of immaturity) or alternatively as a multi-paradigm science. In particular it is the re-emergence or re-appearance of interest in scientific method in sociology and the nature of the relationship between sociological practice and other forms of social life that has provided the focal point of reference for sociological debate. Reconsideration of these issues has produced the diagnosis of a crisis within the discipline.

The idea that sociology is in a 'crisis' seems to me to stem from an unexplicated sense of our failure to interpret social events in a convincing manner, convincing that is both to sociological colleagues and to the wider social community. Implicit in this idea of failure are specific assumptions concerning the expectations people have of a science of society, of sociology, and these need to be made explicit. At the base of the sociological project there is an interest in the provision of awareness and understanding not only of the given present but also of the possibilities inherent in the present for the future. By referring to the future I do not wish to be interpreted as inferring a predictive role for sociology; on the contrary, I merely wish to affirm the open-endedness of social life, its processual, transitional character, as well as allude to the role of sociology as a form of social criticism, as critique. It is in these terms, sociology as a form of critique, that I take Marxian analysis, in particular Marx's critical theory, his critique of ideology, to be directly relevant to the practice of sociology and perceive our task as sociologists to be a revelation of the underlying rationality of the given social order. Hence sociology is to provide a demystification of the social world, to reveal the historically emergent socio-culturally constituted basis of a present which appears as sheer facticity, as a naturally given order. Now my expectations of sociology are not necessarily those of all my colleagues, indeed many may, and do argue in opposition, that where sociology genuinely attempts to be scientific it must also be 'normatively neutral'. Then again others may assert that it is scientificity, sociology's preoccupation with and desire to be scientific, which is at the root of our problems. Here scientific theorizing is treated as a degenerate form of theorizing, and the doing of sociology becomes identified with the 'displaying of mind' (cf. Blum, 1971). For my part it is the Marxian tradition which informs a scientific analysis of the social world and provides therefore a critique of the predominant mode of sociological inquiry.

Within contemporary sociology it is now no longer adequate to merely proceed with the 'doing' of sociological work in the belief that the enterprise is unproblematic, for the very procedures and methods employed, 'domain assumptions' and background relevances, have justifiably become topics of analysis. Reconsideration of the nature of the sociological project, in particular its methodological basis, has not, however, occurred in a vacuum, for similar questions and problems have been posed within Marxist thought and science in general. The most important common denominator in this respect has been the concern with the historical and contemporary meaning of science, in particular with the question of what science might or could mean for human existence. For example in Husserl's (1970), Paci's (1972) and Rieff's (1973) work it is argued that the crisis of science is synonymous with a general crisis of Western culture. Science in general and sociology in particular are perceived to have failed to fulfil the Comtean mission of replacing the old theological culture based upon faith by a positive scientific culture subordinated to the goal of the progressive development of humanity, and Marxism in practice is seen to have failed to provide a solution to the problems of exploitation and alienation inherent in the capitalist mode of production. Hence both sociology and Marxism have been depicted as in a state of crisis.

In sociology the morally and ethically based positive scientific orientation proposed by Comte has been superseded by an approach which Pelz (1974) has observed wishes to 'let facts speak for themselves'. This approach not only accepts the status quo ahistorically and unconditionally as factually unproblematic, but furthermore advances a specific positivist conception of sociological science which assumes continuity with the methodological procedures of the natural sciences. This particular version of a science of society has long been the focus of controversy; for example it is inherent in the Naturwissenschaften–Geisteswissenschaften debate and the writings of Dilthey, Rickert and Weber among others, it constitutes the focus of the phenomenological sociological critique of contemporary sociology and it represents an important topic of analysis within Marxist thought. However, despite critiques and the proliferation of 'alternative' sociologies, the discipline is still dominated by a specific understanding of science and method, positivism is still pervasive.

Sociology's 'original' reflective orientation has then been superseded by an empirical-analytical orientation which contains the potential for furthering the technological domination of social relationships. Recognition of the scientific inadequacy of, and political consequences inherent in, such a position has produced not only the response that we abandon method (cf. Phillips, 1973) but has also prompted sociologists to draw upon resources formerly considered peripheral to the sociological project, viz. phenomenological philosophy, linguistic analysis and, increasingly, developments within Marxist thought. Broadly speaking, criticisms of contemporary sociology have focused upon the elimination of creative theoretical thought from the 'scientific' research process. Sociology through its substitution of mathematically influenced technique for method is depicted as providing, at best, superficial generalizations of commonsense understandings, of confirming the self-evident and objectively given character of the social order. The problems identified with sociological work of this kind have received more attention with the increasing adoption of sociological research by government agencies, industrial and educational organizations, hospitals and welfare institutions (cf. Phillips, 1973, p. 195). To be precise the use of sociological knowledge by governmental, military or industrial organizations has produced the criticism that there is an implicit bias inherent in social science research. However, such criticisms in their preoccupation with the political context have tended to neglect completely the equally significant question of the methodological attributes and limitations of contemporary sociological work (cf. Nicolaus, 1971; Shaw, 1972; Blackburn, 1969). The tendency with such criticisms is to totally reject sociology as a 'bourgeois discipline', to shelter behind political epithets and slogans and to fail altogether to consider the possibility that such a science may have developed because of its efficiency. In a similar vein Sartre has stated that in the United States it is the employer who favours this discipline and who in particular sponsors the research which studies restricted groups as the totalization of human contacts in a defined situation. Moreover, American neopaternalism and Human Engineering are based almost exclusively on the work of sociologists. But one must not make those factors an excuse for adopting immediately the reverse attitude and summarily rejecting sociology on the ground that it is 'a class weapon in the hands of the capitalists'. If it is an effective weapon . . . it is because it contains some truth (1968, pp. 67–8).

In considering the relationship of Marxian analysis and sociology it becomes necessary therefore to guard against the rejection or dismissal of sociology, for the sociological explication of the meaning of the 'social' is not a diametrically opposed position to the Marxian standpoint. If we wish to further our understanding of the nature of the social world and the problems involved in studying it we cannot afford summarily to dismiss a corpus of knowledge dealing with relevant and related issues. This applies not only to the Marxian rejection of sociology but also to the sociological treatment of Marxian analysis.

I shall concentrate in my discussion upon critiques of contemporary sociology emanating from two sources, phenomenological sociology and Marxian analysis respectively. The emergence of a phenomenological sociology, resulting from attempts to translate phenomenological philosophy into a sociological project, has provided an interesting critique of conventional methodological procedures. Phenomenological sociologists have sought to reveal the problems involved when sociologists uncritically accept conventional or given empirical social realities as 'objective', factual realities. They have attempted to persuade sociologists of the necessity of freeing themselves of the 'natural attitude', of the importance of treating social facts as problematical, as constituted or accomplished in a social process. Broadly speaking their project may be described as oriented towards a de-reification of the social world and a reconstitution of the practice of sociology. In the above respects the phenomenological sociological project is compatible with Marxian critiques of contemporary sociology. However, there are substantial differences between the Marxian and phenomenological sociological approaches, in particular the latter's neglect of the dialectical nature of social reality, its preoccupation with the formal structures of consciousness and avoidance of the role of interests in the production of knowledge, and finally its ahistorical approach to an understanding of the social world.

In attempting to re-address the question of the significance of

Marxian analysis for contemporary sociology I have drawn in particular upon three themes: the sociological treatment of Marxian analysis, the methodological problem of the subject–object distinction and the dialectical relationship of social theory to the perpetuation and transformation of everyday life. Re-consideration of the status and relevance of Marxian analysis and related developments, for example phenomenological Marxism and critical theory, to the sociological project does not require that we abandon sociology but rather demands of us a radical analysis of the nature and purpose of sociological work. For me such an analysis is interminable, no matter, as Freud stated, 'how regularly in practice analyses do come to an end'.

1 Sociology and Marxian analysis

Comte, Durkheim, Weber and Pareto were all concerned with establishing sociology as a distinctive social science, delineating in their work both the subject matter and methodology of the new science as well as providing specific examples of sociological study. Within sociology it is generally acknowledged that these nineteenth century thinkers, along with Karl Marx, represent the 'founding fathers' of the discipline. However, in the case of Marx a notable difference is evident in that although his concepts and ideas are to be found in the work of many sociologists, there is in fact in his own work no reference to, or analysis of, sociology either in terms of methodology, subject matter, or substantive study. In this respect the consideration of Marx as a sociologist becomes problematic, as does the nature of the relevance of his work for sociology. One thing is certain, relevance cannot merely be asserted or assumed since the only explicit reference Marx makes to disciplines in the contemporary sense is by way of critiques of both philosophy and political economy plus an assertion to the effect that he recognizes only one science, the science of history. This is not to say that Marx was unaware of developments around him, for as he noted in correspondence with Engels,

> I am studying Comte on the side because the British and French make as much fuss over that fellow. What captivates them is the encyclopaedic about him, the synthesis. But compared with Hegel it is wretched (in spite of the fact that Comte as a professional mathematician and physicist is superior to him, i.e. superior in details; but even here Hegel is infinitely greater on the whole). And this trashy positivism appeared in 1832! (1953, p. 218).

Although Marx does not provide any direct refutation of sociological science his dismissal of Comte's and Saint-Simon's work,

1

including a criticism of the preoccupation with the abstraction 'society', indicates a distinctive opposition to the new social science of society, and adds confirmation to the view that whatever Marx was, he was not a sociologist. However, the subsequent development of both sociology and Marxism in response to particular methodological and epistemological debates, as well as to societal changes, provides us with a very different historical context in which to attempt to make a judgment of the relevance and significance of Marxian analysis for contemporary sociology. One thing is certain, sociology is now rather different from the Comtean conception having developed partly in response to the various interpretations and modifications of Marx's work. In consequence any attempt to reconsider the nature of the relationship between Marxian analysis and sociology must come to terms with not only the several sociological interpretations of Marx's work and the range of different sociologies, but also the existence of an heterogeneous Marxism and an ill-defined Marxist sociology.

Within contemporary sociology three alternative understandings of Marxian analysis may be distinguished. First, Marx's work is treated as an ideological rather than a scientific project. The presence and significance of explicit value judgments in his analysis is taken as a sign of its lack of scientificity (cf. Sorokin, 1928, pp. 544–5). Inherent in this position is an understanding of science as a value-free enterprise which with the assumption that sociologists should emulate the natural scientific study of the natural world has produced demands for accounts of the 'real' world 'out there' which are factual and neutral. A second understanding or treatment of Marx's work is as a legitimating source for new concepts or ideas, the original contextually situated meanings or intentions seemingly being of little relevance in the consequent 'operational' usage by the sociologist. Horton's (1964) discussion of the dehumanization of the concept of alienation provides a critique of this tendency. A variation on this general theme is to be found in the writings of sociologists who assume Marx to be a sociologist and seek to affirm this by prefixing particular sections, themes or aspects of his work by the term 'sociology'; hence the Marxian analysis of the state and civil society becomes the 'sociology of politics', and the analysis of the division of labour, production and commodity fetishism, becomes 'the sociology of the process of production' (cf. Jordan, 1971). Further examples may be found in the work of sociologists with respect to Marx's analysis of ideology and beliefs (which becomes 'the sociology of ideology') as well as in the case of the discussion of social classes and conflict. Finally, there is the understanding of Marx which constitutes the basis of what Gouldner terms the 'liberative potential' of modern sociology, often ambiguously referred to as 'Marxist sociology', 'critical sociology', or 'radical sociology' as distinct from 'bourgeois', 'academic', or 'corporate' sociology.

The most frequently occurring understanding of the relevance of Marxian analysis for sociology is, however, best represented by the notion above of Marx's work as a resource for concepts and ideas which are then developed and applied by the sociologist as he sees fit. The consequence of this has been that discussion of, and extraction from, Marx's work has tended to be substantive rather than methodological, attention being directed primarily towards three specific themes, namely social class and stratification; conflict and social change; and the sociology of knowledge and belief. Few attempts have thus been made to consider the methodological relevance of Marx's work for sociology, a reflection no doubt of the fact that such considerations are not explicitly addressed in his work. In addition the production of a sociological method and techniques of investigation, predicated upon specific unexplicated assumptions concerning the adequacy of the scientific division of labour and consequent methodology for analysis of the social world, has provided 'legitimate' grounds for a dismissal of Marxian analysis and method as ideological, philosophical or unscientific. As a result the conventional range of sociological understandings of the relevance of Marxian analysis has in general precluded analysis or consideration of methodological issues. However, with the erosion of the relative consensus among the sociological community concomitant upon the decline of the functionalist paradigm and the emergence of critiques of positivist and empiricist sociological approaches, the discipline has become more open to what may be termed 'extra-sociological' perspectives, including Marxian analysis, phenomenology and critical theory. The discipline is now allegedly without a governing paradigm for according to Gouldner (1971) the functionalist approach no longer predominates, its domain assumptions have been shown to be inadequate and therefore rejected. A comparable analysis of the transformation of sociology is provided by Friedrichs (1972), reference being made to 'normal' and 'revolutionary' periods in sociology.[1] However, whereas Gouldner places emphasis upon functionalism Friedrichs stresses the significance of 'system', pointing out that

> Here was a single word that not only summed up the essential common denominator that ran through the wide array of functionalist positions, but made implicit functionalists of that broad band of non-theoretically oriented sociologists who were simply searching for a common semantic base to which they might anchor their professional vocabulary. 'System' had an obviously attractive ring . . . [whereas] . . . the 'ism' attached to

'functional' served to remind the cautious that the forest of functionalism was cluttered with snares to catch the unwary, system stood forth as a relatively neutral alternative devoid of apparent substantive content (1972, p. 16).

Friedrichs argues that even though the consensus over the system paradigm was only achieved in the 'decade or two following the Second World War' by the 1960s the passage of events was beginning to give rise to a paradigmatic revolution. Whether the description of the current state of the discipline as one of 'scientific revolution' is warranted is a controversial issue. However, without entering into an analysis of Friedrichs's justification for employing Kuhn's thesis in an analysis of sociology we are able to recognize the re-emergence of methodological questions and problems central to the sociological project. The depth and extent of the controversies surrounding contemporary sociologists are manifest not only in the re-examination of what Gouldner has termed background and domain assumptions but also in the reconsideration of the work of the 'founding fathers' of the discipline. It is now no longer possible to reflect that 'the new Ph.D. [has] no need . . . to underpin each empirical or theoretical venture with his own first principles, his own language, methods, and standards' (Friedrichs, 1972, p. 22). The validity of scientific sociology can no longer be taken to be self-evident. It can no longer be assumed that either functionalism is synonymous with sociological analysis itself or that empiricism equals scientific sociology, for with the re-emergence of Marxian analysis and the development of what may be generically termed the 'sociology of everyday life' (phenomenological sociology and ethnomethodology), 'doing sociology' has become problematical.

Increasing recognition of the fact that knowledge is a social product, produced by a scientific community of social beings negotiating agreements, employing conventions all situated within a specific socio-cultural and historical context has led to criticism of the methodological procedures of conventional sociology (Phillips, 1973). However, although a minority of sociologists have recognized the necessity to re-open the question of the nature of the social and have worked to revise the sociological project, in other cases the absence of a dominant paradigm has resulted in an indiscriminating eclecticism, biographies of the founding fathers, or the growth of a new breed of sociologies, rather than a critical and constructive appraisal of the methodological issues at the centre of the discipline's problems. Thus in the case of Wallace's (1969) analysis of sociological theory 'eleven (plus one) theoretic viewpoints' are considered, representing in the context of his classificatory scheme a mere fraction of the total possible number of sociological theories.

Similarly Martindale (1961), Sorokin (1966), and to a lesser extent Cohen (1968), offer accounts of a range of theoretical schools and approaches without providing any critical comparisons, and alongside works of this kind there is the vast expansion of the Marx, Weber and Durkheim 'business' which all too often has produced interpretations of their work independent of any salient comparisons with other theorists, or theoretical positions.

In addition there has been the emergence of a 'new' group of sociological works drawing upon the writing of Husserl, Schutz, Merleau-Ponty and others in the phenomenological philosophical tradition. A phenomenological sociology and ethnomethodology materialized in terms of a critique of the positivist assumptions inherent in contemporary sociology. Broadly speaking, positivist sociology has been subjected to criticism for assuming a unity of scientific method, 'the common identity of natural and social phenomena' (Walsh, 1972) and accepting the 'reality of the world of everyday experience' as a heuristic fact (Bittner, 1973). Phenomeno-logical sociological analysis has attempted to show the necessity of addressing common-sense assumptions inherent in scientific accounts, establishing a methodology appropriate to the intentional, interpretive and meaningful social world and recognizing the interpretive and indexical nature of sociological work. Phenomenological sociology has therefore provided a theoretical de-reification of sociology and the social world. The sociological acceptance of conventional social reality as an objective reality is an example of scientific analysis operating within the natural attitude. Phenomenological sociologists have emphasized the necessity of sociologists proceeding beyond a mere reinterpretation and elaboration of everyday typifications towards an understanding of the intersubjective process of meaning construction. Such a reorientation requires that the meaning individuals attribute to and the consciousness they have of the social world constitute the 'data' to which sociologists attend.

Given the discussion of 'paradigmatic revolutions', 'new directions' and critiques of well established methodological procedures and techniques, it is not surprising that the discipline is held to be in a state of crisis. Reconsideration of the nature of social reality, the appropriate scientific method as well as the relationship between sociological work and other social practices has provided the context for a renewed interest in the works of the classic sociologists. A return to the writings of the 'founders' of the discipline should not be thought a regressive step providing of course that it does not become a wholly linguistic, interpretational and textual exercise. Rather in the specific case of Marx it provides an opportunity for us to reconsider the nature of his analysis and the adequacy of our sociological understanding of the Marxian project. It offers us the

5

possibility of addressing again not only the question of the relationship of Marxian analysis to sociology but also the relevance and
significance of Marx's work for an enlightened understanding of
issues and problems central to a scientific analysis of the social
world. Unfortunately there is a considerable problem of conceptual
ambiguity in this area, for discussion frequently has revolved around
the question of Marxism and sociology or Marxist sociology without
recognizing that the terms employed do not refer unproblematically
to a determinate corpus of knowledge or a specific group of theorists.
In view of this problem I shall use the term 'Marxism' to refer to
the heterogeneous body of thought developed by followers of Marx,
the term 'Marxian' to refer to views and ideas attributed to Marx,
and 'Marxist sociology' to connote the development and utilization
of Marx's work within sociology.[2]

To begin to assess the influence of Marx's work on sociological
thought we have to understand the nature, development and
significance of Marxist sociology. It was towards the end of the
nineteenth century that Marx's work was first beginning to be
accepted as a profound and original system of sociology. Bottomore
and Rubel (1963) note that Marx's work constituted a resource for
not only those who were in agreement with the orientation and
central assumptions of Marxist thought, for example Ferri on
criminology and Sorel on 'the materialist theory of sociology', but
also for other scholars such as Durkheim and Weber who took
issue with commentaries on Marx's work. Hence on the one hand
Marx's work was treated as a significant contribution to sociology,
as providing 'a series of discoveries which will enable man to
become master of his own destiny . . . [giving] significance to his
life' (Bottomore and Rubel, 1963, p. 51). However, on the other
hand a considerable amount of attention and time was devoted by
sociologists to a critical examination and rejection of Marxian
analysis. Although the beginning of the twentieth century was
accompanied by an increase in the positive influence of Marx's work
on sociology Bottomore argues that by the 1930s interest in Marx's
sociology had waned. Whether the growth of sociological science
modelled on the natural sciences and adopting the doctrine of
detachment and value-freedom accounts for the diminished interest
in a Marxian analysis frequently associated with revolutionary
politics and ideology is a controversial issue. Certainly it seems that
as sociologists began to strive after scientific status the direct
influence of Marx's work diminished although Marxism and
Marxist sociology still remained reference points for sociological
work.

While the idea of a 'Marxist Sociology' represents for some
scholars a contradiction in terms, for others it offers a synthesis of

disparate world-views. For example in the work of Sartre (1968) and Bottomore (1968) the concept of a Marxist sociology is redundant whilst for Lefebvre (1972) it represents a specific sociological domain. In the case of Sartre it is not a question of either rejecting sociology entirely and adopting Marxian analysis nor is it a matter of incorporating Marx's work into the prevailing sociological orthodoxy; on the contrary, sociology has to be subordinated to the methodological considerations of Marxian analysis. Either therefore sociology stands opposed to Marxian analysis or alternatively it must be situated within the Marxian framework which alone can provide the possibility of an understanding of the historically changing totality of social life. Sartre argues that the sociologist

> wants to hold on to the benefits of teleology while at the same time maintaining the attitude of positivism – that is while suppressing or disguising the ends of human activity. At this point sociology is posited for itself and is opposed to Marxism, not by affirming the provisional autonomy of its method – which would, on the contrary, provide the means for integrating it – but by affirming the radical autonomy of its object (1968, p. 68).

In developing a critique of sociological 'objectivism', the removal of the sociologist from the field of investigation, as well as the frequent neglect of history in sociological work, Sartre seeks to 'reintegrate the sociological moment into the historical totalization'. Sociology for Sartre becomes a catalyctic agent in the development of Marxian analysis providing 'information which is capable of developing the dialectical method by compelling it to push its totalization to include this information' (ibid., p. 74). Hence, for Sartre, sociology constitutes a method for Marxian analysis, revealing new relations, discovering new mediations between concrete men and the material conditions of life, which must be integrated into the historical totalization.

In contrast Bottomore has suggested that the integration of Marx's work within sociological thought produces the disappearance of a distinct Marxist sociology. Three possible interpretations of Marxist sociology are examined by Bottomore. First, as referring to the sociology of those thinkers who on other grounds are Marxist in their general philosophical and political outlook; in which case they first have to reconcile the empirical findings of sociological research to their Marxist ideas and then further consider whether a separate Marxist sociology has any viability. Second, the term can refer to all those sociologists who attach prime importance to economic factors, class relations, or group conflicts in the explanation of social events whilst not necessarily agreeing with the

7

conclusions of Marx. Employed in this sense the term would encapsulate the sociologies of such diverse theorists as Weber, Pareto, Coser, Galbraith, Dahrendorf and Rex. In this sense the concept of Marxist sociology becomes almost as meaningless as Kingsley Davis's understanding of functional analysis. Finally Bottomore states that Marxist sociology may refer to a methodology, a persistent critique of the aims and methods of the social sciences. In this form it has of course achieved particular significance, largely through the writing of Lukács, Marcuse, Sartre and Goldmann. However, he concludes that in this sense Marxist sociology becomes 'Marxist anti-sociology'. For Bottomore, therefore, it seems that either the term Marxist sociology is too ambiguous for intellectual discourse or alternatively it connotes an earlier stage in the development of sociology as a discipline prior to the adoption of Marx's ideas in sociological practice.

Lefebvre argues that not only is Marx not a sociologist but what is more 'every positivist sociology presenting itself as "Marxist"' (1972, p. 21) is tending towards reformism. However, whilst being critical of sociology as a conservative discipline which separates knowledge from criticism Lefebvre asserts that there is a sociology in Marx, namely a 'sociology of the family, of the city and the countryside, of subgroups, classes, and whole societies, of knowledge, of the state etc.' (ibid., p. 24). In particular he suggests that Marx's concept of praxis contains many sociological elements, a sociology of needs, objects, knowledge and everyday life. In other words contemporary sociology is not entirely incompatible with the Marxian project. Although it is clear that Lefebvre does not rule out a reconciliation of aspects of Marx's work with sociological inquiry the specific nature of the relationship is left somewhat ambiguous. For example he recognizes that sociologists have interpreted Marx's critical comments on philosophy to refer to the replacement of philosophical concepts by empirical sociological fact, a consequence of this misunderstanding being the 'tug of war between positivism and philosophy, the objective and the subjective, empiricism and voluntarism' (ibid., p. 35). Nevertheless Lefebvre still legislates for the assignment of a specific domain to Marxist sociology, namely the development and accentuation of the critical aspect of Marxian thought to include not only a study of the emergence of forms and 'the way forms react on contents, structures on processes' but also 'the efforts of the working class to transcend the laws of value and of the market – the world of commodities – through revolutionary praxis' (ibid., p. 103). Such a conception of Marxist sociology is hardly controversial for it is an approach of this kind which has represented the most common development of Marxian thought within sociology. Furthermore it does not address, let alone resolve, the question of the relationship between Marxian analysis, Marxist sociology and 'academic' sociology. Lefebvre attempts to deal with this issue in retrospect, stating

> We have tried to discern in these [Marx's] writings a sociological method and area of study . . . we have tried to show in what sense Marx's method implies the project of constituting or re-constituting, exploring or creating a totality (of knowledge, or reality). . . . Marxian thought is not alone sufficient, but it is indispensable for understanding the present-day world. . . . It is part of the modern world, an important, original, fruitful and irreplaceable element in our present-day situation, with particular relevance to one specialized science – sociology (ibid., p. 188).

For Lefebvre therefore it is the Marxian method which is of primary significance. However, when assigning a specific domain to Marxist sociology not only does he fail to attend to the prior existence of just such a field of inquiry within conventional sociology but also he neglects to address the question of a possible incompatibility between Marxian analysis and the predominant forms of sociological analysis (e.g. positivism, empiricism, phenomenology etc.). Hence the possibility that a Marxist sociology might represent a contradiction in terms is obscured by the assumption of its validity and as a consequence the implications for sociological inquiry of a re-constituted Marxian analysis remain undisclosed.

While for some scholars the concept of a Marxist sociology is largely redundant (e.g. Bottomore, Sartre), for others it either holds out the possibility of a re-constitution of Marxism by way of a synthesis of historical materialism with the techniques and methods of research developed by sociologists (cf. Wiatr, 1969; Zivkovic, 1969; Kalab, 1969) or alternatively denotes a specific sociological domain (e.g. Lefebvre). The concept of a Marxist sociology may thus be seen to be exceedingly ambiguous, referring not only to the views expounded above and to the notion of Marx's work as sociology but also to the hybrid of selections and developments of various aspects of Marx's work found in contemporary sociology. The conceptual ambiguity surrounding the sociological enterprise, which this particular example illustrates, is even more explicit in the debates over the crises within academic sociology and Marxism.

The notion of a crisis within Marxism is not new; Bottomore notes that at the end of the nineteenth century, 'it was common to speak of the "crisis of Marxism", a crisis both intellectual and political' (Bottomore and Rubel, 1963, p. 52). Similarly, sociology has frequently been 'on trial', confronted by criticisms of its methodology and scientific status (cf. MacRae, 1964; Stein and Vidich,

1963). Broadly speaking there are three distinct parties to the current debate. First, Marxists who are opposed to and critical of sociology, believing it to be a bourgeois ideology (Shaw, 1972, 1974; Blackburn, 1969; Harvey, 1972). Their analysis provides part of the case for sociology being in a state of crisis. Second, sociologists who are critical of both 'Marxist' sociology or Marxism, and sociology (Gouldner, 1971, 1973; Wiatr, 1969; Zivkovic, 1969; Kalab, 1969). Finally there is a sociological account of the crisis in Marxist thought in general and Marxist sociology in particular (Birnbaum, 1968). These accounts will be analysed in the context of the respective crises.

The crisis in sociology: the Gouldner thesis

The most important account of the current crisis confronting sociology is that presented from within the discipline by Gouldner. The focus of his account is on the decline of functionalism as the dominant paradigm within academic sociology. It is not a general critique of the possibility of doing sociology but rather a concise analysis of the methodological and ideological implications of the functionalist paradigm exemplified by Talcott Parsons's work and seen to be for some time the dominant theoretical orientation in academic sociology in the USA. Necessarily, therefore, Gouldner's work offers a less than complete coverage of the emerging 'crisis in sociology', dealing only superficially with the work of Goffman and Garfinkel and providing only a limited account of Marxism. These somewhat limited terms of reference, however, are stated by the author to be an inevitable consequence of the enormity of the task of analysing the relationship of social theory and society, further questions and issues being conceived as part of a future project.

Gouldner's account may be divided into three sections:
(a) Sociology and the welfare state
(b) Social change and the functionalist convergence with Marxism
(c) The rise of 'alternative' sociologies

Sociology and the welfare state

Gouldner states that Parsonian functionalism typically represents the social theory of a market economy society, one in which the state has little effect and where emphasis is placed upon the philosophy of voluntarism. In such a society the functionalist account of equilibrating mechanisms being spontaneous and natural results of the free play of market forces may be acceptable at both the ideological and empirical level. However, with the growth of state involvement in the economy, health, education and welfare services, the concept of a market economy is displaced by that of a welfare state. This in itself creates difficulties for a sociological theory which lays stress on the stabilizing tendencies of technology, science, the division of labour and moral values rather than intervention by the state. However, such difficulties are further compounded by the welfare state's demands for, and finance of, applied social science as a way of resolving the problems of an industrial society. Gouldner states that 'in 1962 the US Federal Government spent $118,000,000 in support of social science research. In 1963, $139,000,000 was spent. In 1964, $200,000,000 was spent. In the space of three years, then, federal expenditures alone increased by about seventy per cent' (1971, p. 345) . . . such is the pressure of the welfare state on the social sciences for policy-oriented research.

Gouldner further remarks that the consequences of this expenditure within sociology, and for functionalism in particular, are extremely significant. Functionalism has consistently offered an account of, or justification for, the status quo, it traditionally has not been concerned with how one might change the present in order to improve it. It is in this sense that functionalism is placed in jeopardy by the welfare state's need for applied social science. The state requires guidance as to how social conditions can be improved, how the plight of minorities can be alleviated and how the total society can be managed. Hence Gouldner notes the pressures on functionalism to modify certain of its central assumptions and to adapt itself for practical purposes. Specifically, the demand is for causal explanations to facilitate planned and deliberate change in particular social conditions and in addition a social research programme which will expose social problems whilst providing justification of governmental commitments to social reforms. As a result conservative sociological theories offering a justification of the status quo are displaced by liberal reformist sociologies which offer both technological and ideological assistance to the welfare state.

Although Gouldner's account of the genesis of sociology's crisis under the welfare state is an interesting contribution to an understanding of the dialectical relationship between social theory and society it does contain some important omissions. In particular there is a neglect of two significant distinctions: first, that made between sociological theory and empirical research, and second, the equally salient distinction between small-scale (micro) sociologies and large-scale (macro) sociologies. Reference to the former distinction in Gouldner's *Crisis* is brief, the emphasis being on the weaknesses of the respective positions.

If the empiricists had stressed that sociologists are, or should be guided by the facts yielded by properly conducted research, theory-stressing sociologists tended to reply that sociologists are, or should be guided by articulate, explicit, and hence testable theory. From the standpoint presented here, however, both seem to have been at least partially mistaken (1971, p. 43).

However, rather than proceeding to embark upon an introduction to the idea of 'reflexivity' as does Gouldner, it is important to consider the possibility of the differential impact of the crisis on the theoretical and empiricist wings of sociology. Whereas for the former, particularly in the case of functionalism, demands for policy-oriented practical research might be problematic, in the case of the latter no such difficulties need be experienced. Gouldner's critical comments concerning both these aspects are not only accurate but also important, but in one respect they fail to provide the vital link between sociology, the crisis and the welfare state. The demands of the state are for social technologies, that is to say applied social science which lends itself to social reform, and for this, empiricist sociology is peculiarly well equipped, operating as it does within the domain assumptions of the given society. The crisis identified by Gouldner seems to apply therefore not to sociological approaches which adopt a positivist-empiricist approach to social reality but specifically to the functionalist account of the nature of society. While there may be a consensus within the sociological community over the inadequacies of the functionalist position the conclusion to be drawn from this is not necessarily that sociology in general is in crisis but that functionalism in particular has critical limitations. For the sociologist for whom data and empirical research are of primary value such problems may appear to be far less significant, primarily because although theoretical assumptions are present at every stage of sociological work they are frequently unexplicated, implicit and directly compatible with the assumption inherent in much sociological work that the given social order constitutes the 'natural' factual order.

The other distinction glossed over by Gouldner is that between micro- and macro-sociology.[3] Sociological theories may be classified according to their scope either as small-scale (micro) or large-scale (macro), the former concentrating upon individuals and small groups, the latter upon societal institutions or societies themselves. It is this latter type of sociology, the macro-theory of Parsonian functionalism, with which Gouldner is concerned. The absence of any critical discussion of micro-sociology and the problem of the relationship of micro- and macro-sociological accounts to social reality conceived as a totality, devalues Gouldner's general case for there being a crisis in sociology. All that is established is that particular changes within society, especially the growth of the welfare state and its demands for applied social science, have led to a crisis for functionalism in general and Parsonian functionalism in particular. In failing to distinguish effectively between functionalism and other positivistic sociologies (for example empiricism), by overlooking the institutionalized distinction between theory and research, and Merton's compromise 'Middle-Range' solution, and additionally by neglecting the differences between macro- and micro-theories Gouldner's account is more limited than is suggested by his general reference to Western sociology and academic sociology in the USA in particular. Developments in the wake of Gouldner's study suggest that the crisis of functionalism has given way to the more general sociological crisis of scientism, a matter which cannot be considered in sufficient depth at this point but which will be discussed below. It is adequate at this stage to note that within sociology increasing critical attention has been directed towards the general question of the nature of sociological science as well as to the particular problem of the limitations of specific approaches, primarily positivist and empiricist in nature. Critics of contemporary sociology have focused upon both the political (Nicolaus, 1971; Blackburn, 1969) and methodological aspects (Douglas, 1971; Filmer et al., 1972) of sociological work. In some cases there has been a recognition that methodological approach and political interest are related; for example Horton (1971) depicts sociology as an apologetic science which functions to affirm the reified understanding of the social order. He notes that sociology

> incorporates as its topic the reified objectivism of laymen
> rather than the social practice which it hides. This conventional
> attitude is then reified again into a language too obscure for
> laymen to understand. The second-level reification thus
> transforms a commonplace commodity mystification of social
> life into a neutral science of the manipulation and management
> of social life (1971, pp. 176 – 7).

This issue will be reconsidered in the context of both a phenomenological and a Marxian critique of contemporary sociological methodology.

Social change and the functionalist convergence with Marxism

The second limitation of functionalism which has precipitated the current crisis is according to Gouldner its unsatisfactory account of social change. Given the demand for policy-oriented social science to assist in social reforms it becomes mandatory for sociology to be able to offer a theory of social change which is not only credible but which allows for the possibility, even necessity, of managed or

13

planned changes. In these respects Gouldner notes that function-alism is very limited, its orientation being towards explanations of the status quo and its accounts of change being in terms of natural processes or homeostatic mechanisms. In these circumstances it is suggested that functionalism will abandon certain of its domain assumptions and will adopt others, in particular those of Marxism. Hence Gouldner discusses functionalism's adaptation to the problem of accounting for social change through what is termed Parsons's 'drift toward Marxism'. Broadly speaking, he denotes three aspects of Parsons's attempt to confront issues of social change which are indicative of domain assumptions sympathetic to Marxism. These are:

   (i) Vested interests and resistance to change
  (ii) Differentiation
 (iii) Evolution

In the case of the first aspect, Parsons remarks that 'change is never just "alteration of pattern" but alteration by the overcoming of resistance' (1951, p. 491), implying not only the concept of 'vested interests' but furthermore that change takes place through conflict. Gouldner notes that, 'if men have a vested interest in resisting change in order to maintain gratifications will they not tend to labor for change which will expand their gratifications?' (1971, p. 355). He thus introduces the conclusion that the idea of conflict is inherent in social systems. Clearly in these respects Parsons's orientation is not entirely incompatible with that of Marx.

In the case of differentiation Parsons is seen to be moving towards the evolutionary perspective, seeking to provide an explanation of the way in which social systems change in an orderly manner, but again seeming to drift further towards the Marxist position. Specifically, Gouldner argues that Parsons's discussion of differentia-tion resembles Marx's account of the contradictions between the forces and relations of production, the re-orientation in the work of the former – from considerations of equilibrium to those of change – being accompanied by a shift from Comtean to Marxian domain assumptions. Hence it is suggested that Parsons transforms Marx's revolutionary account of change into an evolutionary one.

The final aspect concerns directly the application of similar analytical categories in the work of Parsons and Marx; these are pre-requisites for socio-cultural development and 'aspects' of social activity or of certain historical 'moments' respectively. Parsons's pre-requisites constitute the 'very minimum that may be said to mark a society as truly human' (1964, p. 342) and include technology, kinship organization, language communication and religion. The 'moments' of social activity discussed by Marx and Engels which 'have existed simultaneously since the dawn of history' (1970, p. 50) include the production of material life, technology, family and the mode of co-operation of individuals (social relationships). In addition Marx and Engels stress the concomitant importance of language, that is practical consciousness. Gouldner thus concludes that in the work of Parsons and later Smelser (1968) and Moore (1967) there is a convergence with Marxism in terms of functionalist attempts to account for change. This is consequential in that functionalism, by modifying many of its domain assumptions, becomes less distinct as an approach within sociology, a pertinent result of this tendency being the false claim that functional analysis is synonymous with sociological analysis (Davis, 1967; Fallding, 1972). Even if Gouldner may be correct in his assessment of the latent and unacknowledged influence of Marxism on functionalist sociology his diagnosis of a crisis remains controversial.

The rise of 'alternative' sociologies

For Gouldner a third symptom of the sociological crisis is the emergence of 'new theories', in particular those theories expounded by Goffman and Garfinkel. The development and appeal of their works is seen as further evidence of the growing disenchantment of the 'younger sociologist' with functionalism, as confirmation of the rejection of the old sociological orthodoxy, and as indicative of the likely re-direction of theoretical interest within the discipline. Goffman's dramaturgy, Becker's sociology of the under-dog and Garfinkel's ethnomethodology are held to be sympathetic to the sentiments and assumptions of 'young people oriented to the new Psychedelic Culture, and perhaps even of some of the New Left' (1971, p. 444). Gouldner's optimism that the popular appeal of these perspectives will grow, thereby challenging even further the orthodoxy of conventional sociology, becomes virtually insignificant once we realize that in discussing 'new' developments he completely neglects to attempt to elucidate the connection or relationship between new perspectives and the crisis of functionalism. As a consequence of his exclusive concentration upon the topic of functionalism Gouldner fails to attend to the at least equally significant 'crisis' of methodology in contemporary sociology. An insight into his neglect of this topic can be gleaned from the fact that positivist, empiricist and phenomenological sociologies constitute an insignificant aspect of *Crisis*. In a work devoted to the growing problems confronted in sociology by sociologists there is but a cursory and indirect reference to phenomenology through a brief recognition of the work of Alfred Schutz and its influence on Garfinkel's ethnomethodological studies. Furthermore there is no mention at all of equally important American sociologists such as Peter Berger, Jack D. Douglas or Aaron Cicourel, all of whom in

15

different ways have been influenced by phenomenology and are active in promoting and constructing alternative sociologies. In this context Gouldner's selection of Garfinkel and Goffman becomes problematical particularly in view of his proposal for a 'Reflexive Sociology'. He notes that,

> The ultimate goal of a Reflexive Sociology is the deepening of the sociologist's own awareness, of who and what he is, in a specific society at any given time, and of how both his social role and his personal praxis affect his work as a sociologist (1971, p. 494).

Yet despite the interest in reflexivity Gouldner does not address the question of the limitations inherent in his selection of Goffman and Garfinkel as exemplars of the 'new' sociology, neither does he discuss his avoidance of the methodological question at the centre of the phenomenological and ethnomethodological critiques of contemporary sociology.

Goffman's dramaturgy

Goffman's sociology is concerned with everyday life, in particular with showing the tenuous nature of social life. It is a sociology for 'making out' in the world, where life is a drama and men and women strive to contrive and project a convincing image of 'self' to their audiences. In his work, he is concerned to display the significance of ostensibly insignificant rituals in the preservation not only of identity but also of a semblance of social order. Yet amidst such work there lies the hidden terror of disorder, the constant struggle of people trying to accomplish or manage an identity compatible with an apparent external demand system. Goffman's sociology is about adaption, accommodation and impression-management, its focus is upon the conflicts and contradictions experienced by individuals in social contexts attempting to exercise and preserve some degree of control over their situation despite the pressures exerted by a dominating social system.

Gouldner's critique of Goffman's micro-sociological role theory draws upon much the same material to be found in his earlier discussion of Becker's work (1968). Basically he argues that Goffman is not concerned to change society, or the structure of its institutions, but rather is interested in how people manage through rituals to accommodate and adapt to the dilemmas inherent in the social world. For 'one-dimensional' man it is a theory of 'secondary adjustments', with the offer of 'role-distance' as a refuge from the overpowering social structure. It is the sociology of the new bourgeois, designed for the urban, alienated individual whose 'self' is the consequent and managed product of interactions with many discrete role partners in the company of several different audiences. As Gouldner states:

> A dramaturgical model is an accommodation congenial only to those who are willing to accept the basic allocations of existent master institutions. . . . It is for those who have already made out in the big game . . . those members of the middle class who generally mask their alienation out of a concern to maintain a respectable appearance (1971, p. 386).

Categorically its radical appearance is a deceit, Goffman avoiding explicitly the vital issue of the ways in which definitions of the situation are controlled and managed not equally but differentially by power holders. Indeed, Goffman's view of the social world excludes from consideration particular features of social life which have a direct bearing upon the theme of interaction central to his analyses. The most significant omissions concern stratification, political control and the social distribution and evaluation of knowledge. If Goffman had reflected upon the theatrical metaphor he might have recognized that actors frequently work to scripts, are directed, and thus only interpret their roles or contrive an image within specific limitations. Clearly according to the type of play, script or director these limitations will vary, giving rise to different 'degrees of freedom' and a variety of possible 'dramas'. Since there may be a variety of 'dramas' one should not generalize as does Goffman from the new experience of the educated middle class. It has not been established that role distance is a mode of role playing normally available to all individuals, and premature generalization of such an hypothesis can only lead to an increase in the sociological construction rather than understanding of reality. [4]

Goffman's world, unlike that of Parsonian functionalism, is one in which it does not matter whether men are moral as long as they seem moral; it is the sociology of the hustler, and the confidence trickster. Now although Gouldner's account conveys very well the degree of cynicism in Goffman's work and does elucidate some of the more important limitations, it fails to recognize the reification at the heart of Goffman's analysis. In his work Goffman relies heavily on the role metaphor, analysing human behaviour and interaction in terms of roles and role distance. The role concept is adopted unproblematically and treated as a convenient analytical tool for understanding interaction situations, offering a conceptual resolution to the problem of the individual's relationship to the social structure. However, Goffman's work goes beyond this point in that individuals are treated as a collection of roles and further are credited with a consciousness of their condition. It is explicitly affirmed that individuals promote an image, manage their identity, adopt suitable postures for their various audiences, acting in each case to persuade others to accept an appearance or definition of the situation at face value. Not only then has the analytical tool become reality – no account being offered of the historicity of the concept or the specific social circumstances which give rise to distinct and discrete behavioural expectations and motivations – but furthermore Goffman attributes to people an unparalleled degree of cynicism and detachment. He clearly is in the process of imposing his own disenchantment with men on to the sociological understanding of a disenchanted world.

Garfinkel's ethnomethodology

Unlike the functionalist concern with morality as the basis of social order, Garfinkel stresses the importance of tacit understanding, a world taken for granted as the basis of order. The focus of his work is on the mundane, on everyday life, and like Goffman he avoids the general issues of power and social hierarchy. The latter, although quite clearly excluded by Garfinkel's terms of reference, remain problematical for his analysis. Gouldner correctly notes that in Garfinkel's terms there is no radical difference between sociologists and other men. However, while arguing that all men in society are collectivity members, are doing sociology (both lay and professional), Garfinkel recommends that professional sociologists should be more self-conscious than lay sociologists. If sociologists are, or become, more self-conscious then there can be no denial of difference between sociological and commonsense theorizing. Indeed Garfinkel's own work displays and depends upon the existence of difference. This is clear from the use made by Garfinkel of 'reality bust' techniques to lay bare the taken-for-granted basis of social reality. As such there is an unexamined contradiction in Garfinkel's work between on the one hand the assertion that there is no difference between professional and lay sociologists and on the other the assumption and adoption of the privileged position of the professional sociologist to be able to employ the available resources of sociological investigation to intervene consciously and directly in the everyday world. In particular Garfinkel takes for granted the political, economic and educational resources available to the sociologist in the course of his disruption of other members' social realities, hence neglecting significant characteristics of the social world. Just as we have no warrant to treat those in the media, the 'consciousness industry' (cf. Enzensberger, 1970), as indistinguishable from receivers of broadcasts so when considering the relationship between professional and lay sociologists we must not ignore the possibility of significant differences in social awareness (self-consciousness), privileged access to relatively scarce resources ('materials' and finance for research), and opportunity to intervene (with a specific scientific involvement) in the everyday world. As Gouldner has noted, Garfinkel appears to be totally unconcerned as to how or 'why one definition of social reality becomes prevalent in one time or place or group and another elsewhere' (1971, p. 391).

Garfinkel's ethnomethodology is therefore potentially a method of destroying the taken-for-granted aspects of social reality, a way of stripping the shared cultural base of its cloak of invisibility. In this specific sense, by holding out the possibility of changing consciousness and awareness, Garfinkel's experiments represent radical ventures within sociology which as yet have been left largely undeveloped. Unfortunately when we examine the typical ethnomethodological experiment or demonstration we find in agreement with Gouldner 'a micro-confrontation with, and non-violent resistance to the status quo', a very largely safe and symbolic rebellion which does not recognize any conflictual or political interests within the social order. It consequently becomes 'a way in which the alienated young may, with relative safety, defy the established order and experience their own potency' (1971, p. 394).

A critical analysis of the strategies adopted by ethnomethodologists reveals that their experience of potency is gained not at the expense of the pillars and propagators of the established order but rather through the 'bewilderment, uncertainty, internal conflict, psycho-sexual isolation, acute and nameless anxiety' (Garfinkel, 1967, p. 55) experienced by those who are already victims of social processes over which they have little control. The arenas in which demonstrations have been staged, for example in the families of co-operative students, in conversation situations between friends, at social gatherings such as parties, and in pseudo-experimental situations, all confirm the safe nature of ethnomethodological radicalism. All these situations, with the possible exception of the last, lack any formal or structured hierarchy, an important factor to consider when wishing to account for the reactions of 'bewilderment, anxiety etc.'. In discussions of the place of values and ideology in social science it has been suggested that ideological bias need not be reserved purely for cases of distortion but might also refer to the selection of safe topics for research, those which are politically unembarrassing. Thus the research not done becomes as important as that which has been done. In the case of ethnomethodology the absence of any demonstrations in hierarchical social situations where sanctions may be employed to enforce specific situational definitions is significant. Not only does this indicate the possible presence of political limitations upon ethnomethodological demonstrations but furthermore it raises serious doubts concerning the general validity of Garfinkel's statements about social order. Garfinkel as a professional sociologist has considerable advantages over lay members in that while he is able through his privileged position to conjure up anxiety, bewilderment and uncertainty for them, they with the notable exception of Agnes can cause him little discomfort.[5]

Thus it is clear that although sociology may have a dialectical character, containing both repressive and liberative dimensions, the latter is not applicable to the sociologies of Goffman and Garfinkel. The only sense in which the 'new' sociologies have been critical for conventional sociology is in terms of methodological issues, in particular through the development of critiques of positivist and empiricist approaches. As I have stated Gouldner tends to gloss over the question of methodology, thereby avoiding the controversy surrounding the adoption of the natural sciences as a model for scientific sociological work, as well as the equally significant question of the status of data, evidence and facts and the relationship between observational and theoretical categories. The observations which he does make are, however, of importance. He asserts that the positivist heritage is manifest in contemporary sociological preoccupation with value-freedom and bias, 'modern "value-free" sociology (being) the anomic adaptation of sociological positivism to political failure, an adaptation that commonly takes a ritualistic form, in which pure knowledge or the methodology of map-making tends to become an end in itself' (1971, p. 102). The positivist element in contemporary sociology is therefore manifest according to Gouldner in the pre-occupation with objectivity, perceived to be concomitant with value-freedom, and is a consequence of the failure of Comtean positivism to provide a functional alternative to religion. Hence 'objectivity is not neutrality, but alienation from self and society . . . [it] is the ideology of those who reject both the conventional and the alternative mappings of the social order . . . [however these] "objective" men, even if politically homeless, are middle class and operate within the boundaries of the social status quo' (ibid., p. 103). As can be seen from Gouldner's comments on positivism he is primarily concerned with the moral and political aspect rather than the scientific and methodological assumptions and limitations inherent in the position. Consideration of methodological assumptions in sociological work constitutes the focus of the phenomenological sociological critique of contemporary sociology neglected by Gouldner.

For Gouldner the rise of 'new' sociologies with domain assumptions dissimilar to those of Parsonian functionalism contributes to, and is a symptom of, the crisis of sociology arising from the decline of the functionalist paradigm. Parallel to Gouldner's detailed and critical account of the crisis confronting sociology there are critiques from Marxist writers who denigrate sociology as a bourgeois ideology, as an exercise in mystification. These critiques are import- ant contributions to the debate over the relationship between Marx's work, Marxism and sociology. Two particular critiques will be con- sidered, one being general to social science and sociology – the other focusing specifically on Gouldner's account of sociology's crisis.

Blackburn's critique of sociology as bourgeois ideology

Although Blackburn's critique is frequently directed at sociology in general, it does leave open the possibility of a sociology which is not bourgeois, but which takes up the critical orientation laid down in Marx's analysis of capitalist society. Furthermore the criticism offered by Blackburn from within the Marxist tradition can be seen to be compatible with criticisms from within sociology, notably those of Gouldner discussed earlier. Specifically, Blackburn argues that sociology offers an explanation and justification of the existing social arrangements from which critical concepts are excluded. Thus aspects of sociology are considered to be either consecrating the social order, or alternatively supplying the necessary techniques to run it (i.e. policy-oriented social science). With respect to the concepts employed, Blackburn argues persuasively that critical terms are either excluded or emasculated, his examples including the follow- ing: capitalism, exploitation, contradiction, alienation and class. In the case of the first three concepts sociologists have increasingly tended to use instead such terms as 'industrial society', 'reciprocity imbalance' and 'dysfunction', a good example being Gouldner's comment in a pre-*Crisis* work that 'exploitation is by now so heavily charged with misleading ideological resonance that the term itself can scarcely be salvaged for purely scientific purposes and will, quite properly, be resisted by most American sociologists. Perhaps a less emotionally freighted – if infelicitous – term such as "reciprocity imbalance" will suffice to direct attention once again to the crucial question of unequal exchanges' (1960, p. 167). This quote serves not only to illustrate Blackburn's point but also to indicate the degree of change and quality of a particular sociologist's work, Gouldner's revised version of 'The norm of reciprocity' (1973), omitting the passage quoted above. However, the fate of the concepts of aliena- tion and class in the hands of sociologists has been somewhat different. Both terms have been employed extensively in sociological work, usually in such a fashion as to totally transform their original meaning (cf. Horton, 1964; Broadhead, 1973). The concepts have been 'tested', operationalized, stripped of their former critical value and harnessed to descriptive empirical work. The consequence of

21

such sociological work is the mystification of social consciousness, the blunting of critical imagination and the undermining of the idea that people can ever radically transform society. However, this view of sociology as the theory and practice of containment oriented towards the provision of social technologies to ameliorate social problems is not the monopoly of ex-sociologists or Marxist writers. An awareness of the ideological status of some sociological work is present not only in the work of Blackburn (1969); Shaw (1972) and Nicolaus (1971) but also appears indirectly in the work of both Gouldner (1971) and Giddens (1972b).[6]

Consideration of the following four themes will provide an overview of Blackburn's perception of sociology as bourgeois ideology:

(1) Sociology of development and underdevelopment
(2) Sociology of change and revolution
(3) Alienation, the destruction of a concept
(4) Social science and bourgeois ideology

The ideological character of sociology is according to Blackburn explicit in the case of discussions of 'advanced' and 'backward' countries, in that although it is recognized that the gap between them is growing, sociologists can state that 'there is no contradiction between the interests of the underdeveloped countries and those of advanced countries' (Aron, 1971, p. 24). Similarly, Parsons in an essay uncharacteristically titled 'Polarization of the world and international order' offers as a policy recommendation 'that every effort be made to promulgate carefully considered statements of value commitments which may provide a basis for consensus among both have and have-not nations' (1967, p. 475). Unfortunately despite the work of Marxist scholars and general sociological critiques of convergence theory, sociological accounts of the relationships between developed and underdeveloped societies emphasize the importance of technology and industrialization rather than neo-colonialism, exploitation or military interventions.

The second theme, concerning the sociological treatment of change and revolution, follows on directly from the last topic. In agreement with Gouldner, Blackburn notes that the dominant school of social theory has been that of functionalism, a theory which sought to explain integration, social order and stability rather than change, each part of the social system or society being analysed in terms of its contribution to the maintenance of the status quo. However, unlike Gouldner who seeks to analyse the way in which functionalism has been adapted to account for change Blackburn contrasts the equilibrium theorists with the 'so-called conflict theorists', arguing that the difference between the two positions is insignificant as both are oriented towards integration. Thus it is implied, for example, that the work of Dahrendorf (1959) on the institutionalization of conflict is compatible with that of Coser (1956) on the functions of social conflict. However, Blackburn's position is unlikely to provoke much opposition, for the conflict-consensus distinction is now treated within sociological circles as a myth (cf. Giddens, 1972a). Blackburn concludes, echoing Bottomore's earlier statement,[7] that sociology has no adequate theory of social change or revolution and thus confirms the necessity for a Marxist rather than sociological analysis of society.

Consensus among sociologists over the third theme is unlikely to be any more widespread than in the case of the earlier themes for although many sociologists have recognized different interpretations and applications of the Marxian concept of alienation, and even in a few cases the evaluative emasculation of the concept, the conclusions which are drawn from such observations vary considerably. For example whereas Horton and Broadhead request a return to the critical meaning of the term along the lines of its meaning within Marxian analysis, Feuer (1963) argues that the concept is of little use in social analysis, that it 'remains too much a concept of political theology which bewilders rather than clarifies' (p. 146). Therefore even though the doctrine of value-freedom has been subjected to criticism and sociologists have re-examined the meaning of the concept of alienation the attempt to restore the concept within sociological discourse meets opposition either from those who engage in operationalizing the concept (cf. Seeman, 1959; Nettler, 1957; Keniston, 1968) or from those who deny its relevance in any form to sociological work.

The final theme, of social science and bourgeois ideology, is really the crux of the matter. It ought to be noted from the beginning that Blackburn attributes to all the social sciences an ambition to become value-neutral, a goal which has for sometime now been rigorously criticized within sociology. Indeed Gouldner's critique of the myth of a value-free sociology, published seven years before Blackburn's essay, was so well received that he was led to publish a further article warning of a possible over-reaction leading to the substitution of an alternative myth.[8] Clearly, therefore, Blackburn's comments do not apply universally within sociology. Indeed many of his statements and criticisms of sociology are perfectly compatible with critical analyses by sociologists of their own discipline. Another example of this tendency is provided by Blackburn's assertion that within sociology a confused account of the method of the natural sciences is presented as the appropriate model for social science. This is a point of view held not only by Gouldner but also by many phenomenological and ethnomethodological sociologists. Similarly he states that sociology is guilty of reification, accepting at face value the thing like character which social relations appear to possess, assuming 'axiomatically that everything is exactly as it appears' (Blackburn, 1969, p. 207). This specific criticism although perhaps valid for sociological approaches which treat the given social order as a 'factual' and objective social order is not applicable to sociology as a whole. In particular it is not relevant to sociological research which treats data, evidence and facts as problematical, work which focuses upon either 'facts as social accomplishments' (cf. Zimmerman, 1974) or analysis which recognizes the interrelationship of theoretical and observational categories (cf. Hindess, 1973). Blackburn's analysis is primarily focused upon the implicit political interest inherent in sociological research and as a result it omits from consideration any discussion of the at least equally important methodological basis of sociological work. In consequence he does not attend to the emergence of critiques of contemporary sociology by phenomenological sociologists or ethnomethodologists and therefore remains unaware of criticisms of the 'objectivist' position by sociologists. The account offered by Blackburn is in consequence limited in significance in so far as it treats sociology as a discipline universally characterized by an assumption that 'things are as they appear'. Clearly it is not the case that sociologists uniformly approach the study of social reality in such a manner, for as Berger states, 'the first wisdom of sociology is this – things are not what they seem' (1966, p. 34). Indeed many of the problems associated with doing sociology, for example the unexplicated nature of the relationship between the everyday empiricism of common sense and the abstracted empiricism of much sociological research (cf. Wright Mills, 1970), which makes the status of the sociologist's findings uncertain vis-à-vis commonsense understandings, constitute important topics of investigation and analysis within the discipline.

Blackburn tends to treat sociology as an homogeneous discipline which legitimates and reifies the given social order; hence its classification as bourgeois ideology. In contrast I believe the absence of a dominant paradigm and a universally acceptable methodology within sociology makes the question of the discipline's effect and function more complex than Blackburn's simplistic analysis allows. In asserting that sociology constitutes a bourgeois ideology Blackburn tells us nothing about the nature of ideology, science or reality and totally neglects the question of the methodological heterogeneity of the discipline. His purpose is clear, namely to reduce and simplify the issue to a loaded choice – sociology or Marxism.

Shaw's critique of Gouldner's *Crisis*

Shaw's general critique of sociology is very similar to Blackburn's in that the discipline is seen as part of bourgeois ideology, offering social control technologies capable of resolving the contradictions of the capitalist mode of production to the satisfaction of those with vested interests in the system. Like Blackburn's critique it concentrates primarily upon the political consequence of sociological work and merely glosses over the question of the methodological character and inadequacy of sociological practice. Again sociology is viewed as bourgeois ideology providing legitimation and reinforcement for the status quo. Ideologies for Shaw are 'world-views which, despite their partial and possibly critical insights, prevent us from understanding the society in which we live and the possibility of changing it' (1972, pp. 33–4). In these terms sociology is seen to be ideological because it is limited by the limits of bourgeois society. However, we may ask whether any theory or doctrine provides us with a comprehensive understanding of the society in which we live as well as the knowledge to change it. Shaw assumes that Marxism meets these requirements but he fails to offer the criteria by which he is able to distinguish between an ideological and a non-ideological understanding. Since he rejects the positivism of contemporary sociology as 'an ideology of empirical social research' which stresses 'the objective, external character of social reality and the naturalism of social study' (ibid., p. 35), the work of Weber for its 'cultural relativism and subjectivism' as well as phenomenology (as ahistorical) and ethnomethodology for abstracting individuals from 'systematic social relationships', it can only be assumed that his unexplicated Marxist analysis is predicated upon a method which avoids these limitations. The onus is on Shaw to display the method.

Gouldner's project, of which Shaw is critical, attempts to lay bare the relationship between social theory (including Marxism) and society as a first step towards a display of the impossibility of a 'pure' sociology. His intention is to work towards the construction of a reflexive and humane sociology. In that Gouldner's work demands a rejection of normal academic sociology and the undertaking of a new praxis there is some ground for agreement with Shaw. However, the salient difference rests with the fact that while for the former a liberating sociology is a possibility liberation for the latter can only be achieved at the expense of the discipline itself. While recognizing the importance and severity of Gouldner's critique of contemporary mainstream sociology Shaw's work manifests a concern that the discipline has not been completely rejected as totally bourgeois and repressive. For Gouldner there is still the possibility of doing a liberating sociology. In rejecting the optimism explicit in Gouldner's work Shaw's critique offers only one possibility for a radical sociology – 'it will have to go "back" to the crisis of nineteenth century bourgeois thought before it can solve its own problems' (1972, p. 39). In particular it will have to go back to Marx and to Marxism, which as Shaw argues is in one sense a sociology in that it seeks to explain the logic of capitalist society and the dynamic of the class struggle. However, such a re-examination will in Shaw's terms lead to the abolition of 'sociology in the specific sense'. This raises the crucial issue of the relationship between Marxism and sociology, implicit in Shaw's work.

The position adopted by Shaw on this vital question is that first the relationship between Marxism and sociology is not overt, and second that Marxism is not represented within sociology and cannot therefore be seen as sociological. Unfortunately Shaw does not clarify his Marxism, although Gouldner (1972) has attributed to him a Lukácsian orientation, nor does he address the general problem of the heterogeneity of Marxism. Consequently his statement concerning the relationship between Marxism and sociology is difficult to assess; much depends upon an answer to the question, 'Whose Marxism?' Shaw seems to ignore the fact that at one extreme Bukharin and Adler acknowledged the compatibility of Marxism with sociology, while at the other both Goldmann and Lukács have reacted to, been influenced by, and exerted influence upon, the development of sociology. He may consequently, as Gouldner has suggested in a reply to the critique, be said to be over-reacting to sociology, attempting to 'safeguard something he calls "Marxism" from subversion by something called "Radical Sociology"' (1972, p. 89). While disagreeing with the generality of Shaw's polemic against sociology his comments on the attitude of sociologists to Marx do have considerable validity. Not only has sociology extracted elements of Marx's thought from out of its context but it has also redefined and applied them in such a way as to misrepresent the original work. Hence within contemporary sociology Marx is frequently presented as a conflict theorist, attention being directed primarily towards his analysis of social class and social change, as well as alienation, ideology and the sociology of knowledge. These aspects are frequently referred to as Marxist sociology, a term representing very well the ambiguity, confusion and uncertainty surrounding the relationship between Marx's work and sociology. However, in conclusion, rather than agreeing with Shaw's prognosis of the disappearance of sociology, I believe we have to critically analyse both sociology and Marxian analysis so that we can understand the nature of their relationship and begin to construct a more comprehensive science of society. It is no more valid to dismiss sociology as bourgeois ideology than it is to assume that Marxism is merely dogma. What is required is a reconsideration of the relevance of Marxian analysis for sociology accompanied by an examination of the significance of developments within sociology for Marx's work.

Marxism and Marxist sociology

One of the difficulties which sociologists have with Marx is that, since the problems which concerned him and his contemporaries were not primarily, or only, sociological, it is difficult to translate his ideas directly into sociological language and hence to say where Marxist sociology stands (Rex, 1973, p. 162).

However, despite all the difficulties and ambiguities, sociologists still employ the term Marxist sociology, often refer to Marx's work as though interpretation is unproblematical and frequently evaluate Marxism as though it constitutes a unified body of knowledge. Now as far as Marxist sociology is concerned there are no grounds for assuming that it constitutes an homogeneous body of knowledge. On the contrary it represents a diffuse selection of topics and themes drawn out of context from Marx's writings and interpreted to provide compatibility with the sociological project in hand. As a result Marxist sociology displays only the selective substantive relevance of Marx's work for sociology, its methodological significance is lost. Three positions may be delineated concerning the relationship of Marxism to sociology:

(i) Polarization

(ii) Integration and assimilation

(iii) Convergence

The first position refers to Marxism and sociology as two distinct bodies of thought which are completely opposed and developing by way of reaction to one another. Within sociology this position manifests itself in criticisms of Marx's work and Marxist publications as ideological and biased. The emphasis in this type of criticism is frequently upon the social scientist's need to be value-free and objective, and in these terms Marx's work is found lacking and thus judged to be unscientific. The appropriate position within Marxism is that to be found in criticisms of sociology as bourgeois ideology, a criticism which stresses the inevitability of the disappearance of sociology along with the capitalist mode of production.

The second position is the most commonly occurring one within sociology, namely that Marx and Marxists have made a useful and significant contribution to the sociological project. The nature of their work is interpreted and transformed in such a way that Marxist sociology is frequently seen as a sub-system of sociology dealing with specifically critical issues such as inequality, industrial strife, social conflict and change, and it is in these respects therefore that Marx's work has become particularly relevant in sociology. Frequently this position rests upon the separation of the sociology from the philosophy, from the economics in Marx's work. Sociology becomes a synthesizing subject with Marx's work as one of the basic

27

ingredients. It must be stressed that the assimilation and integration of Marxism into sociology has not been completed; this may be confirmed by the continuing existence in sociology of interest in such dichotomies as consensus and conflict theory, sociologies of order and control, or order and change. Recognition of this unfinished task is often the first stage of an unnecessary attempt to develop a synthesis. A particularly salient example of this tendency can be found in van den Berghe's (1967) synthesis of dialectical and functionalist sociology, a work which treats Dahrendorf's *Class and Class Conflict in an Industrial Society* as an authoritative source for an understanding of the methodological basis of Marx's work. Another example appears in Lenski's (1966) monumental attempt to bring together in a meaningful way the diverse contributions of various theorists classified as functionalist or conflict in orientation, his intention being a theory of stratification incorporating both consensual and conflictual elements. In both cases an understanding of Marx as a conflict theorist constitutes a significant aspect of their synthesis and no attempt is made to address the adequacy of such an understanding. The reading of Marx's work implicit in the second position outlined here has given rise to Birnbaum's identification of a crisis in Marxist sociology. His account will be considered below.

The third and final position is that of a convergence between Marxism and sociology. This notion is predominant in the work of sociologists from eastern Europe in particular, although it does feature in the work of Gouldner and a minority of other western sociologists. Of these three positions, the second more nearly represents the present relevance of Marx's work within contemporary sociology and as such serves as a useful starting point for discussion. Most of the significant issues can be considered through a critical analysis of Birnbaum's work on Marxist sociology.

The crisis of Marxist sociology: Birnbaum's thesis

Two specific conditions are proposed by Birnbaum as indicators of the crisis; first that the reality to which the system of thought originally referred has changed so much that the concepts and categories are now inapplicable to the new situation, and second that the system of thought has developed to its limit, the categories being incapable of further transformation. These conditions are recognized to apply generally to any theoretical system in crisis; however, a third condition is noted as being peculiar to Marxism alone, namely its claim to represent a total system of thought, not merely a description but a prescription for action within society.

One difficulty with Birnbaum's subsequent analysis is the conceptual ambiguity surrounding his own use of the terms 'Marxist sociology' and 'Marxism'. Ironically Birnbaum not only recognizes that he has 'made rather free use of shorthand expressions like "Marxist sociology" and "bourgeois sociology" ' but furthermore states that he is aware of the significance of his over-simplification.

> I understand quite well that these are in fact shorthand, that the systems of thought at issue are complex and varied, that the two types of sociology interpenetrate, and that there are serious conflicts and great differences within each grouping as well as between them (1968, p. 348).

If Birnbaum had clarified this issue his subsequent discussion of the crisis within Marxist sociology would have been far more significant for assessing the contemporary relevance of Marx's work for sociology. However, the object of the exercise is not to judge Birnbaum's or related work at the semantic level; rather the above serves to illustrate merely one of the difficulties involved in determining what is in crisis. Unlike Gouldner's analysis in which the crisis for functionalism is spelt out, Birnbaum's leaves open to dispute the sense in which Marx's work or that of any of his followers may be said to be in crisis.

Three particular developments are recognized as creating a crisis for Marxist sociology:

(i) Changes in the class structure

(ii) Emergence of 'neo-capitalist' and socialist societies

(iii) Exploitation of the third world

It is argued that capitalism has not developed along the lines predicted by Marx, that polarization has not occurred, and furthermore that the working class has not become impoverished. Whilst acknowledging the continuing existence of disparities in wealth, income and access to particular social facilities, Birnbaum asserts that any analysis must now give recognition to the political efforts of the workers' movement and their relative success in assuring an increase in standards of living. Additionally the occupational structure has become more complex since Marx's time, with the growth of a middle strata of administrative, technical, maintenance and service workers, seemingly making obsolete the prediction of polarization, and raising serious doubts as to the relevance and validity of Marxist definitions of social class.

The second development precipitating a crisis for Marxist sociology concerns first the increased role of the state in capitalist society and second the emergence of socialist societies. In the case of the former, Birnbaum's position is that the state has become embedded in the economy co-ordinating and directing the development of the society, nationalizing strategically important industries, and reducing considerably the significance of private property. The increasing role of the state within the economy and the separation of

29

ownership and control are recognized as indicators of a change within capitalism sufficiently significant to enable us 'to speak of a "neo-capitalist" society type which has largely replaced the older type of capitalism' (1968, p. 350). Neo-capitalist society is a society for which Marx's analysis is deficient; hence the diagnosis of a crisis in Marxist sociology.[9] Related to this particular development is the emergence of societies in which industry and the economy are totally controlled by the state, where there is virtually no private ownership of the means of production. The existence of such socialist societies and the recent availability of sociological research confirming the reappearance of a class structure, inequalities and privilege within them, has according to Birnbaum cast doubt on the importance attributed to private property in Marx's work and that of Marxists in general (cf. Djilas, 1966; Lane, 1971; Parkin, 1971).

Finally there is the issue of exploitation and the third world, an aspect which Marx of course does not analyse in any significant detail and which in Birnbaum's terms raises problems for Marxist analysis. It is noted that, although the third world may be said to constitute a global proletariat and that the relationship between 'developed' and 'underdeveloped' societies may be recognized as exploitative, the industrial working classes of the developed societies are themselves accomplices in the exploitation of their counterparts in less developed societies. Furthermore he observes that the conflicts existing in these situations are nationalistic, focusing directly upon the liberation not of a class but of one nation from the domination of another, and that therefore Marxist analysis, depending as it does upon generalizations drawn from an analysis of a developed society, is inevitably deficient.

Birnbaum's treatment of these three developments implies the self-evident nature of their critical status for Marxist sociology. This is surprising in view of his recognition of his own free use of the term Marxist sociology, an admission implying knowledge of different readings of Marx as well as differences within Marxism. Finally the developments are themselves considered to have an unproblematic status, an assumption which is difficult to share in view of the ongoing debates both within and between Marxism and sociology on these particular issues. It is of course very clear that many significant changes have occurred since Marx's lifetime but the exact nature of the changes and their status vis-à-vis Marxian analysis is more problematic than Birnbaum allows. Marx's work cannot be assessed by a simple comparison of a 'prediction' with a description of a given empirical social situation, for social thought as meaning, value, belief and understanding is inherent in social situations, participates in their production and is transformed by their emergence.

Characteristically the developments considered thus far are substantive in nature, and indicative of the meaning of Marxist sociology for most sociologists. However, Birnbaum does recognize the importance of the relationship between Marxism and bourgeois thought and, in an albeit brief closing section, the significance of methodological issues. Now although he emphasizes the similarity of sources at the base of Marxism and bourgeois sociology, in particular Saint-Simon's work, he in general fails to account for the separate and mutually critical development of the respective systems of thought, in particular the detachment of empirical technique from a moral-political standpoint in sociology. The emulation of the natural sciences manifest in this particular stress on value-neutrality had consequences not only for the relationship between sociology and Marxism but also internally for the development of the latter system of thought. For example, within Marxism there were scholars who accepted the positivistic world-view and thus sought closer affinities with sociology (e.g. Max Adler). However, in general and particularly within sociology Marxism has been recognized either as a form of vulgar materialism, as with Weber's critique of 'orthodox' Marxism, or alternatively as a political ideology, a revolutionary doctrine devoid of any scientific status. A clear example of the latter view is to be found in the work of Durkheim:

Undoubtedly, even in its most utopian forms it never disdained the support of facts, and has even in more recent times increasingly taken on a definitely scientific turn of phrase. . . . Yet how can one fail to note the enormous disparity between the thin and meagre data it borrows from science and the extent of the practical conclusions that it draws – which are, nevertheless, the core of the system? (Giddens, 1972c, pp. 155–6).

And further, on Marx's *Capital*,

What an abundance of statistical data, historical studies and comparisons would be required to solve any one of the vast numbers of questions that are covered there! . . . The truth is that the facts and observations assembled by the theorists anxious to document their affirmations are hardly there except to give form to the arguments. The researches they have carried out were undertaken to establish a doctrine that they had previously conceived rather than the doctrine being a result of the research. . . . Socialism is not a science, a sociology in miniature—it is a cry of misery . . . (Giddens, 1972c, pp. 156 – 7).

Thus in the present, Marxist sociology has in a sense the worst of

31

both worlds; within sociology it is frequently regarded with suspicion as committed and ideological and therefore not value-free, objective or scientific; and within Marxism it is seen to be a compromise with bourgeois sociology, and therefore a form of revisionism. Finally, before considering some of the specific areas of sociology in which the crisis of Marxist sociology is apparent Birnbaum notes that a further indication of the authenticity of the crisis is the process of differentiation within Marxism. He states, 'We confront not a uniform set of Marxist ideas but a number of Marxist traditions differing from country to country and indeed sometimes from group to group within the same country' (1968, p. 353). Two comments can be made about such a statement. First, this is equally true of bourgeois sociology, to which Birnbaum has referred as an apparently unified system of thought. Second, and more importantly, the above statement occurs in a paper discussing the crisis in Marxist sociology and Marxism, in the course of which general reference has been made to the aforementioned as coherent and unified systems of thought. In fact, identification of a crisis rests for Birnbaum with the inability of the 'system of thought' to account for particular historical developments, an observation which, in view of his failure to address the question of the heterogeneity of Marxism and Marxist sociology, is of little significance. There is in Birnbaum's analysis therefore a contradiction between on the one hand the assumption that Marxist sociology constitutes an integrated and unified system of thought in a state of crisis because it is unable to account for specific historical developments, and the statement that another index of the crisis is the fragmentation and differentiation of the system of thought.

Birnbaum attempts to draw support for his crisis hypothesis from an analysis of specially selected areas of Marxist sociology, including the culture-material base relationship, Marxist anthropology, and methodology. In the first of these three areas he is critical of the existing sociological interpretation of the Marxian analysis of the base-superstructure relationship, observing that it is derived primarily from vulgar Marxism. According to Birnbaum the resurrection of the early works of Marx and Engels has led to a reorientation within Marxist theory, the result of which has been a reconsideration of the culture-material base relationship. However, despite the accuracy and relevance of many of Birnbaum's observations, one must question the contemporary nature of the controversy over the culture-base relationship, as this particular topic has preoccupied Marxists almost continuously; therefore contemporary discussion of this issue can hardly be interpreted as indicative of an impending crisis. Also this particular topic cannot be considered in isolation from a re-examination of the totality of Marx's work, a task made all the more urgent by the availability of apparently dissonant texts. For example it is clear that the Marx of the *Grundrisse*, in the course of preparing notes for his magnum opus, was concerned to consider the culture-material base relationship most cautiously, asserting for example 'that certain periods of the highest development of art stand in no direct connection to the general development of society, or to the material basis and skeleton structure of its organization' (1972, p. 44). Reorientations within Marxist theory of any kind appear to Birnbaum, however, as components of a crisis in that as innovations they are regarded as introducing assumptions and methods derived from other philosophical systems and methodologies, thus raising the important question of the possible transformation of Marxism and a concomitant reduction of its definitive status.[10] Of course the assumption that Marxism has a definitive status is in itself questionable when one considers the variety of interpretations and developments of Marx's work. What is not in dispute, however, is that the reorientations within Marxist analysis have led to the re-opening of many issues at the centre of the relationship between Marxian and sociological analysis.

The penultimate area, Marxist anthropology is controversial within both Marxist and sociological analysis. Specifically it concerns the ontological and anthropological assumptions implicit not only in Marx and Engels's own work but also in that of contemporary Marxists and sociologists. All sociological theories operate either implicitly or explicitly with a view of *man* which allows for the influence of social factors on the development of human potential, although the extent to which man is considered to be entirely a social product varies considerably from theory to theory. With Marx the basic assumption is that man is a sensual and active being, both the product and producer of history. As such one may distinguish between man existing within a determinate mode of production and potential man, the former being the victim of social forces and pressures, suffering from a condition of alienation resulting from a specific mode of production, and maintained by social institutions and historical processes. This is man the product of history, man incapable of seeing either the possibility or the presence of his role as the producer of history. On the other hand potential man is the sensual and active being, with the capacity to be able to do as Marx expressed, somewhat romantically, 'one thing today and another tomorrow, ... hunt in the morning, fish in the afternoon, rear cattle in the evening, criticise after dinner' (Marx and Engels, 1970, p. 53). This is a view of man which allows for the possibility of a communist society, one in which there is more free time and leisure, where the possibilities for human development provide for the realization of man's potential. However, only through liberation from the alienating capitalist mode of production is it possible for man to realize his potential and this according to Birnbaum will only materialize with the development of a revolutionary praxis. The neglect of the development of a revolutionary praxis according to Birnbaum's analysis stems from two factors: first, Marx and Engels's greater preoccupation with the social institutions and historical processes maintaining alienation, and second, the emergence of an implicit theory of human malleability. As Birnbaum notes,

> In the absence of revolutionary Praxis, and in the light of the evidence of the corruption of much of the revolutionary Praxis undertaken hitherto, a despairing conviction has possessed Marxist sociologists: men are capable of assimilating any injury and any insult (1968, p. 371).

For Birnbaum the consequences of the 'malleability hypothesis' are first that the unilinear theory of liberation requires modification and second that Marxists must reconsider their view of the significance of work. If one accepts the malleability hypothesis it is then necessary to allow for the fact that there are differences between human cultures and historical societies and consequently that no single pattern of human liberation can be postulated. From this point of view each historical configuration is recognized as producing a distinctive human type making necessary a revision of the Marxist view of man. Consideration of this latter aspect forces one to confront the second of Birnbaum's consequences, the significance of work in Marxist theory. Marxist sociology according to Birnbaum is handicapped by an acceptance of the romantic notion that work constitutes the privileged form of human self-expression, and that in view of the innovations and changes within society it is now necessary to revise Marxist anthropology based as it is on the image of homo faber. It is argued by Birnbaum that Marx and Engels envisaged man's liberation from the deformations associated with 'machine work . . . [in so far as they envisaged it concretely at all] in something like the assumption by every man of the totality of work functions fragmented in the division of labour' (1968, p. 372), and that since developments of the productive forces under the capitalist mode of production have changed the nature of work that a new view of the problem is essential to further progress in Marxist sociology.

Although one may accept along with Birnbaum that the productive forces have changed since Marx's time and that in turn the nature of work is now rather different one cannot accept his account of Marx and Engels's hopes for man's liberation. The implication of Birnbaum's argument is a return to the status quo ante, a reversal of the division of labour, and a recombination of all the formerly fragmented functions with each man the master of all tasks. Yet reading Marx, it is apparent that not only was he aware of the changes imminent within the productive process of his time but also of the future changes necessary to provide for the possibility of human liberation. For Marx a society in which man might be free from alienation was one in which labour was necessarily no longer an essential part of the productive process, where the creation of wealth would depend on the development of science and technology. Rather than offering a romantic notion of work Marx, in the *Grundrisse*, asserts that there must be a reduction of the necessary labour time to a minimum, enabling all members of society to develop 'their education in the arts, sciences etc., thanks to the free time and means available to all' (1972, p. 142). Contrary to Birnbaum it may be claimed therefore that Marxist anthropology is perfectly adequate for understanding the contemporary nature of work although it is accepted that a restricted reading of Marx's writings might lead to Birnbaum's criticisms. As with the crisis surrounding the analysis of the culture-material base relationship, the nature of man is controversial not only for Marxian but also sociological analysis and will therefore feature as an element in the discussion to follow.

Finally Birnbaum considers a methodological issue which appears to be critical for Marxist sociology, concerning specifically the concept of praxis. As such he touches upon the heart of the matter, the relationship between Marxism, Marxist sociology, and academic sociology. For Marxism, praxis refers directly to the unity of thought and action, to the fusion of theory and practice, to action based upon knowledge gained not merely for understanding but in order to change the world. Thus praxis involves an anticipation and apprehension of the future, the goal being the eventual abolition of the division of labour and the fulfilment of human potential. As such, praxis is a concept which implies that a totally detached or value-free and objective science of society is impossible and therefore represents a critical concept for sociology. Birnbaum argues that the concept presents even greater difficulty for Marxist sociology because it is dependent for its very existence upon the continued practice of sociology which in turn is a consequence of the division of labour. Hence for many Marxists the idea of a Marxist sociology is a contradiction in terms as it is a product of the very division of labour within knowledge which through revolutionary praxis will be abolished. Equally Marxist sociologists have the problem of reconciling empirical or positive components of their work with other aspects of Marxism critical of the reifying and objectivist tendencies of sociology.

Birnbaum concludes that the crisis of Marxist sociology in its methodological aspects is part of the general crisis of the social sciences. Specifically this crisis is twofold. First, the social sciences were initially created to apprehend human history in full whereas a total capitulation to the scientific division of labour has prevented this, leading to a fragmented description of a fragmented reality. Second, social science through the division of labour, the separation of mental from manual labour and the concomitant monopoly of knowledge, along with the employment by social scientists of positivist approaches to the study of social reality, has become another instrument of domination rather than liberation. Thus the methodological crisis of Marxist sociology reflects the parallel debate within sociology crystallized in the critique of positivism and the concern with reflexivity.

The lessons to be drawn from Birnbaum's analysis are simple yet important. First, any discussion of Marxism, Marxist or academic sociology, must proceed from an open acceptance of their individual heterogeneity; the question 'Whose Marxism?', and for that matter 'Which sociology?', is crucial. Without such guidance one cannot begin to evaluate assertions that assumptions foreign to Marxism have been introduced, thereby reducing its definitive status. Assuming Birnbaum's awareness of the differences between Althusserian and Lukácsian Marxism, as well as the difficulties with interpretations of Marx's work, it is surprising to find in his analysis statements referring to Marxism as an homogeneous body of knowledge. Second, it is apparent that the problems of a Marxist sociology, in particular those of determinism and determination, the nature of man, and the concept of praxis, can only be resolved through a working out of similar difficulties within academic sociology. In this respect Gouldner's case for a convergence between Marxism and academic sociology is worthy, at the methodological level, of a qualified acceptance.

The convergence of Marxism and sociology

Gouldner's work on Marxism is located first in *The Coming Crisis of Western Sociology* and second in an essay published in *For Sociology*. (Gouldner (1974) has subsequently developed *The Two Marxisms* by elaborating upon the tensions between a Marxism$_1$, emphasis being upon the importance of socio-economic structures, and a Marxism$_2$, emphasis on the importance of consciousness and will, etc.) It is in the former work that he is most concerned with the relationship between Marxism and sociology and hence this must constitute the focal point of the discussion although the latter text dealing with a defence of sociology and an account of the division within Marxism will also warrant consideration. For

Gouldner, Marxism and academic sociology are both recognized to have developed from what is termed 'Western sociology'. In other words, the sociology of Karl Marx and Comte's pure sociology are both seen to be derived from Saint-Simon.

One part of sociology, 'Marxism', moved eastward and became at length, after World War I, the official social science of the then new Soviet Union. The other part which I will call 'Academic Sociology', moved westward and came to a different kind of fruition within American culture (1971, p. 20).

From such a position, Gouldner commences to track the separate paths of development of the 'two sociologies', the growth of their distinctive intellectual paradigms and opposition to one another, and then later their convergence. The assumption by Gouldner that Marxism represents the sociology of Karl Marx is in itself very surprising, revealing a slack use of terms which later contributes to the confusion over a convergence between academic sociology and Marxism. Had Gouldner explicitly acknowledged the problem of distinguishing Marxism, academic sociology and Marxist sociology from one another then his account would be more valuable. In consequence one is forced to read between the lines to comprehend the significance of any apparent convergence between Marxism and sociology, remembering to allow for the heterogeneity of the respective bodies of knowledge and the existence of a 'buffer state' in Marxist sociology.[11]

Nevertheless Gouldner's account although suffering from many limitations is still of interest, specifically because of his identification of three aspects of a crisis for Marxism, two of which are recognized as central to the 'convergence with sociology' hypothesis. The three aspects are:

(1) The growth of neo-Marxisms
(2) The ideological function of Marxism
(3) The academization of Marxism

Gouldner argues that the designation of Marxism as the official theory and ideology of the Soviet State and Communist Europe has had the consequence of blunting its critical impulse, critiques of communist states and movements no longer being possible. Second, the growing détente between the USSR and the West is recognized to have created an additional need for internal stabilization within the former, and thus to have brought about a further dwindling of the critical and revolutionary component of Marxism. In each case Gouldner is referring explicitly to Marxism in the USSR and other communist countries, and does not distinguish between what may be described as official Marxism and prevalent alternatives. Certainly it cannot merely be assumed that crises and developments in Soviet

37

Marxism are common to Marxism in general, although it may be argued that the heterogeneity of the latter has increased partly in response to the rigidities associated with the former doctrine. According to Gouldner a consequence of developments in both internal and international politics has been the need for a sociology oriented towards the problem of the integration of society and that this has opened the way for a convergence between Marxism and functionalism. In particular Parsonianism is identified as especially 'congenial to those who, like some in the Soviet Bloc, are more concerned with the problem of stabilising their society' (1971, p. 457). Thus Gouldner asserts that many Marxists in the Soviet Union and elsewhere in the Communist Bloc are showing a great interest in academic sociology. While this is partially correct it does not allow for the different degrees of freedom experienced by sociologists in the Communist Bloc, Polish and Yugoslavian sociologists being much freer from state control than their Soviet colleagues. Furthermore, although there has been a growth of sociology in the Soviet Union under the guidance of the Institute of Concrete Social Research and its first director Alexei M. Rumyantsev (now dismissed), its development has been consistently controlled by the party and subject to its ideology. For example, Rumyantsev was replaced as director early in 1973 in a reorganization intended to make sociologists more responsible to party officials. Furthermore politicians in the Central Committee demanded that the word 'concrete' be eliminated from the institute's name, a sign that its research should be less empirical and more congruent with the official ideology. In addition, in 1970 the Academy of Social Sciences of the Central Committee produced a report condemning a sociologist for ideologically deficient work, for departures from the social-philosophical foundations of Marxism. Finally, one other unusual aspect of sociology's position in the Soviet Union is that many of its findings are kept secret, the institute distinguishing between 'open' and 'closed' bulletins. Thus while one may assert that empirical sociology is all but established in Eastern Europe it must be remembered that this applies more to Poland and Yugoslavia, the Soviet Union being far behind this vanguard.

Therefore, although Gouldner's account of the emergence of a non-theoretical 'concrete' sociology heavily dependent upon the positivist frame of reference and oriented towards the demands of the state is partially correct, it does not address the important differences between sociology in the USSR and the West, nor the significance of the differences within the Communist Bloc. Furthermore, a more general limitation concerns the shift in focus in Gouldner's analysis, from Marxism in the earlier part of *Crisis* to Soviet Marxism in particular in the concluding sections. Although this is explicit in his account, criticism is justified in that there are frequent general references to the 'Crisis of Marxism' based purely upon the analysis of a specific Marxism, namely the ideology of the Soviet State. Where the context is more general, as with his listing of problems confronting the Marxist thesis, for example the 'new' middle class, the separation of management from ownership, and the absence of increasing misery for the proletariat, or where referring to the growth of neo-Marxism, the analysis is deficient in not offering an account of either the answers, solutions, or interpretations offered by Marxist scholars to these problems or the consequences for the relationship with sociology of any increase in heterogeneity. In practice Gouldner's account of the crisis and later convergence of sociology and Marxism becomes a specific account of functionalism in the USA and Marxism in the USSR and their respective responses to demands for policy-oriented, socially relevant social science. In many respects his terms of reference lead one to expect no more and yet frequently he makes more general claims for his analysis, seemingly referring to sociology and Marxism in toto.

His work on *The Two Marxisms* (1973) is a development of brief references to the increasing heterogeneity of Marxism to be found in *Crisis* and other essays. There is in this work a continuation of the crisis theme in that Marxism is held to be divided into basic schools, 'scientific' and 'critical' respectively. The former include Marxist scholars who accept the view that Marx was a scientist and that Marxism is a science, for example, Althusser, Poulantzas, Godelier and della Volpe. Opposed to these are the advocates of critical Marxism, stressing the continuities between Marx and Hegel, the young and the old Marx. Included in this group are Lukács, Gramsci, Sartre, Goldmann, and the 'Frankfurt School'. Now although Gouldner offers a lucid and interesting account of their respective differences, he unfortunately does not seek to relate their contributions to the parallel division within sociology between the positivist-empiricist and phenomenological orientations.[12] Only through consideration of this issue does it become possible to arrive at a full understanding of the relationship between Marxism and sociology and a possible re-assessment of the relevance of Marxian analysis for sociological inquiry.

Summary

A critical reading of analyses and accounts of Marxism and sociology provides a very clear understanding of the reasons for the idea of a Marxist sociology being surrounded by controversy and ambiguity. Rarely is any attempt made to address the issues in their full complexity or to recognize the open-endedness and interrelationships of the crises confronting Marxist and academic sociology. Significantly, as yet, few attempts have been made to consider the consequences of the critique of positivism within sociology, or the concomitant emergence of a phenomenological sociology, for the relationship of Marxist to academic sociology or Marxian to sociological analysis (cf. Horton, 1971). However, the resurrection of the debate over the 'young' and the 'old' Marx, and the controversy over the question of the 'unity' or 'break' in his work, has provided a context within which a long overdue reconsideration of the relevance of Marxian methodology for sociological analysis can begin. Until sociologists reconsider the relevance and significance of Marxian analysis for sociology, a step requiring a change in orientation away from the substantive and descriptive aspects of his work towards those of methodological import, it is unlikely that we will be able to develop further our scientific understanding of the social world or adequately conceptualize the interrelationship between the problems confronting Marxism and sociology and the contradictions within society.

Sociological readings of Marx's work have usually drawn upon or emphasized its substantive significance for sociology and where this has not been the case Marxian analysis has been crudely classified as functionalist or conflict oriented. In fact within sociology there is not one but several Marxs, the existence of which lends considerable credence to the diagnosis of a crisis for Marxist sociology. Of course this 'crisis' must be dissociated from the source material; it cannot merely be assumed that Marxian analysis is in crisis because sociologists drawing upon Marx's work and Marxist analyses have constructed a body of knowledge which is ambiguous, internally inconsistent, or theoretically and methodologically sterile. The way forward is through a critical assessment of the classification and development of Marx's work within both Marxist and academic sociology, the intention being to re-open the question of the nature and meaning of a science of society in order to display the relevance of a Marxian analysis to the problems associated with a sociological analysis of the social world.

To achieve this end it is necessary not only to re-examine the sociological interpretation of Marx, and consider the significance of the emergence of 'radical' sociologies such as ethnomethodology and phenomenological sociology, but also to reject the fragmentation of Marx's work into history, philosophy, economics, sociology and political science. The rejection of a 'fragmented' Marx raises the question of the underlying unity of his work and the extent of its compatibility with a sociological analysis far removed from the Comtean positivism of which Marx was so critical. The essential unity of Marx's critique of political economy and the capitalist mode of production is inherent in the constant thematic presence of a critical analysis of both the reificatory nature of 'scientific' and common-sense understandings of social reality and the underlying social relationships which produce reification. His is an analysis which locates the knowledge and beliefs manifest in a given discipline in the context of the historical stage of development of the particular mode of production. That is, it seeks to account for the creation of knowledge, the belief in the universal natural status of an in fact socially created order by way of a consideration of the relationship between existence and consciousness, the separation of mental and manual labour, and the increasing alienation inherent in the capitalist mode of production. As Bottomore noted of Marx, 'His own science of society . . . is closer to the present concerns of sociology than is the theory which gave its name to the discipline' (1963, p. 30).

Marx the sociologist revisited

Having partially dismissed earlier in this chapter the false identification of Marx as a sociologist it is now necessary to reconsider the judgment on rather different terms. Although Marx's writings are addressed to political economy and not sociology his method and critique are of direct significance for sociologists attempting to achieve a scientific understanding of the social world. Marx analyses not only the nature of the social world, society and social relationships, but also the relationship between scientific and common-sense accounts and the underlying social context. This, however, does not make Marx a sociologist, for the essence of his work is still considerably different from the predominant contemporary sociological approaches to the study of social relationships and society. Yet there seems to be a growing recognition and realization among sociologists of the significance of Marx's work for sociology. Undoubtedly this has not always been the case; for example Parsons's seminal text *The Structure of Social Action* (1937) is based primarily on the work of Pareto, Durkheim, and Weber, relatively little discussion being devoted to the relevance of Marx's work. Timasheff's *Sociological Theory* (1961), a work offering an account of the discipline's nature and growth, devotes complete sections to Pareto, Weber, Durkheim, Cooley and Thomas, whereas Marx is dismissed in the course of a few brief paragraphs as an economic determinist. However, times have changed, now. 'No one . . . who set out to repeat Parsons' exercise by examining the major theoretical preoccupations of modern sociologists, could afford to ignore the marked revival of interest in the original work of Marx and Engels which has occurred over the past twenty years' (Banks, 1970, p. 1). The nature of the revival of interest in Marx's work has in general, however, prevented much progress towards a more comprehensive understanding of the problems confronted in attempting a scientific study of society, for the emphasis has frequently been on 'empirical tests' of selected statements extracted out of context, or alternatively upon historical and textual accounts of his writings, the intention being finally to reveal 'what was really meant'. In some respects textual analysis is necessary; first, to determine the location and meaning of newly available works and second, to provide some kind of evidence for unsubstantiated assertions. However, for sociology the requirement at this time must be an assessment of the methodological and analytical relevance of Marx's work, a task which must begin with the methodological controversy at the heart of the discipline.

Within contemporary sociology methodological interest has been focused upon two significant and interrelated issues:

  (i) The nature of social reality

  (ii) The relationship between sociology and social reality

The nature of social reality

The question of the nature of social reality is basic to the work of any sociologist, it constitutes the most important domain assumption. As such it defines not only the character of the subject matter but also the appropriate methods to be employed in studying any given social phenomenon. Within contemporary sociology these issues, inherent in the Naturwissenschaften–Geisteswissenschaften debate, appear at the centre of the controversy between positivist and phenomenological sociologists, the former treating social phenomena and social reality as comparable to natural phenomena, the latter through their critique of this established sociology, offering an alternative definition of social phenomena which stresses their qualitative differences from natural phenomena, social reality being depicted as continuously constructed and produced by individuals in the course of interaction.

The relationship between sociology and social reality

This issue has generally been addressed either in terms of the value-freedom versus value-commitment debate or alternatively with reference to the distinctions between pure and applied sociology on the one hand, and social engineering on the other. In this work, assessing the relevance of Marxian analysis for sociology I will draw attention in particular to the socio-culturally situated character of sociological work, the relationship between knowledge and interests, consciousness and existence, and theory and practice. This does not prevent sociological work from being scientific; on the contrary only by recognizing the inevitable location of sociology and sociological work in determinate yet transitory socio-historical contexts will it be possible for us to reflect upon the grounds of our understandings and hence to arrive at knowledge of the dialectical nature of social reality and the relationship of sociological work to social reality.

In the following chapters I will therefore attempt, through an examination of the above issues, to address the question of the methodological and analytical importance of Marxian analysis for sociology. Consideration will be given to an analysis of contemporary sociological readings of Marx's work to illustrate the source of some of the main misunderstandings surrounding the topic of Marxian analysis in sociology. Additionally the question of an 'alternative' sociological approach, phenomenological sociology, will be examined in so far as it has provided an important non-Marxist critique of the reificatory nature of positivist-empiricist sociological approaches. Finally I will discuss the significance of two developments, phenomenological Marxism and critical theory, both of which have emerged from Marxian analysis and constitute alternatives to a conventional sociological approach to a scientific analysis of the social world.

2 Sociological readings of Marx

The continuing reappearance of Marx's work both as a critique of and resource for sociological work is a testimony to the impetus which has been derived by sociologists from writings which do not explicitly address sociological issues and problems per se. Indeed this is one of the unchanging characteristics of sociological work, its dependence upon interpretations of the classics, the drawing upon readings of Marx's, Weber's or Durkheim's work as resources for sociological writing. Latterly, however, the intellectual base of the discipline has been developed by the emergence of phenomenological and ethnomethodological alternatives to conventional sociology, predicated upon existentialist and phenomenological philosophy. Although to some extent continuous with Weberian and interpretive sociology these 'alternative' approaches denote a radical departure from conventional sociological procedure.

Any familiarity with sociological analyses or descriptions of the vast stock of classical sociological writings will reveal the considerable range and variety of readings and interpretations. This is especially evident in the case of Marx's work both within sociology and Marxist thought. My interest here lies primarily in attempting to provide some clarification of the limitations and problems of particular sociological readings of Marx's work.

Reading Marx

It cannot be assumed that all sociologists have read or do read Marx's work. More often than not it appears that Marx's work is 'read' through the writings of others who pre-package it for sociological consumption. Indeed for most of the sociological community a 'second-hand' reading is an inevitability consequent upon the cultural barriers of language and time. Hence although the desirability of Althusser's reading of the French translation supplemented by the 'original' German Marx may not be disputable the possibility may, for many, be remote. In view of this we ought as sociologists to try to be aware of what reading of Marx we are guilty. To do this we must critically address the limitations inherent in the sociological interpretation and reconstruction of Marx's work. Given the problems of translation, the intrusion of secondary sources making available differing interpretations and readings, plus the predilection within sociology to treat Marx's work as a resource from which hypotheses, data or concepts may be extracted at will, the existence of several Marxs within the discipline is understandable. As Althusser has noted, 'The intellectual "technocracy" lives by this kind of confusion, securing its full time employment with it; for nothing takes so long to resolve as a problem which does not exist or has been badly posed' (Althusser and Balibar, 1970, p. 184).

The reading offered here is one seeking to avoid the failure of so many sociological readings of Marx, namely the neglect of any critical analysis of the methodological assumptions inherent in the sociological adoption of specific aspects of Marxian analysis. Marx's work represents a critique not only of political economy but also of the reificatory nature of social science in general. A sociological reading of Marx must therefore produce a critique of sociology. My reading is more guilty than Althusser's in that it cannot guarantee to 'divulge the undivulged event'; at best it attempts to provide for the possibility of inquiring into the analytical and theoretical problems at the heart of sociology. Marx's works are to be read critically and theoretically for possible sociological inference. They are to be analysed and discussed in order not only to promote a reconsideration of the received sociological interpretation of Marxian analysis but also to facilitate a re-examination of sociological inquiry and its attendant problems.

Four specific sociological readings of Marx's writings will be addressed. They are:

(1) Marx the conflict theorist
(2) Marx the functionalist
(3) Marx the determinist
(4) Marx the action theorist

1 Marx the conflict theorist

Perhaps the most common understanding and portrayal of Marx's work within sociology is as 'conflict theory'. Typically it is presented as the 'radical' alternative to the 'conservative' consensus theory derived from functionalism, thus providing for the possibility of such dichotomies as coercion-integration, control-order, consensus-conflict and change-stability.[1] The focus in this section will be upon Dahrendorf's (1959) reading of Marx in so far as it has frequently served as the sociological reference point for understanding the relevance of Marxian analysis not only for contemporary society but also for the practice of scientific sociology.

Dahrendorf's treatment of Marx rests squarely within the positivist-empiricist tradition of academic sociology. His explicit purpose is to test particular propositions in Marx's analysis, specifically those in the area of class and class conflict, in the light of changes in industrial societies since the end of the nineteenth century. Such a project relies not only upon an assumption of the unproblematical nature of operationalizing Marx's work but also rests upon an implicit faith in the self-evident nature of the empirical reality to which the work is purported to refer and against which it is tested. For Dahrendorf the reading of Marx's work is not a daunting task, being as he states a 'thorough reader . . . [there] is no reason for despair' (1959, p. 8). Nor is there apparently a need to address the question of how the reading is accomplished. Even the task of writing the unfinished chapter on class appears to be regarded as a feasible project unlikely to inflict violence upon the original text. Dahrendorf's neglect of these issues, and his failure to address the problems which arise from them, is indicative of his disdain for the 'pathetically preliminary discussion of the possibility of a sociological science' (ibid., p. ix).

Although concerned to scientifically test Marx's work Dahrendorf provides no account of either his concept of science or the procedures to be employed in the testing of given propositions. What is patently clear therefore is that his work is predicated upon the assumption of an unproblematic scientific method common to the community of sociologists and hence, as part of a shared stock of knowledge, not requiring explication. As a result his sparse references to science become particularly interesting and important, revealing his dependence upon a specific conception of social science as the grounds for his critical reading and rejection of Marx's work. For Dahrendorf the terms 'theory', 'empirical test', 'refutation' and 'science' are used in sociology in the strict sense of the methodological characteristics of an empirical discipline. He states that,

At least logically, physics, philosophy, and sociology are subject to the same laws – whatever may render one or other of these disciplines empirically preferable in terms of exactness. I cannot see why it should not be at least desirable to try to free sociology . . . and weld it into an exact social science with precisely – ideally, of course, mathematically – formulated postulates, theoretical models, and testable laws (ibid., p. ix).

In Dahrendorf's terms there are therefore no particularly crucial or distinctive characteristics of social science in general nor sociology in particular which make necessary any discussion of the question of methodology. His infrequent references to science are assertive and affirm that sociological method should be considered as uncontroversial. Now although Dahrendorf is reasonably clear about his adoption of Popper's conception of science proceeding by way of falsification, he fails to attend to the equally significant question of the discovery of 'facts'. On the question of when empirical evidence is deemed significant to the refutation of a given theory and how it is to be harvested Dahrendorf is silent. Indeed his satisfaction with ad hoc examples to 'confirm' the rejection of propositions and hypotheses is most unsatisfactory. One clear example of this occurs in the course of his consideration of the validity of Marx's analysis of revolution. Accepting for the moment the adequacy of his reading of Marx on this topic attention may be given to the question of the empirical testing of a given proposition.

Dahrendorf focuses upon the assertion that may be found in Marx's work that the class struggle will intensify as the condition of the proletariat deteriorates, eventually producing a revolution. This particular hypothesis is dismissed as a result of an observation that revolutions and revolts do not occur when conditions have reached an extreme level but on the contrary once the extremity and the associated lethargy have passed. By way of empirical evidence he notes that 'The revolts and revolutions in the recent history of Eastern Europe (June 17, 1953; Poznan, Hungary) have confirmed this hypothesis quite convincingly' (ibid., p. 132, n. 10). Remarkably, Dahrendorf fails to consider the special problems posed for an 'application' of any reading of Marx's work on capitalist society to societies in Eastern Europe which have adopted Marxism in practice as an ideology (cf. Marcuse, 1971). The complexity of the relationship between events in Eastern Europe and the role of Marxism in the construction, legitimation and critical rejection of social conditions and relationships is totally neglected by Dahrendorf. The empirical evidence he draws upon apparently requires no sociological explication or analysis; its status as exemplar is regarded as self-evident. Given Dahrendorf's clear concern for scientificity it is exceedingly strange that no consideration is given to the problem of observation and interpretation of such controversial social events. Additionally the analysis he offers is subject to limitation in so far as the conceptual differences between a revolt and a revolution remain unaddressed. Too much can be made of this one example, yet it does serve to indicate the ad hoc nature of Dahrendorf's procedures for 'testing' the sociological propositions and hypotheses which he claims to have extracted from Marx's work.

A further controversial aspect of Dahrendorf's work follows directly from his emulation of Schumpeter's (1961) unwarranted reduction of Marx's work to sociology, economics and philosophy. It is ironic that Schumpeter should accept uncritically the prior existence of specialized social sciences as the basis of his reading of Marx, for the Marxian project represents a critique of the very division of labour from which the contemporary social sciences have emerged. Why Schumpeter neglected this central issue is difficult to understand; the answer probably lies in the institutionalized nature of the scientific enterprise, in particular the consequences which follow the advance of the division of labour within the social sciences. Habermas (1974a) has argued that as a result of the disengagement of sociological and economic elements from a basically philosophical framework 'three basic themes are from the outset excluded from rational examination' (ibid., p. 205). These are:

> The prior integration of the economic and sociological aspects, separated analytically, to form the unity of one single object, the society as totality; second, the dialectical conception of society as a historical process is also excised, a process which in the conflict of specifiable tendencies drives forward to produce one situation out of the other; and finally, a relation between theory and praxis which Marxism explicitly incorporates into reflection (ibid., p. 205).

Consequently Schumpeter reduces Marxian analysis to the status of a positivist-empiricist science and neglects the critical and practical orientation of the Marxian theory of society. Similar limitations and omissions can be located in Dahrendorf's analysis. In his case the primary distinction to be employed in assessing Marx's work is the distinction between hypotheses and theories which permit empirical test, which by way of empirical observation may be falsified, and theories which cannot be empirically tested. The latter which Dahrendorf depicts as irrefutable in principle are termed philosophical' and include statements of the order that capitalist society is the last class society, or that communist society leads to a total realization of human freedom. Propositions of the former kind, to be regarded as sociological, include those concerning the relationships between social classes, class conflict and structural change.

Dahrendorf argues that whereas sociological propositions may be falsified or rejected by the tools of science, philosophical propositions can only be denied or disputed, not refuted scientifically. The question which arises here is whether the sociological-philosophical distinction is appropriate. However, perhaps more significant than the conceptualization of the distinction is the question of its very legitimacy, for it would appear that the distinction between the two sets of propositions hangs not so much on the actual availability of empirical material refuting specific propositions as upon the impossibility of 'imagining' empirical data which could falsify propositions regarded in consequence as 'philosophical'. Any interest that is aroused by the nature of the philosophical-sociological distinction and the role of 'imagination' in Dahrendorf's work is thwarted by his failure to reflect upon the social structuring and construction of his own and other sociologists' imaginations. In contrast Wright Mills (1970) addresses the question of the sociological imagination directly, stating that it 'enables us to grasp history and biography and the relations between the two within society' (p. 22). Whereas Dahrendorf assumes sociological science to be unproblematical Wright Mills treats sociology as a discipline moving in three directions towards a theory of history, a systematic theory of 'the nature of man and society' and 'empirical studies of contemporary social facts and problems'. For Wright Mills the meaning of sociology is an issue worthy of discussion rather than dismissal and the question of science is considered to be vital not only for the development of sociological thought but for the social world as a whole. He argues that the physical and biological sciences are being displaced as 'the source of serious reflection and popular metaphysics in Western societies' by the social and psychological sciences, in particular that the 'sociological imagination is becoming . . . the major common denominator of our cultural life' (ibid., p. 21).

The contrast with Dahrendorf's work is stark, for Wright Mills treats science in its cultural context, recognizes its limitations, addresses critically the 'bureaucratic techniques which inhibit social inquiry' and attempts to develop a programme for fulfilling the promise of social science. Dahrendorf's project is explicitly focused upon specifically delimited substantive issues and problems. Although his project is therefore not primarily concerned with methodological questions, in making a distinction between sociological and philosophical propositions in Marx's work the onus is on him to explicate the nature of his conception of science, sociology and the relationship between theory and empirical data. To be fair, in his later works some of these issues are indeed considered, interestingly in a more open and less conclusive fashion. For example in his postscript to *Homo Sociologicus* (1973) Dahrendorf clearly recognizes that sociologists are far from agreeing that the discipline is an empirical science. Rather it is acknowledged that there are many sociologists who deny such a possibility whilst others admitting

49

of the possibility stress the role of sociology as interpretive analysis. Hence for some sociologists the 'distinction between testable and speculative statements' is unrecognized and consequently unproblematical for their 'reading' of Marx. Dahrendorf's later work is in fact sympathetic to the perspective of 'philosophical sociologists', there being an explicit recognition of their significant presence within, and service to, European sociology.

Nevertheless in his important text on Marx Dahrendorf treats the question of the relationship between theory and empirical observation in a manner consistent with other sociological works which accept as unproblematical the natural-social science continuum. Science for Dahrendorf is essentially an empirical project and yet he provides no account of the grounds upon which observations or data are based, nor guidance as to how Marx's 'sociology' was dissected from the total work. His conception of social science is situated squarely within the positivist-empiricist tradition representing 'an attempt to connect many loose threads into a net with which we can "catch" an important sector of social reality' (1959, p. 119).

The critique of Marx

Five major indices of social change are regarded as significant since the end of the nineteenth century and critical for Marx's analysis. They are:
(1) The transition from capitalist to industrial society
(2) The change in ownership and control
(3) The increasing differentiation of the working class and the rise of the middle class
(4) Increases in social mobility
(5) The institutionalization of class conflict
The mere fact that these changes are not recognized to be uncontroversial within sociology, and for some not problematical for Marx's analysis in any case, complicates any evaluation of Dahrendorf's work. For example it cannot be accepted that, 'It emerges clearly from Marx's writings, and has never been doubted by his interpreters, that the concept of revolution meant for him the sudden and rapid upheaval of a social structure' (ibid., p. 130). Not only may it be argued that this is inadmissible from the standpoint of Marx's own writings (although what he meant will remain a matter for speculation) but what is more important is that the issue constitutes a topic of debate for his interpreters and is not a matter that may merely be resolved through assertion. In Marx's work the meaning of the concept of revolution is not especially clear; however, in Dahrendorf's writings it is even more vague and

ambiguous, frequently being used synonymously with the concept of revolt. It is reasonably clear that Marx was concerned among other things with both revolutionary and social change in general. However, in Marx the concept of revolution is used to refer not only to sudden or rapid change but also to gradual and peaceful change. It is employed in references to the constant and continual changing of the means of production, the so-called revolutionary bourgeois mode of production, as well as to denote major and important qualitative changes in the very nature of a given mode of production, as for example in the transition from feudalism to capitalism.

It is indeed far from clear that a significant qualitative change could only be achieved rapidly, and violently. Rather there are grounds for believing that Marx entertained the possibility of gradual and progressive changes. For example Fischer notes that although Marx frequently referred to the necessity for 'the peoples' revolution to smash the machinery of the State, he also stressed the 'possibility of a peaceful revolution in America, England and Holland' (1973, p. 132). Similarly Lobkowicz (1967) notes that 'one may object that when speaking in 1843 of a "revolution" Marx did not have in mind a violent uprising. . . . We shall even see that "revolution" never unambiguously implied violence for Marx' (p. 283). Implicit in this position is the view that for Marx human practice was itself necessarily revolutionary, in other words that men and women are constantly involved in transforming the social world, acting purposively, changing their environments and achieving 'new' (re-)admirations or understandings of their social relationships independently of engagement in violent struggle. However, Dahrendorf's reading of Marx allows only for violent, revolutionary and rapid change, and excludes altogether from consideration the recognition by Marx of the possibility that change may occur through the extension of social democracy and legislation. In this way the development of the caricature of Marx as a conflict theorist begins to take form.

Oblivious to the inherent unity of the Marxian project and its relationship to sociology as a critique, Dahrendorf focuses exclusively upon class and class conflict in Marxian analysis and attempts to extract out of context sociological concepts, hypotheses and propositions from Marx's work on the capitalist mode of production. Adoption of a 'conflict theory' reading and the preoccupation with social class to the exclusion of other related topics not only misrepresents the scope of Marxian analysis but also reduces its relevance for sociology. In particular such a reading fails to incorporate or address the consensual aspects of Marx's work, the analysis of situations in which open class conflict is neither manifest nor imminent. There is in addition a striking omission of any discussion of ideology, or false consciousness and their possible significance in the production of social situations which appear to be consensual. The result of Dahrendorf's reading of Marx is in consequence a development of the conflict theorist characterization to the neglect of possible insights into consensus and integration situations. Such unimaginative readings are behind the unnecessary and futile attempts to produce syntheses of the so-called conflict and consensus positions.

For example in Dahrendorf's terms there are 'two faces of society', two schools of thought, one stressing integration and values, the other coercion, conflict and interests. He argues that both integration and coercion theory should be used by sociologists, both being seen as valid 'or rather, useful and necessary for sociological analysis' (1959, p. 163). The consequences of his reading of Marx have been far reaching in that not only has the idea of Marx as a conflict theorist been powerfully reinforced but sociologists have turned their attention to the task of reconciling the consensus and conflict positions produced through such readings. It is to be regarded as unfortunate that Dahrendorf's analysis and reading of Marx's work has constituted an unproblematical resource for sociological work. Only by critical analysis and consideration of his work as a topic rather than a resource can sociologists re-address the question of the relevance of Marx's work for sociology and protect themselves against the re-production of unwarranted distinctions.[2]

2 Marx the functionalist

Within sociology there has been a continuing debate as to the nature of theory and methodology, evidenced by the coexistence of different schools allegedly representing different conceptions of the discipline. Until the middle of the 1960s the question of sociological analysis was focused almost exclusively upon the topic of functionalism as a scientific method. The central thesis in this area has been Kingsley Davis's (1959) assertion of functional analysis as synonymous with sociological and scientific analysis itself. The intention behind his contribution was to conclude the debate over not only sociological methodology but also functionalism, by resolving the question of the relationship between sociology, science, functionalism and other positions within the discipline.

In terms of the relationship between Marxian and functional analysis three distinct positions may be considered:
  (a) Marxian analysis as functionalist
  (b) Marxian analysis as inclusive of functional analysis
  (c) Marxian analysis and functionalism treated as forms of systems theory and as elements for a synthesis

Lockwood's thesis

Lockwood, in a paper which discusses some of the implications of criticisms of functionalism, proposes a thesis which indirectly provides the grounds for a classification of Marx as a functionalist. Qualifying Davis's position that all sociological analysis is functional, Lockwood stresses the necessity of distinguishing the general functionalist position from the more specific form, namely normative functionalism. The latter is representative of the most predominant and controversial form of functional analysis within sociology, its chief exponent being Parsons. The characteristics of normative functionalism are recognized to be as follows:

(i) Social integration constitutes the focus of analysis

(ii) Integration is attributed to common values

(iii) Analysis of stability is necessary to, and hence must precede, the analysis of social change

Alternatively what is termed general functionalism is concerned with analysis of the relationship between the 'parts' in contrast to the 'actors' in a social system. Its focus is upon the question of system, as opposed to social integration. Hence in general functionalism there is no necessity for a prior commitment to stability, integration or harmony; the analysis is instead concerned with the inter-relationship of the structural elements or 'parts' of the system.

Lockwood proceeds to show that some critics of functionalism, namely Rex (1961) and Dahrendorf (1968), may have been less effective as a consequence of their preoccupation with the question of normative functionalism and neglect of general functionalism. Ironically it is argued, not uncontroversially in the case of Rex's analysis, that their respective positions are derived from a standpoint, namely Marxist, which itself is functionalist. That is to say that both Rex and Dahrendorf, according to Lockwood, fail to consider the structural basis of change, how some conflict gives rise to change whilst other forms do not.

> Both Dahrendorf and Rex arrive at their respective positions through a generalization of Marx. Yet it is precisely Marx who clearly differentiates social and system integration. The propensity to class antagonism (social integration aspect) is generally a function of the character of production relationships (system integration aspect) (1964, p. 249).

For Lockwood therefore it is structural contradictions, that is to say system conflicts rather than power conflicts (social conflicts), that are decisive in Marx's account of change. In conclusion Lockwood's position is somewhat ambiguous in that one implication is that Marx's analysis may be regarded as general functionalist in orientation. And yet nowhere is there an explicit affirmation that Marxian analysis is functionalist; rather, in response to the observation that general functionalism fails to formulate an answer to the question of the source of contraditions in social systems, Lockwood asks: 'Does the Marxian view contain the elements of a more general sociological formulation?' (ibid., p. 250).

The most obvious example of a sociological reading of Marx's work which does explicitly classify the analysis as functionalist occurs in Fallding's (1972) proposal of 'one sociology'. Predicating his argument upon Davis's earlier controversial remarks on functional analysis Fallding crudely depicts Marx as having been opposed to the dysfunctional society and for the functional society. Asserting that Marx's analysis of social structure rests upon typically functionalist considerations Fallding's account serves to exemplify the authoritative and legislative sociological statement. The caution and doubt which characterizes Lockwood's paper is absent; there is no recognition of the possibility that it might be Marxian analysis which is inclusive of functional analysis. However, Lockwood and Fallding's analyses do have one attribute in common. Both fail in analysing Marxian analysis to consider the significance of consciousness, man's role in shaping history, in reproducing, albeit under constraint, his social world. Of course this is a polemical issue in Marxist thought, but it is an issue that is alive and present in Marx's work and conspicuously (and significantly for Lockwood and Fallding's respective comparative purposes) absent from functionalist analysis. Besides failing to consider the question of consciousness in their comparison of Marxian and functional analysis, both neglect the related problem of reification, the assumption that structures may be treated and considered independently of their production through norms, values, culture and action. It is the totalizing focus upon the structure-action-consciousness interrelationship which distinguishes Marxian analysis from functional analysis. Marxian analysis provides for the possibility of treating reification as a topic of inquiry through the consideration of structures not as ends in themselves but rather as socially and historically constructed and created parameters subject to and requiring transformation. Whereas functional analysis typifies the reificatory nature of much sociological work, Marxian analysis allows reification to be treated as a possible and necessary topic not only of inquiry but also for action (cf. Horton, 1971).

Synthesis

One of the developments to emerge from the contrasting of 'consensus and conflict' or 'integration and coercion' theories has been the felt need on the part of sociologists to formulate some kind of synthesis. One attempt only will be considered here, van den Berghe's (1967) theoretical synthesis, the basis of Lenski's (1966) attempt to formulate a synthesis of conservative and radical theories of social stratification. In his attempt to synthesize functionalist and Hegelian–Marxian dialectical positions van den Berghe relies heavily upon received interpretations of the 'two traditions' in which he has an interest. Both the functionalist and Marxian positions are, as in Dahrendorf's work, deemed to be adequate in accounting for 'one of two essential aspects of social reality and thus complementary to one another' (1967, p. 293). Hence the production of a synthesis holds out the promise of a grasp on reality, in toto. Interestingly van den Berghe observes that the failures and weaknesses of orthodox Marxism have led many sociologists to 'throw out the baby with the bath water'. However, his subsequent discussion of the Marxian position is similarly misguided, his account of the Hegelian–Marxian dialectic being a product of a reading of Marx's analysis derived apparently from Dahrendorf's work.

What emerges from van den Berghe's account is a degree of misunderstanding not only of the dialectic and change in Marx, but also a narrowly based dependence upon the conflict theory reading to the total exclusion of all other possibly relevant readings. The identification by van den Berghe of limitations to the Marxian dialectic, namely that it does not account for all the possible sources of change and secondly that its value is in any case subject to limitation as a consequence of its dependence upon a dualistic view of social reality, exemplifies the sociological misunderstanding of both the concept and the method. Ironically, van den Berghe does not offer any explicit account of his understanding of the dialectic and change in Marxian analysis; rather he asserts that such a critical examination is 'out of place'. If an attempt to develop a synthesis of the dialectical and functionalist approaches does not constitute an occasion for a critical examination of the respective approaches we can only wonder when such an analysis might be regarded as relevant and necessary. To merely assert that such an examination is unnecessary because 'there is no point in beating the dead horse of orthodoxy' or that 'the task has been successfully accomplished by countless people' (1967, p. 299), is to evade the issue. Van den Berghe's comments indicate not only an apparent lack of knowledge of the controversy surrounding the concept of the dialectic in Marxian analysis but also a far from satisfactory conception of what it is to do sociological work. The question of the dialectic is basic to his synthesis and it requires some degree of explication; a footnoted reference to Dahrendorf's specific analysis of Marx's

55

work on class and class conflict is not really adequate for van den Berghe's intended synthesis. His work is predicated upon the false assumption that the definitive understanding of Marxian analysis has already been successfully accomplished and can therefore be employed unproblematically as a resource for sociological analysis. Van den Berghe appears content to rely upon the conflict theory interpretation of Marx's work; class struggle, polarization and revolutionary social change, as *the* reading. This is understandable, although not acceptable, for if the question of alternative readings had been addressed the search for a synthesis might well have been recognized for what it is, namely unnecessary.

Confusion over the concept of the dialectic is not confined to van den Berghe's work alone; on the contrary, sociologists in general seem to have found great problems in coming to terms with the fact that it represents both a methodology and a theory of society. For example, Schneider (1971), referring to the dialectical 'bent' or 'bias', surely not the most appropriately neutral of terms, asserts that the concept has traditionally been 'troublesome' for sociologists. He attempts to ease the problem and reduce the ambiguity surrounding sociological usage by providing a taxonomy of the dialectic in contemporary sociology. Schneider identifies seven meaning-clusters in the uses of the term:

   (i) Unanticipated consequences
  (ii) Goal shifts
 (iii) Adaptions that, once made, inhibit more effective developments
 (iv) Development through conflict
  (v) Phenomena of the type of contradiction, paradox, negation
 (vi) The 'contradictory logic of passion' in particular
(vii) Dissolution of conflict in coalescence of opposites

The existence of these meaning-clusters points for Schneider to the fact that the dialectic has no exact meaning in sociological usage, a conclusion which may well encourage a further rejection of the term as being sociologically irrelevant. Schneider's discussion of the dialectic, in particular his comments on its inexactness of meaning and absence of method for sociology, exemplifies the inappropriateness of attempting to transform or modify the dialectic for use in a positivist-empiricist sociological approach. As Albrow has noted in his critical comparison of what are termed the dialectical and categorical (positivist-empiricist) paradigms, the two approaches 'are genuinely antithetical because they depend in their use on how we choose to view and hence construct the world in which we live' (1974, p. 198). The discussion of dialectic in sociology offered by Schneider exemplifies the manner in which sociologists have consistently transformed radical and critical concepts into scientistic descriptions. The dialectic in Marxian analysis is a method of criticism as well as a theory of social reality. Its focus is not only on 'what is', namely the given appearance of society or the social world, but also upon what is latent, hidden, imminent or becoming. Necessarily, a dialectical analysis goes beyond the mere appearance of reality to reveal the relationship between the nature of society and its ideology. As has been noted by Broadhead the reference in Schneider's work to the absence of a dialectical method for sociology is mistaken. If it appears that 'sociologists have no dialectical method to follow, it is because by and large, they eschew the opportunity of critical social analysis' (1973, p. 45).

We can argue therefore that the distinction within sociology between consensus and conflict or order and change perspectives is primarily a product of a gross misunderstanding of the nature of dialectical analysis and social reality. There is no need for two schools of thought or perspectives, or for that matter a synthesis, for a Marxian analysis attends in a structural and historical sense to both stable and recurrent processes as well as to situations of qualitative change in social structure. The adoption of this position raises the question of reification, in particular the issue of the productive and creative role of subjectivity in constructing the social world. It has been argued by several commentators (Lobkowicz, 1967; Habermas, 1972; Wellmer, 1971) that in Marx's work there is an ambiguity or tension between on the one hand determinism, or an emphasis upon laws and tendencies working with iron necessity, and on the other voluntarism or an acceptance or focus upon the active role of subjectivity. Indeed recognition of deterministic elements in Marxian analysis has led to both the development of a phenomenological Marxism oriented towards subjectivity and to the attempt to reconstitute a genuinely critical theory of society. Both these developments, as I will attempt to establish, are of direct relevance to sociology. At present the active role accorded to subjectivity by Marx remains neglected; sociological readings tend instead to portray Marx as a determinist.

3 Marx the determinist

Marx fell into the dialectic trap by advancing his own brand of one-sided determinism as an antithesis to Hegel's idealism. Clearly Marx's economic determinism (and hence much of the complex theoretical edifice built upon it) is as untenable as the idealism of Hegel (van den Berghe, 1967, p. 299).

The determinist reading of Marx's work has predominated in sociology, being implicit in both the conflict and functionalist readings. Before discussing the question of a determinist reading of Marxian analysis, however, consideration must be given to the general question of determinism in sociology. One sense of the term is associated with sociology's scientific status, specifically the adoption of the assumptions of recurrence and the ordering of empirical phenomena over time. Both are deemed to be central to a scientific explanation and essential characteristics of logically deterministic theories. In other words for many sociologists any attempt at scientific explanation necessarily implies determinism. This usage of the term determinism is methodological and represents a basic rule of intellectual procedure, namely that the investigator should seek to relate elements in his analysis to one another in terms of sequences of dependency. Implicit in this usage, the understanding of determinism as a rule of thought and research, is a belief in the validity and necessity of the distinction between the logical and existential uses of the term in social science work. In other words determinism does not necessarily imply any thesis about reality, 'the primary application of the term . . . is to theories and only derivatively does the term apply to extralinguistic systems' (Rudner, 1966, p. 90). It is this derivative usage, the second sense of the term determinism, which has aroused controversy in sociology.

Determinism in sociology when applied to extralinguistic systems such as society, social structure, interaction, etc., infers that whatever has or is happening 'cannot not happen'. Things could not have been otherwise, it is held to be in the nature of events that given consequences materialize in the given form. This particular understanding is evident in Bendix's (1961) emphasis upon modern social science's success in showing that man is a creature of habits, drives, and social roles. It is typical of the Parsonian functionalist characterization of man, or rather the actor, as the reflex of a constraining, socializing social system in which functional requirements, internalization of roles, and social control mechanisms serve to guarantee consensus and conformity. Determinism in these instances is nothing less than a reference to the one-sided nature of the relationship between man and society, the individual and social structure. The image presented in such accounts of the society–man relationship is indeed Berger's (1966) puppet theatre where the puppets cheerfully act out their assignments, it is the Durkheimian conception of society as not only external to, but also readily internalized by, the individual. It is of course recognized that this conception of the society–man relationship has been subjected to criticism within sociology in particular because of its over-socialized conception of man (cf. Wrong, 1970). However, notwithstanding criticisms and developments of methodological alternatives to conventional sociological approaches the deterministic reading of the society–man relationship has provided the sociologist with a mandate to view as relatively un-problematic the meanings, understandings and interpretations of individuals in their respective social contexts. The focus for sociological attention has then been upon the society, the social structure, reality, the facts, the world 'out there', in other words the determining framework from which all other things follow and which itself awaits discovery and comprehension. In consequence sociologists typically have treated other men purely as objects, ignoring completely the constructive, creative and productive aspects of human activity. As Blumer (1962, pp. 184–5) has noted,

> Sociological thought rarely recognizes or treats human societies as composed of individuals who have selves. Instead they assume human beings to be merely organisms with some kind of organization, responding to forces which play upon them . . . these forces are lodged in the make-up of the society as in the case of 'social system', 'social structure', 'culture'. . . .

Now although symbolic interactionist approaches do accord an active, constructive and interpretational role to human beings the identification of social life with symbolic interaction has led to other significant problems. In particular, as Lichtman (1970, p. 77) has noted of this approach,

> it is overly subjective and voluntaristic, lacks an awareness of historical concreteness . . . abandons the sense of human beings in struggle with an alien reality which they both master and to which they are subordinate. It is a view which tends to dissolve the concept of 'ideology' or 'false consciousness' and leaves us, often against the will of its advocates, without a critical posture toward the present inhuman reality.

Nevertheless symbolic interactionism and phenomenological sociology although themselves subject to criticism, as Lichtman and Horton (1971) have emphasized, provide useful and necessary critiques of sociological determinism. For example the neglect in sociological work of the role of consciousness, awareness and intention in the constitution of social reality, has served as the focus of the phenomenological sociological critique, as has the insensitivity of sociologists towards the implication of their determinist positions for the very possibility of doing their own work. The paradox of the external determination of the sociologist's own account has of course been treated extensively within the sociology of knowledge but in such a way that the critical question of the dialectical nature of social reality has been neglected and superseded by the unexplicated rationale that some men are less subject to existential determination than others. The technocratic-authoritarian implications of the sociologist's attempt to pull himself out of the existential-determinist quagmire by his own bootstraps has produced on the one hand retreats into relativism and on the other various shades of scientifically disguised political paternalism.

Sociological readings of Marx's work as deterministic rest primarily upon an understanding of the account of the capitalist system, or for that matter any system, as economically determined. It is an imaginative rather than symptomatic reading. Indeed it might be felt that fictional would serve as a more appropriate epithet, for it is difficult to comprehend the claim that there is a sole or exclusive emphasis upon economic factors in Marx's work even though it may be accepted that 'the only science Marx dealt with critically was economics' (O'Neill, 1972, p. 241). It is clear that both Marx and Engels were aware of the problem of economic determinist readings of their work. However, our problem is not to achieve the 'essential' Marx for there is no sense in which that is possible given the present terms of reference; rather it is to recognize the controversy and ambiguity surrounding the issue of determinism and the consequences of particular readings for an understanding of the sociological relevance of Marx's work. Of course it is important to recognize that the problems of determinism in Marx emanate in part from the texts. Indeed as Engels noted,

> Marx and I are ourselves partly to blame for the fact that the younger people sometimes lay more stress on the economic side than is due to it. We had to emphasise the main principle vis-à-vis our adversaries, who denied it, and we had not always the time, the place or the opportunity to allow the other elements involved in the interaction to come into their rights (1962, Vol. II, p. 490).

It seems self-evident therefore that the possibility of ambiguities over the question of economic determinism in Marx's work should be treated as a topic. This is in direct contrast to the procedure of those sociologists who apparently have no need to read Marx, having resolved to their satisfaction all the controversial aspects pertaining to the analysis, and who are therefore able to accept as unquestionable its uncontroversial status as a resource for sociological work. Sociological readings offering a deterministic account of Marxian analysis tend to emphasize the economic factor but in addition reference is frequently made to technological or historical antecedents (Lenski, 1966; Timasheff, 1964 edition). In each case special emphasis is placed upon Marx's references to laws working with 'iron necessity' towards an inevitable conclusion, to the eventual displacement of the capitalist society and to the natural character of the laws of capitalist production. In developing some of these points attention will be focused upon first the question of determinism, determination and the base-superstructure relationship, and second the issue of science and positivism in Marx's analysis.

As has been noted the view of Marx as a determinist, a mono-casual theorist, places emphasis upon his preoccupation with particular external factors to the exclusion of others and to the neglect of the individual's activity in producing history or constructing social reality. Whether or not one can find textual reference for such readings is immaterial for one can also 'discover' alternative references and statements. The question clearly is not 'Which reading of Marx is the reading?' but rather 'Can there be a sociologically relevant reading which is compatible with the emancipatory interest inherent in the Marxian project?' To date, sociologists have tended to ignore the problem, inherent in a deterministic reading of Marx, of praxis, that is man's activity in the world based upon a knowledge of that world. Readings which attribute a determinist position to Marx render unimportant the role of consciousness as a basis for action and sunder the dialectical relationship between political activity and theoretical work in his analysis. This brings us to the threshold of the distinction that is made between determinism and determination, between on the one hand a praxis that is completely determined and on the other one which is situated historically through the determination of its possibility yet where the present and future possibilities for action are open. Lefebvre's (1972) reading of Marx adopts such a position, distinguishing between determination and determinism in terms of a proposal that, although history does provide social structures, systems or forms which may be seen to exert influences upon any present, within these parameters creative activity on the part of individuals and classes is possible. Significantly such activity may not only be seen to be made possible by the specific socio-economic context, but critically for the determinist position; action is itself constitutive of the transformation of the particular social context. Action is not determined per se; even the problems men face, the situations they confront have to be recognized to be problems, to exist as situations for action to be a possibility. It is not so much the case that men take on only those problems that they can resolve as that they can only take on those problems which they can identify. Necessarily therefore the question of consciousness whether 'true' or 'false' becomes important to the understanding of action and its situated character in the social structure.

Perhaps the most significant 'recent' discussion of the question of determinism and the role of economic factors in Marx's analysis has come from Althusser (1969). In attempting to reveal the misconception inherent in the debate over the problem of determinism in Marxian analysis Althusser has produced the concept of over-determination. He situates the determinist account within a decontextualized reading of parts of Marx's analysis as an exact mirror image of the Hegelian dialectic. Whereas for Hegel the politico-ideological is portrayed as the determinant of the economic, determinist readings of Marx, 'inverting' Hegel, substitute another simple principle, namely material life or the economy as the determinant. Economistic and technologistic 'deviations' of this kind are for Althusser still entrapped within the Hegelian problematic and in consequence do not adequately represent the importance and originality of Marx's work in providing the foundation for the science of history. Therefore Althusser proposes 'a new conception of the relation between determinant instances in the structure-superstructure complex which constitutes the essence of any social formation' (1969, p. 111). This new conception involves basically two principles:

(i) The relative autonomy of the superstructures and their specific effectivity

(ii) The determination in-the-last-instance by the (economic) mode of production

Hence although the economy is determinant in the long run, Althusser argues that history asserts itself through local tradition, international circumstances and the various forms of the super-structures. That is to say that the economy has a critical influence but that its influence will be mediated in and by different forms, through different structures. Althusser's reading of Marx has met with the increasingly characteristic hostile reception especially from 'critical' or humanist Marxists. However, in addition to Marxological polemics there has been the important observation that the concept of over-determination which Althusser employs to refer to the cumulative effect or outcome of contradictions in the many social practices constituting a given social formation, implies the substitution of a pluralist position for the monist conception evident in many determinist readings of Marx. This is interesting for the concept is, as Althusser acknowledges, already dormant in Engels's references to the relative autonomy of the superstructures vis-à-vis economic conditions. Unfortunately even a strained reading of Engels or Althusser on this issue will fail to provide any further indication of the degree or circumstances of the autonomy of the superstructures, or any hint as to the nature of the mediation of the economic in-the-last-instance. To be sure there are references to the distinct practices, their respective contradictions and manifestations in given social formations as well as admissions of the differing forms of over-determination and variations in the structure in dominance. However, all that Althusser succeeds in doing is to replace the specific problem of economic determinism by an ambiguous alternative in which all the elements, both structure and superstructures, are interrelated in terms ultimately (or should it be initially?) of the economic. By rejecting the active, and creative role of man in history, Althusser closes off a possible solution to the problem of a determinist reading of Marx and at the same time obstructs the construction of a more adequate theory for his explicit political purposes.[3]

An alternative way to read Marx's work with its emphasis upon economic factors and production is to consider that reference is being made to the fact that the production of existence is basic, that is the production of those things which provide for the possibility of the reproduction of existence.[4] In an important sense the preoccupation with the economic determinist reading is indeed trite, for who would disagree that subsistence, shelter and clothing are vital to human existence? This, however, is only part of the story, for language too is basic and perhaps critical in distinguishing man from other beings. Refraining for the moment from considering the question of ontology, if the economic is to be emphasized then recognition must be given to the fact that the form which production takes is not alone determined by economic considerations but rests with the nature of social organization, culture and many other factors. Hence we are led to confront the enormity of scope of the dialectical relation between human beings and the social world. Human beings are active beings situated in a world which is not only economically structured but also socially, politically and intellectually structured. We receive, interpret and internalize a language and culture, are constrained by, construct and re-act back upon an objectified social world. Hence both social interaction and isolation are situated within a determinate socio-cultural and historical context which includes significant others (physically present and absent) with differential access to, interpretation or understanding of, and control over scarce and relatively freely available social resources. As Lichtman has noted,

> Human action can be understood neither independently of the meaning which the actor gives it, nor simply identified with his own interpretation. Human beings may act under the belief that they are productive, free and equal when the opposite is the case. Defining their activity as they comprehend it will lead us to misconstrue their act. . . . Human beings can only act toward the world on the basis of some 'understanding' but it does not follow from this that their activity, or the world, possesses the character which they 'understand' it to have (1970, p. 77).

The relationship between the base and superstructure in Marx's work need not be read as inferring simplistically that the economic factor determines all others (cf. Mitchell, 1971, p. 101; Williams, 1973). On the contrary not only may the relationship be subject to lags, complications and reciprocal effect, but the reference to economic factors, production, work or industry may well be taken as paradigmatic for all forms of social interaction, a reference to the production and construction of social reality in general.

Science and positivism

The determinist reading of Marx's work attributes a positivistic conception of science to his analysis. Such a reading begs the question of the nature of science in the analysis, indeed avoids the very issue of the status of the latter as science or criticism, or science and criticism. This specific issue is central not only to the assessment of the sociological import of Marxian analysis, in so far as the latter's status is controversial, but exists also as a continuing debate within sociology itself. References to science in Marx are not particularly revealing for although mention is made of science, scientific method and methodology it is frequently in inconclusive terms. Where the question of science is addressed directly then almost by implication determinist readings have drawn support, leaning heavily upon the 'inevitability' of developments, the 'iron' laws of history or the apparent 'natural' character of social factors in Marxian analysis. Indeed a positivistic-deterministic reading of Marx's work can fairly simply locate specific selected textual grounds to 'legitimate' its interpretation. The problem with this, however, is that first it ignores other readings of Marx's writings which place emphasis upon the importance and centrality of the critique of ideology in his analysis, that is to say the rejection of 'facts' as they immediately appear, are presented to us, or are mediated by formal categories; and second such a reading omits to recognize or address the vital question of a possible underlying tension within the Marxian project between ideology critique and 'positivistic material determinism' (cf. Habermas, 1972).

Marx's analysis is genetically speaking situated within the developing capitalist mode of production for which the natural sciences were becoming increasingly significant both as factors of production and as ideological structures. Within such a context Marx sought to critically assess and supersede economic accounts and explanations and their mystifications of the capitalist mode of production. Furthermore his analysis was oriented towards the removal of the very reality of the capitalist mode of production. It was directed not only against 'false' accounts or ideologies but also the 'false' realities themselves. Undoubtedly there are fairly plausible grounds for arguing that Marx's analysis is in particular respects positivist in orientation, a consequence possibly of the common line of descent of Marxian analysis and positivism from the Saint-Simonian school. Indeed it is proposed (cf. Lichtheim, 1971) that Marx might have been more influenced by Comte than he was aware for the latter played a large part in Saint-Simon's later writings. However, such a standpoint is not uncontroversial; certainly to assert glibly as Nisbet (1970) does that Marx's search was compatible with Comte's and Spencer's quest for an objective sociology is to neglect the former's contempt for the development of Comtean social science. Marx's references to the natural sciences, and acceptance of positivistic-deterministic reviews, have of course lent credence to the view that there exists a positivistic Marx, whose emphasis is purely upon a scientific understanding and description of a specific mode of production and its laws of development. This conception is further confirmed for many readers by the reference to the future unity of the sciences of man and nature, the unification being seen to arise as a result of the sciences of man emulating the natural sciences. Such readings neglect to attend to the contradiction between on the one hand a positivistic conception of science in which human beings are reduced to the status of objects, and on the other the necessity for direct intervention in the historical process, requiring active, conscious subjects, to fulfil the latent promise within humanity. It may be argued that an emancipatory concept of science requiring a change in both social and natural sciences represents a pre-requisite for the possibility of any action to modify or alter the course of history. Here of course is the dilemma. The lack of consistency in Marx's vacillations on science, indeed throughout his works, has produced a polarization of Marxist thought into either early and late, young and old Marx, or alternatively critical and scientific Marxism. On the one hand there are those theorists who conceive the capitalist mode of production to be subject to the iron laws of history and as such suffering inexorable decline. Alternatively, 'critical theorists' have tended to emphasize far more the necessity of active intervention, the importance of recognizing that men make history and need to be made aware of the possibility of doing so rather than surrendering to the constraints imposed by an acceptance of a technicist and positivistic conception of science and history.

Given the past and present state of sociology it is not surprising that a positivist reading of Marx has received preference over possible alternatives. Specifically Marxian analysis has been treated as offering an account of society as a social system in which the mode of production, or the economy, is regarded as the basic determinate of all other spheres of social life. The attractiveness of such a reading is that it attributes equal insignificance to consciousness, subjectivity and creative action in Marxian analysis as exists in much conventional sociology. Ironically the very same reading of Marx's work has even been forthcoming from sociologists ostensibly critical of positivistic tendencies within sociology (e.g. Walsh, 1972).

This reading of Marx's analysis of action as the product of material interests alone, and man's consciousness as a direct reflection of objective conditions, follows from particular assumptions concerning the nature of Marx's ontology (man as homo faber), the preoccupation with Marx's at times ill-conceived concept of class, replete as it is with ambiguity, as well as the problem of the under-development in his analysis of the social structure-action-consciousness dialectical relationship. The absence of any significant discussion of dialectics in Marx's work is clearly in part a factor responsible for the subsequent ambiguity and controversy surrounding the relation for example between the forces and social relations and conditions of production, facilitating in fact a mechanistic interpretation of the latter. Both the reduction of interaction to labour and the treatment of productive work as the paradigm for the generation of all social categories provide a firm basis for determinist readings. Indeed, the treatment of work or production exclusive of for example meaning, interaction or language as the basic category of analysis exemplifies for many the extent to which the Marxian concept of science is oriented towards the natural sciences and further serves to indicate the degree to which an objectivist illusion intrudes at times into his historical and social theory.

If revolution, change and freedom from the constraints of a particular mode of production are historically necessary and inevitable then the role of an active consciousness becomes virtually insignificant, and the liberating function of the class struggle, the creative and constructive nature of social interaction is neglected in favour of the system-breaking function of objective class antagonisms. Certainly just such a view gains confirmation from Marx's approval of a reviewer's comments, that

> Marx only troubles himself about one thing: to show, by
> rigid scientific investigation, the necessity of successive
> determinate orders of social conditions, and to establish, as
> impartially as possible, the facts that serve him for fundamental
> starting points. For this it is quite enough, if he proves, at the
> same time, both the necessity of the present order of things, and
> the necessity of another order into which the first must inevitably

pass over; and this all the same, whether men believe or do not believe it, whether they are conscious or unconscious of it.

Marx treats the social movement as a process of natural history, governed by laws not only independent of human will, consciousness and intelligence, but rather, on the contrary, determining that will, consciousness and intelligence . . . (Marx and Engels, vol. I, 1962, p. 454).

Against this position it may of course be argued that Marx and Engels's occasional use of scientific terms, what Wellmer (1971) refers to as Marx's 'flirtation with positivism', may represent nothing more than a strategy to facilitate the dispersion of their ideas. As such there need be no inherent contradiction between the apparently scientistic character of historical materialism and the ideology critique of political economy. However, the problem with this rationalization of Marxian analysis, emphasizing the critical unity of the work, is that it underestimates the significance of science for both Marx and Engels. It is apparent that their science was more than a carrier of an ideology critique, that there was a felt necessity to situate the analysis and critique of the capitalist mode of production within the hegemonic scientific problematic. As Engels affirmed,

Marx would protest against the economic 'political and social ideal' which you attribute to him. When one is a 'man of science' one does not have an ideal; one works out scientific results, and when one is a party man to boot, one fights to put them into practice. But when one has an ideal one cannot be a man of science, for one starts out with preconceptions (quoted in Godelier, 1972, p. 82).

The compatibility of this statement with the sociologist's conception of his particular role is striking, but of course too much importance can be attached to remarks of this kind, particularly when consideration is given to the question of Marx and Engels's relationship as well as (and perhaps of greater significance) the near irrelevance of their respective self-conceptions to the possible and actual ramifications and interpretations of their works. However, Engels's comment does serve to further illustrate the problematical nature of the status of Marx's work; science or criticism, or science and criticism. Some theorists certainly regard Marx's science as having overcome the traditional dualism between the empirical and 'speculative' approaches, it being argued that the analysis begins neither with brute facts nor remains content with simple inductive generalizations but studies in effect whole structures, social situations taken in their totality, conceiving every existing form in its change, as

67

being in transition (Markovic, 1968; Colletti, 1972). In this conception Marx's work is scientific, a method of critique and revolutionary practice. Alternatively, Wellmer (1971) regards the union of the science of historical materialism and the critique of political economy as inherently contradictory in that in contrast to the ideology-critical approach of the latter, the interpretation of history implies an objectivist conception of revolution.

The question of science and criticism in Marx's work is in many respects comparable to the controversy surrounding the status of science in sociology. For as in readings of Marx's work there is disagreement over his concept of science and its relevance in general to the analysis, so in sociology there are debates over the appropriate methods of procedure for studying social reality some of which bracket the very assumption that sociology must proceed scientifically (cf. Blum, 1971). Both the heterogeneous nature of Marxist thought and ambiguities and discrepancies in Marx's analysis, and the continuing debates over value-freedom and commitment, phenomenology and positivism, and Naturwissenschaften and Geisteswissenschaften in sociology, testify to the complexity of a scientific analysis of the social world and the problems involved in attempting to comprehend the nature of social reality.

4 Marx the action theorist

In some respects it may be argued that the close relationship between logos and praxis in Marxian theory obviates the need for any distinct theory of action. Alternatively the absence of a theory of action may be held to account for the problem in Marxian theory of the relationship between structure, revolutionary action and consciousness. Sociological readings of Marx's work have rarely dwelled upon the issue of action however; indeed Parsons's statement that 'on the sociological level, Marx is one of the symbolic "grandfathers" of the theory of action' (1961, p. 361) is in itself novel. That this perspective on Marx has remained largely undeveloped by sociologists is not surprising in view of the more explicit treatment accorded to social action by Weber. However, there have been two recent readings of Marx's work as action theory by sociologists, namely Cohen (1968) and Poggi (1972).

Cohen reads Marx as treating the social actor as a calculating strategist, as employing a highly simplified model of instrumental rationalism derived from the means-ends schema of the classical economists. This is especially ironical in view of Marx's critique of the liberal-utilitarian belief in the absolute autonomy of the individual. For Marx the latter is not the starting point but the product of social development. Then again, contrary to his assertion that there is little in the young Marx of value to sociology Cohen leans heavily upon an idealist-historicist reading to account for the emergence of social relationships. The latter are portrayed as emerging as a necessary product of man's interaction with the material world and represent the constraints upon men in any given situation. Likewise the dialectical process is diluted to refer to the 'development of any social system . . . from the development of one type of situation into another, each chain in the link being forged by the solution which results from the previous situation' (1968, p. 80). Hence the dialectic is reduced to the 'logic of each situation'.

Cohen's explanation of the development and transformation of each system is predicated upon a conventional interpretation of the base-superstructure relationship, namely that the logic of economic situations determines that other social situations (the superstructure) assume particular forms. As with several other sociological accounts of action and system (Parsons), or 'subjective' and 'objective' aspects of reality (Berger and Luckmann), from action Cohen produces determinism. Consciousness, intention and meaning figure nowhere significantly in Cohen's account; rather, where the question of 'false consciousness' is addressed it is as a problematical category denoting a departure in Marx from the assumption of instrumental rationality. Faced with this difficulty of accounting for false consciousness Cohen adopts a basically conspiratorial conception of ideology as an instrument for the maintenance of privilege, the specific implication being that ideology may be manipulated to produce false consciousness in others. By treating ideology only as a theory that is produced or constructed to generalize and mystify special interests, primarily class interests, Cohen neglects other significant aspects of the term in Marxian analysis. In particular he fails to attend to Marx's use of the term ideology to refer to false representations of history; that is, ideology as illusion or distortion independent of class interest. The basic question of the relationship between existence and consciousness and the inevitability of illusory representations and understandings of reality are not discussed by Cohen.

On reflection therefore we may well argue that it is Cohen's account of Marx's work, not Marxian analysis, which is 'too simplified to be acceptable as a basis' for sociological inquiry. The significant omission of any discussion of the complexity of the base-superstructure, logic of economic situations – logic of political, legal, ideological and cultural situations in Cohen's work – and most critical of all the failure to attend to the debate over the question of the dialectical relation of consciousness and social existence in Marxian analysis, make his account less than adequate for an understanding of the sociological relevance of Marx's work.

By way of a contrast Poggi's analysis addresses the very issues neglected by Cohen Action is seen to emerge through man's ability to contemplate and reflect upon his own activity, this being accomplished through consciousness. In turn consciousness is regarded as a process of the making of man's activity into an object. The particular base from which man is able to conceptualize his activity as action, as an object, is his selfhood, a concept not analysed by Marx but central to the analysis of, for example, Mead. Both selfhood and consciousness are therefore treated as being socially mediated, as products of social relations. Although consciousness is integral to the establishment of man's selfhood, it in turn is regarded as a social product which can only be expressed through the social medium of language. As Marx and Engels have stated,

> Man possesses 'consciousness', but, even so, not inherent, not 'pure' consciousness From the start . . . [it] is afflicted with the curse of being 'burdened' with matter, which here makes its appearance in the form of . . . language. . . . Consciousness is therefore, from the very beginning a social product, and remains so as long as men exist at all (1970, pp. 50–1).

For Poggi the consciousness of individuality contra Cohen is analysed as a product of social development not its pre-requisite. Individuality only arises when the subject engages in relations with others whom he recognizes as similar yet irreducible to himself. Hence as with Mead, whose work may be seen to be compatible with or derived from this aspect of Marxian analysis, man is only able to relate to himself through his relationships with other men. Poggi's reading reveals not only the poverty of conventional sociological accounts but furthermore addresses the neglected question of the methodological basis of Marx's analysis of society and social reality in general as distinct from the capitalist mode of production in particular. Recognition of the creative element in Marx's latent concept of action sets Poggi's analysis apart from most other sociological accounts (another exception being Lefebvre's). Marx analyses reality as man-made, offering full recognition to the creative role of human action, in particular man's ability to transcend the givenness of a specific situation It is the creative character of action which provides it with the property of 'objectness', namely through its production via labour of 'bits of reality that are not present in nature' as well as the construction of two classes of other objects, namely ideas (representations, concepts, linguistic structures, theories and symbolic structures) and relations (social relationships). Emphasis of the material basis of the latter is perhaps required in view of the predilection to treat social relations as secondary to 'concrete' material objects. As Marx observed, 'men [not only] produce cloth, linen, silks . . . [but] also produce the social relations amid which they prepare cloth and linen' (Marx and Engels, 1953, p. 47).

Action then has the character not only of transforming nature in providing for the possibility of existence, but also whilst sustaining and reproducing the subject it actually modifies him and his social relationships. Human action has the property, as Marx has noted, of acting back upon the individual.

Not only do the objective conditions change in the act of reproduction, e.g. the village becomes a town, the wilderness a clear field, etc., but the producers change, too, in that they bring out new qualities in themselves, develop themselves in production, transform themselves, develop new powers and ideas, new modes of intercourse, new needs and new language (1973a, p. 494).

Now to emphasize the significance of action in Marx's work is not to ignore the fact that men are not entirely free arbiters of their own actions. On the contrary, reading Marx it is clear that the products of previous activity, that is to say the social contexts (including knowledge, beliefs and values) which are the product of previous actions, represent limitations upon the choice of action in the 'present'. Hence although man's activity has a degree of open-endedness, prior activity is determinate in constituting in part the given context of any particular human action. Choices still exist, however, as to whether the individual acts or not, whether action is oriented to changing the world or merely affirming it. According therefore to Poggi's reading, for Marx reality does not determine action, yet action is determinate in terms of the pre-existent reality. This reading with its focus upon the topics of the nature of man and the relationship between nature, culture and social reality in Marx's analysis is unusual in that sociological interpretations of Marx's work usually stress class, ideology or conflictual aspects of the social structure. As such Poggi presents a reading which demonstrates that, although the prophetic-deterministic components in Marx's work may have been neutralized, much of sociological value remains silent and unrecognized in the Marxian position.

Summary

In each of the readings of Marx's work discussed above it is apparent, with the possible exception of Poggi's account, that a specific aspect has been extracted and treated as being representative of the general relevance of Marxian analysis for sociology. The readings have as a result a somewhat arbitrary character in that they stress conflict or change or functionalism, or again economic determinism, as the defining characteristic of Marx's contribution to sociology. Not surprisingly Marxian analysis is not treated or read as a critique of conventional sociological procedure, rather it is seen to constitute a possible resource for doing 'normal' sociology. In contrast to such readings I will treat Marxian analysis as a critique of socio-logical science, as embodying the basis of a methodology appropriate to a scientific study of the socio-cultural historical world. Marx's work stands therefore as a stimulus to inquiry, exemplifying the need continually to re-examine critically ideas and reflections upon social reality, their constitution of, as well as production by, that reality. Although the relevance of empirical descriptive aspects of Marxian analysis has been reduced by the passage of history the critique of ideology and the methodological basis of Marx's work remain vital to a scientific understanding of the social world.

3 Phenomenological sociology — an alternative sociology ?

The re-awakening or re-emergence of doubt, uncertainty and criticism over the question of sociological methodology has thrown into relief a great many problems which have long been neglected by sociologists. Sociological research has tended to be conducted as though for all practical purposes basic methodological problems and questions have been satisfactorily resolved. Where sociological work has addressed problematical topics and issues – for example the question of the nature of social phenomena, social reality or society – then the discipline has frequently been regarded as in a state of crisis. In turn the existence of a crisis within sociology has been depicted as a sign of a possible 'revolution' (cf. Goldthorpe, 1973), indicative of a 'paradigm shift' (cf. Friedrichs, 1972) or a characteristic of 'normal' sociology (cf. O'Malley, 1970). At the focus of most discussions on the inadequacy of conventional sociological methodology there has been a debate over the suitability of positivism, neo-positivism and empiricism for a scientific understanding of the social world. Concomitant with the development of critiques of positivist and empiricist sociology a claim has been made for the emergence of an 'alternative' position, namely a phenomenological sociology. However, the subsequent development of phenomenological sociology and ethnomethodology has been disappointing, tending to result in an addition to, rather than a replacement or thoroughgoing amendment of, established sociological approaches. One consequence of the emergence of a phenomenological sociology and ethnomethodology has been a further increase in the internal diversity of the discipline. This is further compounded by the fact that the 'new' developments themselves are differentially evaluated by sociologists as not sociology, as new terms for old practices, or by a minority as more humane or moral ventures than conventional sociological approaches.

From the outset it is important to recognize that I shall not be considering the relationship of phenomenological philosophy to either sociology in general or to the concept of a phenomenological sociology in particular. The relationship of phenomenology to sociology is a complex one, the problem being magnified by the heterogeneous nature of both 'disciplines' (cf. Phillipson, 1972). I will concentrate upon the idea of a radically 'new' sociology, a phenomenological sociology, derived from the phenomenological philosophical clarification of the sociological task. The emergence of a distinctive phenomenological sociology has both contributed to, and been a product of, the declining credibility of conventional sociological approaches. In particular, phenomenological sociology provides a critique of sociological approaches which minimize the differences between the socio-cultural and physical worlds. One important consequence therefore of the appearance of a 'new' sociology has been a re-consideration or re-vision of the assumptions, methodology and nature of sociological work. At the focus of such re-considerations has been the question of the significance of the distinction between natural or physical phenomena and social phenomena, the natural or physical 'world' and the socio-cultural 'world'.

Typically, the phenomenological sociological critique of conventional sociology has emphasized the latter's naïve acceptance of the natural sciences as a model for social science. Positivistic sociology's use of the natural science paradigm is seen to depend upon a crucial assumption, namely that social phenomena and natural phenomena do not possess qualitatively distinctive characteristics. Developing from Schutz's work, the phenomenological sociological critique emphasizes that such an assumption is unjustifiable in so far as it is predicated upon a basic misapprehension of the characteristics of the natural and social worlds. Natural or physical phenomena unlike social phenomena have no intrinsic meaning structure and therefore provide the scientist with a freedom to observe and construct explanations external to and independent of the particular phenomenon under investigation. Conversely the sociologist is investigating a world that is constituted by meaning and necessarily therefore has to rely upon meanings and interpretive procedures drawn from the social world to offer any account of social phenomena. For the social scientist the phenomena subjected to analysis or examination are already structured. Social phenomena are characterized by and only recognizable because of their meaningfulness for members in the social world. In contrast the natural scientist is attending to phenomena that are cognitively unstructured; the phenomena with which he is concerned may therefore be invested with meanings or subjected to interpretations in the secure knowledge that no inherent meaningfulness or intentionality is being neglected or occluded. Although therefore the natural scientist in dealing with natural or physical phenomena is engaged in a social activity, working within a scientific (and social) community with specific socio-cultural assumptions, the relationship between the phenomena, themes, topics or problems under investigation and the investigator is of a different order to the relationship between the sociologist and social phenomena.

Phenomenological sociology rejects the idea, inherent in sociological approaches which adopt the natural science paradigm, that the social world constitutes an object world divorced from the interpretive procedures of members (both professional sociologists and lay members). Rather the social world is treated as the product of human activity, interpretation and intention, as a subject world. Hence although it is accepted by phenomenological sociologists that the world takes on a factual appearance this is merely taken to be indicative of members' externalizing and objectifying practices rather than representative of any defining characteristic of the social world. Perception of externalization and objectification as taking place primarily through language has produced a preoccupation in phenomenological sociology and ethnomethodology with accounts, descriptions, conversations and talk. The social world is treated as a linguistic and cognitive world and the task of sociology becomes one of describing the processes by which the social world is constructed through accounts, readings, understandings and interpretive procedures.

In striving to offer a critique of conventional sociological procedure phenomenological sociologists have tended to discuss, perhaps as a result of an over-reaction to what is taken to be positivism, only the differences between natural and social phenomena. Surprisingly little or no consideration is given to the fact that the natural world is only known or grasped through language, belief, and understandings, each of which is intrinsic to the social world. Furthermore, no attempt is made to consider the mode in which the natural world is experienced, nor for that matter is there any recognition of the inextricable linking of natural and social worlds, in particular the latter's very dependence upon the former for specific material resources essential to its existence. This is not problematical for all phenomenological analysis as Paci (1972) attempts to reveal in his discussion of Marxism and phenomenology (drawing upon the writings of the later Husserl). To argue for a reconsideration of the distinction between natural and social reality is not to deny the validity of the phenomenological critique of conventional sociology's acceptance of the natural science paradigm. It is, however, to raise the question of the nature and purpose of sociology and further to cast doubt upon the phenomenological sociological account of the processes by which the social world is constructed. It is sufficient to note here that the articulation of natural and social worlds is central to Marxian analysis as is the dialectical relationship between thought and existence, being and consciousness. These concerns constitute the focus of analysis of both phenomenological Marxism and to a lesser extent critical theory.

The question of the nature of social reality is for sociology a source of considerable controversy. Whereas conventional sociologies are concerned with social action, recognizing that the parameters of a given action are not purely 'social' in nature, being also responsive to ecological, climatic, physical and biological factors, phenomenological sociology has tended to neglect the question of action, what people do, so to speak, and has concentrated instead upon accounts, conversation and talk about what has been and is being done. Hence in the work of phenomenological sociologists there is a curious absence of any discussion of power, force, stratification or structure other than in terms of a 'sense' of power, etc. (Clegg (1975) addresses and attempts to remedy this omission.) The question of the sources of accounts, their mediation, control, manipulation or transformation must, in the absence of any apparent work in these areas, be regarded as uninteresting to exponents of the phenomenological sociological approach. The position adopted here is that the social world includes or incorporates the description, evaluation and conceptualization of both social and natural or physical events, social and natural or physical phenomena. Although the social world is in part (re-)constructed by socially organized activities on the part of members, such activities are not only interpretational or linguistic but also materially creative. In other words the meaningfulness or understanding of the social world is not achieved purely through language, interpretation or consciousness but also through material transformation of the natural or physical environment. Given that the focus of sociology's interest is society, specific existing and historical societies, the scope of a phenomenological sociology may be regarded as supplementary, but not an alternative, to the predominant concern of conventional sociology. That the sociologist's concern should be other than it is, is not purely a methodological question but raises in addition the issue of the moral and political nature of the sociological enterprise.

As it is, phenomenological sociology has, through its critique of positivistic sociology, increased sociological interest in the taken-for-granted nature of social reality wherein everyday accounts take on a natural appearance and situations are constructed such that it appears that they 'could not be otherwise'. It has increased awareness of the nature of the social world and by reminding sociologists, and perhaps members too, that it is constituted by their activities and practices in the course of their being-in-the-world, holds out the possibility of a remedy for some of the methodological problems confronted in sociological practice.

In so far as the focus of the phenomenological critique has been upon positivism the tendency within sociology has been to disown or play down the latter position, to distance work from the positivistic stance. As a consequence a typical reaction to the phenomenological critique has been a qualified agreement combined with an apparent confusion or puzzlement as to the relevance of such a critique to mainstream sociology (frequently depicted as non-positivistic, if empiricist). Much hangs here on the question of the nature of positivism, making necessary some specification of the suppositions allegedly entailed in a positivistic approach. The following characteristics are generally attributed to positivism in sociology:

(1) The assumption that the 'scientific method' is that employed in the physical world, and further that it is applicable to the study of the social world.

(2) The goal of sociological inquiry is to formulate laws or generalizations with a view to being able to offer predictions along the lines evident in the natural, physical sciences.

(3) That facts and values are distinguishable for the purposes of scientific analysis and that sociology should deal with the former.

(4) The doing of sociology is regarded as independent of the social world investigated, or rather, and perhaps more appropriately, it is not perceived to be an activity in the social world, involved inevitably in a constitution of the (or a) social world.

(5) The assumption that science itself is not problematical and does indeed represent an appropriate mode for analysing or seeking to understand the social world.

At the most general level the phenomenological sociological critique focuses upon the assumption within positivist-empiricist approaches of the relevance of the methodological procedures of the natural sciences for sociology, calling into question not only the adequacy of these procedures for the study of social reality, but in addition opening up the whole issue of a scientific sociology, the conception, attendant problems and possible alternatives. Frequently reference is made to the work of Durkheim in order to both situate and legitimate the methodological basis of contemporary sociological positivism. Generally this is achieved through an acknowledgment of the Durkheimian proposal that social facts be considered as things, as entities in their own right.

It is argued that for Durkheim this rule – treat social facts as things – is the first and most fundamental aspect of sociological inquiry (cf. Walsh, 1972). It is a rule which from a phenomenological sociological standpoint might be re-phrased as follows: 'Persist in the naïve attitude when analysing the nature of social phenomena.' Now although Durkheim's work is often regarded as the infrastructure of contemporary sociology's mainstream positivism we must exercise caution in our judgment, for Durkheim also writes, 'If then we agree with certain scholars that social reality appears to the individual under the aspect of constraint, we admit with the others that it is a spontaneous product of reality' (1964a, p. 124). Durkheim's methodological proposal that social facts be treated as things seems to have been transformed within sociology and taken to infer that social facts are things. Although it may be the case that sociologists have tended to attribute 'thing-like' status to social reality and social phenomena we should be careful to avoid misrepresenting or mis-interpreting the continuities with Durkheim's work.[1] Consideration has to be given not only to the significance of interpretations of Durkheim's sociology in shaping the nature of the discipline in the present but also to the specific question of the typification of Durkheim as a positivist. I intend to consider here only the latter question.

Walsh (1972) offers an account of varieties of positivism in sociology which attributes to Durkheim the major influence in establishing the framework for positivistic approaches. Now although Durkheim does urge sociologists to recognize that 'social phenomena are things and ought to be treated as things' (1964a, p. 27) one cannot proceed from this statement to a categorical critique of his work as manifestly oblivious to the emergent nature of social reality. For his reference to social phenomena as having the character of 'things' occurs in the context of their scientific treatment, the specific emphasis in Durkheim's work being upon what is given, what is presented to the scientist as being 'there' in the world, rather than how it comes to be, or appears as given. Yet recognition is at the same time given to the possibility that social reality is constituted as a consequence of the development of certain ideas. Now although Durkheim relegates the latter proposition from his immediate consideration on the grounds that ideas are not immediately given, stating that 'they cannot be perceived or known directly, but only through the phenomenal reality expressing them' (ibid., p. 27), his sociological methodology is more contingent than Walsh's comments allow. For example Durkheim in discussing the external character of social facts states, 'If this exteriority should prove to be only apparent, the advance of science will bring the disillusionment and we shall see our conception of social phenomena change as it were, from the objective to the subjective' (ibid., p. 28). Durkheim's work may therefore be more appropriately read as offering a beginning for sociological inquiry rather than a categorical assertion of a determinate sociological method. Certainly it cannot be denied that Durkheim fully recognized that the result might emerge that 'social phenomena do not possess all the intrinsic characteristics of the thing' (ibid., p. 28). It is clear that the attempt to develop phenomenological sociology is based upon the belief that such a result is either now emerging or alternatively has existed albeit unrecognized for some time.

What is phenomenological sociology?

The problem of defining or describing the boundary and essential nature of phenomenological sociology is not unlike that of defining Marxist sociology or sociology in general. There is no one phenomenological sociology; in fact the question is still posed as to whether such an orientation is at all possible for it is at times regarded as a contradiction in terms (again not unlike the concept of a Marxist sociology). Several theorists have, however, addressed themselves to the task of formulating a phenomenological sociology either to replace conventional sociological approaches or to complement them (cf. Heap and Roth, 1973; Psathas, 1973; Filmer et al., 1972). Generally the concept of a phenomenological sociology is predicated on Schutz's attempt to formulate a phenomenology of the social world although other phenomenological sociologies coexist with the Schutzian position, e.g. reflexive sociology, ethnomethodology, existential phenomenological sociology.

Misleadingly, phenomenological sociology has been distinguished from conventional sociologies by the emphasis given to the former's preoccupation with the 'world of everyday life'. The implication of this programme is that the focus of study for a phenomenological sociology must fall entirely on the mundane, the trite and taken for granted, as opposed to the rare, irregular, controversial or intriguing. Reference to the 'world of everyday life' should be treated as indicating the necessity to focus upon and study assumptions and areas of potential social inquiry which have generally remained in neglect in sociology. Moreover this is not merely a recommendation for broadening sociological inquiry but serves in fact as criticism of conventional sociological approaches which ignore the topic of the sociologist's own involvement in, and dependence upon, the everyday world as a resource for his work. The inclusion therefore of the topic of the everyday world within sociological inquiry is not merely optional, or just interesting, but vital and necessary as constitutive of the outcome of any sociological work. From the phenomenological perspective the foundation of any inquiry – sociological, psychological, natural, or social science – is in fact the understanding of everyday life; therein lies the source of social meanings central to and implicit within inquiry. To argue for a phenomenological sociology is not, however, to restrict inquiry to what is referred to as the micro-level of analysis. As will be made clearer below, such a distinction may be seen as itself a manifestation of a sociological fallacy or reification which a phenomenologically oriented sociology contrives to render illusory. However, it may be noted that phenomenological sociologists have tended to neglect certain areas of inquiry, to focus upon specific themes and issues and thus have artificially restricted the domain of phenomenological sociological work to what are regarded as 'micro' issues or levels of analysis.

Studying social reality

That the social world is a social product resulting from the individual-society dialectical process is by no means completely uncontroversial, and yet it is not an unacceptable position within conventional sociology, its most respectable and receptive presentation being found in the work of Berger and Luckmann (1967). Phenomenological sociology is, however, less compatible with conventional sociological approaches than Berger and Luckmann's synthetic approach suggests. Specifically, it advances a critique of what is taken to be the conventional approach to the study of social reality through a display of the methodological differences, assumed to be unrecognized by sociologists indulging in positivist-empiricist approaches, between the social and natural sciences. The following topics, central to the phenomenological sociological critique, will be considered:

(1) The 'natural attitude' of conventional sociology
(2) The subjective-objective distinction
(3) The macro-micro fallacy

In discussing the 'natural attitude' of conventional sociology, phenomenologists have placed great emphasis upon the assumptions implicit in sociological work, namely the covert use, or taken-for-granted acceptance of common-sense understandings of everyday life which serve to provide sociologists with the possibility of being able to meaningfully account for, or employ, the social meanings which serve as their 'data'. These meanings are employed by sociologists as resources, to account for, or describe, social settings. Phenomenological sociologists and ethnomethodologists in particular have stressed the necessity of studying such meanings as topics in their own right. This issue is closely related to the subject-object distinction to be considered below.

Douglas (1971) argues that within conventional sociology the phenomenological sociological critique has been neutralized in terms of the macro-micro sociological distinction. Adherents of structuralist, systems theory, comparative or statistical rates type approaches have attempted to construct a defence of their respective positions by claiming independence for 'macro-sociology' from the emergent phenomenological sociology which is in turn depicted as 'micro-sociology'. However, as Douglas shows in each case 'macroanalysis' is dependent upon empirical evidence, itself derived from, and situated within, an understanding of everyday life. Consequently whether it is a sociology dependent upon survey research, social rates, or historical data, common-sense understandings of everyday life are shown to be implicit in each and every case. In fact, in order to further the possibility of scientific sociological knowledge Douglas states that,

We must stop treating macroanalyses *as if* they were scientific arguments, that is, arguments based on carefully done, systematic observations of concrete phenomena. Above all, it means that we must stop treating such structural analyses as if they somehow constitute '*the* sociological imagination' and make use of 'hard data', while those who do systematic observations of everyday life and analyse from these observations the meanings of things to the members are treated *as if* they were 'reductionists' making use of 'soft data'. The truth is the exact opposite (1971, pp. 11–12).

The demand therefore is for a rejection of the absolutist or objectivist standpoint within sociology, a critique of the notion that there exists only one general set of criteria for scientific validity (viz. the natural sciences) and further a critique of the view of man as an object causally determined by factors independent of his own volition. On the latter point it is interesting that sociologists fail to see the irony of their treatment of man as an object, preferring instead to contrive a 'special place' for the intelligentsia, men of knowledge, or social scientists beyond the perspectivity of ordinary citizens. This is not to deny an hierarchical distinction between the knowledge and understandings of sociologists and that of laymen but rather to draw attention to the fact that the grounds of the distinction have rarely been fully explicated. It is not enough to trade on the authority accorded to scientific work and scientists in bureaucratic industrial societies nor is it sufficient merely to refer to the presence or absence of expertise according to social group membership. The possibility of sociologists conceptualizing and even being able to assist in the treatment of people as objects, people management, is a consequence of the nature of our contemporary

81

society in which social relations take on, as Marx noted, the form of a relation between things. It is our responsibility to attempt to understand and transform this situation by first recognizing that sociology is not a scientific humanism, is not facilitating universal social understanding or enlightenment but rather perpetuates social divisions, theoretically justifies and draws upon reificatory understandings of social reality and thereby provides a scientific gloss for specific socio-cultural and historical social relationships which appear as naturally given. The proliferation of sociologies of knowledge has not provided an adequate forum for consideration of the complex issues involved in this area for the intent has been to repair or restore the sociological edifice, to justify the greater status of the sociological understanding vis-à-vis the layman's understanding rather than to critically explain or account for it.

The phenomenological sociological proposal is that the sociologist should adopt a theoretic stance, stand back and reflect upon the everyday world in order to be able to re-admire or re-view the experiences taken for granted. Hence, contrary to the individual living within a life-world that is pre-given, for whom the meaningful structures of this (his or her) life-world are not questioned, the phenomenological sociologist strives to engage in a process of phenomenological doubt. In other words he attempts to make explicit to consciousness that which is latent in everyday life. Clearly the orientation of the sociologist differs in a significant respect from those individuals he studies, for whereas the latter have a practical and personal biographical interest in their situation in terms of living in it, for the former the interest is in making a study of the 'others' ' life-world and the interest is structured not only by personal biography but also by the scientific tradition and community. In the doing of this work, however, the sociologist necessarily engages in activities which closely resemble those of people engaged in mundane situations, specifically the perceiving, constituting, and accounting for objects in the world (the others in 'their' life-worlds).

The nature of the situation outlined here is indeed critical for phenomenological sociology in that an explication of the meanings in a given social setting only becomes possible through the assumptions of everyday life and it is to the latter which the phenomenologist wishes to direct attention. In other words the sociologist must consider his own assumptions, made in the course of, and providing the very possibility for, the analysis. That this task is potentially an infinitely regressive one is not especially critical for it is readily acknowledged by exponents that a presuppositionless understanding of everyday life is impossible. What in fact is secured by 'bracketing' is a possibility of the sociologist showing or revealing the grounds upon which the process of explication is allowed temporarily to come to rest. What is sought is then the open recognition of an infrastructure of common-sense assumptions in the sociologist's work, assumptions not dissimilar from those made by members in the everyday world, to be addressed and made a topic of study.

The contrast with conventional sociology is striking, for whereas in phenomenological sociology subjective experiences are regarded as related to the processes of externalization and objectification through which the social world is produced in the form of 'society', 'community' or 'organization', and hence requiring study, for the former, human experience is frequently depicted as too subjective and inaccessible to be studied, resort being made instead to second-order conceptualizations in which the nature of the relationship to first-order conceptualizing remains unaddressed. As a consequence, employing meanings derived from his own life-world, treated in a taken-for-granted fashion, the sociologist is able to manufacture conceptualizations of a social world (unspecified) which are later employed or carried over to an analysis of other specific social worlds. How concepts are constructed or created, and of what 'object' they are the concept, is problematical for such a sociology in which universal conceptual consensus is absent and knowledge of the relationship between language, objects, and concepts limited in the extreme.

Subjective-objective distinction

The terms subjective and objective have not enjoyed an unambiguous usage in sociological debate. In one sense the terms are employed evaluatively, objective connoting true, scientific, rigorous and real, apparent to Any Man, whereas the term subjective by contrast denotes arbitrary, biased, unscientific and personal opinion. Subjective becomes in this sense a term of virtual condemnation, taboo for an aspiring science. To further confuse the issue there is one other sense at least in which the terms are employed in sociological discourse which is not manifestly evaluative; namely, where the terms are explicitly adopted to refer to different levels of analysis. In the second sense 'subjective' refers to an analysis which focuses upon the understandings or conceptualizations of the social world by members within it, it is an orientation which is concerned to establish the essential importance of meaning in the study and construction of social phenomena. In contrast 'objective' becomes applicable to a level of analysis which focuses upon the assumed emergent products of social interaction between members of the social world, treating the products as entities amenable to study independently of their constitution by members.

Characteristically within sociology the objective mode of inquiry (objective in both senses discussed above) has been considered as the scientific way to proceed in doing social science. However, within the ranks of the discipline there is considerable controversy over this particular issue,

> In some quarters objectivity has fallen into ill repute and is explicitly denounced; in many parts of the discipline the problem of objectivity is treated as insignificant and uninteresting; and even where the criteria of objectivity are adhered to in the inherited sense much less is made of it than used to be the case (Bittner, 1973, pp. 109–10).

Whilst agreeing with Bittner that objectivity has become a topic of discussion and controversy within sociology it is difficult to accept his view that the discipline has retreated from a position of more stringent objectivity to a lesser stance. That this is taken to be the case and further considered as a possible consequence of influences emanating from a phenomenological sociology is highly controversial and requires explication.

Bittner's paper seeks to establish the inappropriateness of the positivist idea of objectivity deriving from a misunderstanding of the relationship between social and natural reality. Basically three reasons are offered for abandoning the positivist approach. First, there is the question of the methodological contrast between natural and social sciences; second, it is argued that positivist objectivity impedes the construction of a science of social reality by not facing up to the tasks involved, in other words that its 'impartially objective depiction and analysis of the actually existing state of affairs as a functioning social order is in effect nothing else but a defense of this order' (ibid., pp. 114–15). Finally Bittner argues that conventional sociological approaches involve a contradiction in terms in that the objects of study are inherently devoid of objective meaning as demonstrated for example by the ethnomethodological revelation that 'factual realities of socially organized settings are throughout permeated by the ways-in-which-they-are-known, and derive, keep, and change their meanings with it' (ibid., p. 116). Acceptance of this view within sociology is not uncommon although it is frequently qualified by sociologists' persuasive retrievals of omniscience and claims of privileged status for the scientific character of their particular accounts vis-à-vis other acknowledged indexical accounts (cf. Goldthorpe, 1973). For Bittner, such claims to privileged status are unfounded in that the only grounds which are envisaged to warrant the elevation of the sociologist's account above that of the man-in-the-street, require the possible substitution of objective for indexical expressions. And as Garfinkel has shown

> Wherever practical actions are topics of study the promised

distinction and substitutability of objective for indexical expressions remains programmatic in every particular case and in every actual occasion in which the distinction or sub-stitutability must be demonstrated. In every actual case, without exception, conditions will be cited that a competent investigator will be required to recognise, such that in that particular case the terms of the demonstration can be relaxed and nevertheless the demonstration be counted an adequate one (1967, p. 6).

Consequently, as Bittner argues, in attempting an objective study of society some relaxation of the canons of objectivity is inevitable and indispensable. However, the consequences predicted by Bittner, namely the defeat of the conceit of privilege, do not necessarily follow, for it is still possible, even accepting all that has been stated, to regard conventional sociology as something more than merely one folk construction among others. Sociologists may still lay claim to superior information on topics investigated both in terms of quantity and reliability. Indeed it may be argued that the very position advanced by Bittner presupposes the possibility of legislating at the very least how not to do sociology, as well as offering an explication of social reality couched in terms which raise the question of the extent to which his own account may be perceived to be implicitly accredited with privileged status vis-à-vis the possibly contrary accounts of other sociologists and laymen. Caution must, however, be exercised in judging Bittner's work for it is not so much the case that he is opposed to objectivity as to what is referred to as positivist objectivity. Indeed the goal of his analysis may be seen to be the reconstitution of a science of society able to take full account of the objects of inquiry as constituted by human beings for human ends. By being true to the phenomenon an objective sociology becomes possible, but in order to be able to achieve such a reconstitution of the discipline the particular characteristics of social reality must be recognized.

One common problem which follows from a basic misunderstanding is that a phenomenological sociology is perceived merely to call for descriptions of social settings or situations as they appear to those involved, in other words to provide mere unanalysed impressions. Bittner refers to this position as abortive phenomenology noting that it constitutes above all a failure of realism, an inadequate understanding of the nature of everyday life and in particular manifests an ignorance of the essential significance of intersubjectivity for phenomenological sociology. Here there is an open acknowledgment of the tensions within phenomenology, tensions which may either give rise to work offering a 'fruitful theory of social reality' (e.g.

Schutz) or alternatively may lead merely to studies of the 'appearing' of reality in consciousness. It is the latter which has led to the consideration of a phenomenological sociology as solipsistic. The error in this evaluation can be displayed through a brief consideration of the 'subjective dimension'.

The phenomenological sociological approach, it is true, seeks to remain open to the phenomena themselves; however, this is not to say that 'society is entirely "in the mind" and has to be understood as being what people think it is' (cf. Goldthorpe, 1973, p. 455). Rather it refers to the fact that presuppositions about situations or events must be suspended, beliefs, theories and preconceptions considered as topics in their own right and thus critically analysed. Because individuals' assumptions (both sociologists and laymen) structure the(ir) world(s), if phenomena 'in the world' are to be analysed then such assumptions must also be examined. The world cannot be experienced or known in a 'raw' form, free from interpretation, for it is a world of intersubjectively constituted meaningful objects and relations which are in the world not in the mind of the observer. Phenomenological sociology like Marxian analysis does not divide the subject from the object of study; the objective, objectivity, is a subjective or intersubjective construction. As Pelz (1974) has noted of objectivity 'it has no necessary existence apart from inter-subjective conventions' (p. 145). The social world is not 'out there' with characteristics, attributes and appearances independent of individuals experiencing it, it is constituted through intersubjective communication and action. Phenomenological sociology focuses upon neither the subject to the exclusion of the object nor the object to the neglect of the subject but rather is concerned with the dialectic of the active perceiving subject and his experience of the objectiveness of social reality through intersubjective communication and understanding.

The macro-micro distinction – a sociological fallacy?

Within sociology the macro-micro distinction works to allow the sociologist to shift the focus of his investigations or interest from the 'hard data' of social structure (macro) to the 'soft data' of individual and group experience of social reality (micro). The ambition of many sociologists has been the achievement of a synthesis of these different 'levels' of analysis, an ambition as yet largely unfulfilled although there have been some interesting attempts, notably by Parsons and by Berger and Luckmann. Nevertheless the predominant feature of contemporary sociology has been the stress upon the macro-level as the 'more objective', scientific and relevant approach to the study of society. Micro-analysis has in consequence been regarded as secondary, either supplementing and filling out macro-analyses with the analysis of small-scale, delimited areas of inquiry, or alternatively as a subjectively situated analysis eliciting members' understandings of social situations and hence less important in sociological inquiry. Consequently the qualified and minority recognition accorded to phenomenological sociology has been limited to an acknowledgment of its micro-sociological relevance and implied impotence as far as macro-sociological issues are concerned. The ramifications of the phenomenological critique of the reificatory nature of positivist-empiricist sociology for the very macro-micro distinction are glossed over.

This evaluation of the relevance of a phenomenological sociology raises two questions, first, concerning the macro-micro distinction itself, namely its validity, and second, whether phenomenological sociology can contribute anything to the macro-societal level of analysis. Wagner (1973) in his analysis of the scope of phenomeno-logical sociology argues by way of Schutz's 'unfinished' *Structures of the Life-World* (Schutz and Luckmann, 1973) that a phenomeno-logical orientation in sociology is not restricted to the micro-level, for it provides in principle for the analysis of social phenomena from small-scale situations to large-scale structures.[2] Specifically, analyses of three types of interaction situation are to be found in pheno-menological sociology; these are referred to by Wagner as social-psychological, micro-sociological, and finally, the larger contexts of concrete interactional situations. It is the primary importance of the latter aspect, the felt necessity to produce a viable theory of inter-subjectivity, which distinguishes Schutz's contribution above all others. The recognition that social interaction, social contexts, are situated within a broader social and cultural configuration with both historical and structural dimensions does indeed denote an attempt to provide for the possibility of a phenomenological sociology com-ing to terms with supposedly macro-issues. Interestingly this very claim for Schutz's work may be taken as confirmation of his desertion from phenomenology.

In attempting to justify the relevance of phenomenological sociology to other than micro contexts Wagner stresses the import-ance of the conception of social structure as processual, dynamic and intersubjectively constructed in Schutz's work. It is this conception which provides for a critical and de-reified understanding of such everyday conceptualizations as society, institution, and class. With Weber, his demand is for a reduction of social abstractions to their concrete social core, for

. . . in sociology, concepts like 'state', 'cooperative', 'feudalism', and similar ones, in general designate categories of specific kinds of human interaction; thus, it is its task to reduce them 'to understandable' action, and this means without exception: to the actions of specific single individuals (Weber quoted in Wagner, 1973, p. 67).

It is therefore not the case that phenomenological sociology need be restricted to micro-levels of analysis although it is perhaps debatable that just such an impression is communicated by the apparent reticence of phenomenological sociologists to explore macro-areas of sociological investigation.[3]

In the terms of a phenomenological sociology what is required is a realization that facts about society and social phenomena are intersubjectively constituted by individuals engaged in meaningful interaction. Hence concepts like 'state', 'cooperative' or 'society' may be interpreted as meaningful, intersubjectively constituted terms employed to describe the emergent, apparently purposive and intentional behaviour of social wholes which in effect represent the products of aggregations of individuals acting to achieve their particular ends or goals. The message of a phenomenological sociology may be stated thus: 'we must avoid postulating "society" again as an abstraction vis-à-vis the individual' (Marx, 1973b, pp. 137–8). To adopt such a position need not, however, lead to a rejection of social wholes as necessary and significant topics for sociological study; it does not require the championing of methodological individualism in opposition to methodological holism. It is not a case of individuals or wholes but rather that both individuals and wholes are real, in other words the doctrines of 'holism' and 'individualism' are not necessarily incompatible. 'Only when the holist adopts the doctrine that wholes must have aims does the clash begin, for this makes the individualist appear to be denying aims, and thus existence, to wholes' (Jarvie, 1972, p. 157). The major problem with phenomenological sociological analyses of the relationship between subjectivity and objectivity or individual and society is that the critical discussions of sociology which are indirectly or directly provided offer only a theoretical de-reification (cf. Horton, 1971). Antitheses like holism-individualism, objectivity-subjectivity or macro-micro, are not purely theoretical in character, as Marx notes:

the resolution of the *theoretical* antitheses is *only* possible *in a practical* way, by virtue of the practical energy of man. Their resolution is therefore by no means merely a problem of understanding, but a *real* problem of life which *philosophy* could not solve precisely because it conceived this problem as *merely* a theoretical one (1973b, pp. 141–2).

As with the Marxian critique of the categories of political economy we should in analysing sociological works be aware of the relationship between sociological conceptual and methodological distinctions and the reified character of human reality in a given determinate socio-historical epoch. For Marx, economic categories are only the theoretical expressions, the abstractions of specific determinate social relations of production conceived by political economists independently of the historical movement of production relationships. That we as sociologists experience as contradiction distinctions between the objective and the subjective or holism and individualism is perhaps, as Pelz (1974, pp. 150–2) has noted, a symptom of social unease.

Phenomenological and empiricist sociology

Whereas for some sociologists the advent of a phenomenological sociology has been seen as an alternative to empiricist sociology, for others the 'new developments' have been regarded as potentially reconcilable with conventional sociological approaches. [4] The focus here will be on accounts which argue for compatibility between phenomenological sociology and conventional sociological approaches. In the case of Shearing (1973) a rather simplified account is offered of the common ground between positivist and phenomenological sociological perspectives, both being interpreted as taking into account the idea of society as a gestalt and necessarily therefore having to reconcile the institutional order (macro) with elementary forms of social behaviour (micro). Unfortunately whilst considering the difference of emphasis between the two perspectives in terms of the phenomenological preoccupation with the question of the constitution of the appearance of an objective reality and the positivistic emphasis on description of the objective reality, Shearing seems to ignore the critical issue of their quite different interest in the concept of society and what follows from this for his claim for a 'reconciliation'. To be fair it is clear that the difficulties arising from Shearing's work are consequent upon the adoption of Berger and Luckmann's analysis as exemplifying the phenomenological sociological perspective. If Shearing had treated their work critically it might have been possible for him to develop the question of the differences and compatibilities between positivist and phenomenological sociology and therefore to avoid terminating his analysis with an abrupt conclusion which glosses over significant problems. Indeed Shearing's brief statement of the similarities between Parsons' work and Berger and Luckmann's invites the comment that the latter's work although perhaps sensitive to phenomenology (largely through Schutz) is in fact situated squarely within the conventional sociological tradition, representing a synthesis of Durkheimian and Weberian perspectives, flavoured with Marxian analysis, and vaguely reminiscent of Parsons's own earlier attempt in *The Structure of Social Action* (1937) to fuse and synthesize distinct sociological approaches. By way of a final observation on a paper which offers directions toward a phenomenological sociology, the omission of any reference to the work of Schutz, arguably the only theorist to attempt to develop a coherent phenomenological sociology, is strange indeed.

In contrast the orientation of Strasser's (1967) work is towards the potential service that 'pure' phenomenology can render to empirical human science. His intention is to demonstrate the compatibility of phenomenological and empirical human science through first the establishment of the fact that phenomenology makes use of empirical data, and second by way of a purification of empirical human science from the 'prejudices' of empiricism, objectivism, and scientism.[5] For Strasser, phenomenology, ' . . . by laying bare a fundamental structure of human experience . . . provides the framework for empirical research' (ibid., p. 503). The implication of this position is that the rigorous character of phenomenology is far from being a threat to the existence of an empirical science of society; indeed it seems to represent the very precondition of such a possibility. The problem of objectivity which has for long been central to sociology is, in Strasser's terms, seen as a pseudo-problem, for cognition or knowledge is not independent of interests. As Habermas notes, ' . . . the attitudes towards technical control, towards an understanding of life's activities and towards emancipation from the quasi-natural forces of history and society determine the specific points of view from which we are first able to conceive reality as such' (1970, pp. 47–8). Only when the dialectical nature of human science, its self-reference, has been accepted and acknowledged will it become possible to understand that a human science, sociology, is never finished and yet, despite this qualification, can be an empirical science. For Strasser the stream of stimuli manifest in experience from which knowledge emerges are not abandoned, considered irrelevant or disallowed; on the contrary they constitute the starting point of analysis and are to be subject to 'correction'. Specifically they are subject to phenomenological philosophy, an approach which seeks not to destroy the results of empirical approaches but rather to draw attention to the limitations involved, namely that experience and evidence are not infallible and indeed should be considered problematical. The development of any inquiry then becomes a matter of explicating not only the 'what' but also the 'how' of experience.

Strasser's request is for a philosophically sensitized sociology which will recognize that at times both the philosopher and sociologist are interested in aspects of the human condition, for a sociology which will in effect acknowledge the mutually reinforcing, complementary nature of empirical and philosophical inquiry in the study of man. Specifically the demand is for a phenomenologically oriented sociology.

In the case of John Goldthorpe's (1973) examination of the claim that phenomenological sociology represents an alternative to positivist, empiricist sociologies, the focus tends to be upon ethnomethodology. However, given the purposes at hand sectarian differences are not critical, for although ethnomethodology may be distinguished from particular conceptions of a phenomenological sociology, many of Goldthorpe's observations and criticisms are appropriate in the present context. In a critical review, Goldthorpe attempts to show that phenomenological sociology has not accomplished a paradigm-shift within conventional sociology, the 'revolution' never got off the ground. The phenomenological project is portrayed, first, as in no sense novel, Goldthorpe arguing that it is perfectly consistent with critiques emanating from within the ranks of conventional sociology. Second, it is asserted that in any case phenomenology is not sociology and that therefore criticisms emerging from such a source are irrelevant to the discipline. There is in Goldthorpe's review therefore both a denial and an institutionalization of phenomenological sociology, contrast and assimilation.

Perhaps the most outstanding feature of his paper is, however, the continual emphasis upon the necessity for a 'corrective' and 'revelatory' sociological understanding. This is coupled with an apparent insensitivity to the questions which arise from such a pursuit, namely 'corrective of whom or what, by whom?', 'relevatory to whom through whose good offices, in what interests, by which individuals or groups?' Goldthorpe does not consider that the goal might not be either desirable or, alternatively, possible through the conventional sociological armoury of quantitative methods, manipulation of socially constituted 'data' and empirical 'testing'. His account displays a lack of any recognition that what is specifically required within the discipline is a thorough thinking through – not once and for all, but continually – of the salience, validity and purpose of adopted procedures. Unfortunately, for Goldthorpe, the methodological admission that

> . . . no matter how far back one goes in further reducing (or bracketing) one's phenomenological 'reductions', there inevitably comes a point at which one either accepts total solipsism and the impossibility of 'knowing' anything or grounds his thought in some presupposed (commonsensical) experience (Douglas, 1971, p. 22)

serves the purpose of neutralizing the phenomenological sociological criticism of conventional sociology's presuppositions. As a result the importance of the phenomenological stance is seen to be its revelation of the complacent and blinkered nature of sociological inquiry. The prescription, that we critically examine the taken-for-granted nature of assumptions as directly relevant to scientific work, is considered merely as a variation on the value-freedom theme and as such acceptable so long as it is recognized that the whole issue is answerable not in general terms but only instance by instance according to the sociologists' individual interests.

Goldthorpe summarizes the phenomenological sociological critique uncontroversially as stating that sociological methodology needs must differ from that characteristic of the natural sciences. He situates the debate not alone in the contemporary sociological context but also correctly recognizes the long-standing nature of this particular dispute in late nineteenth, early twentieth century German thought.[6] However, two counter-arguments are proposed by Goldthorpe, one referring to an empirical issue at the base of the phenomenological sociological position, the other to conceptions of the nature of sociology as a discipline, its scope and purposes. The first issue, concerning empirical assumptions implicit in the phenomenological standpoint, deals with the question of the validity of the empiricist treatment of interaction situations, specifically assumptions concerning shared, culturally based values and definitions. For Goldthorpe the validity of the phenomenological position and its recommendation that social interaction should be treated as problematical, rather than as an inevitable consequence of pre-existent value consensus, is seen to depend upon the crucial issue of the degree to which, if at all, individuals may be considered as 'programmed' by their culture, and by implication the extent to which the 'programme' is available or 'known' to the investigator. The implication of this position is not the 'cultural dope' hypothesis, but rather that norms and roles may not always be subject to differential interpretation, that in certain circumstances consensus over meanings and definitions may exist.

Goldthorpe's proposal that in certain social circumstances there may be a considerable consensus over cultural meanings and values raises interesting questions as to the possible limitation of both phenomenological sociology and ethnomethodology. However, in another sense his review 'talks past' the phenomenological position in that the latter is primarily concerned with drawing attention to the fact that the sociologist takes interpretive procedures for granted and that therefore his activity is not dissimilar from that of the layman, both falling victim to the natural attitude. The phenomenological position demands that interpretive procedures themselves become topics of analysis and that the sociologist accept that although he may take these procedures for granted they are important, having a bearing on the work in hand, and thus constitute a necessary aspect of the field of study (not necessarily for the same sociologist but certainly for other sociologists). As Strasser has noted, 'Purification of experience from empiricist, objectivistic and scientistic prejudices cannot be the task of the empirical scientist alone' (1967, p. 526).

In contrast to Goldthorpe who tends to limit the significance of the phenomenological critique of the taken-for-granted nature of interpretation in sociological investigation I contend that only by recognizing the necessity of making interpretive procedures a topic of sociological inquiry will the sociologist achieve a greater understanding not only of methodology but also the objective character of everyday life. Through the acceptance of interpretive procedures as a topic of study not only will it become possible to distinguish between situations and contexts in which interpretations, meanings and definitions are held in common from those that are not, but more significantly minimal provision will have been made for an understanding of the genesis of the differences between situations (whether intersubjectively 'negotiated' or 'programmed'), and equally important how a distinction is made recognizable both to 'members' and sociologists alike. Until the necessity for such work is recognized it will not be possible to consider criteria for deciding, recognizing or accounting for the possible variations in the contextual determination of social meanings.

The second argument propounded by Goldthorpe is perhaps the most basic of all and concerns the justifiability of the phenomenological conception of sociology's programmatic purposes; namely, is the concern of sociology purely with social action and interaction? Implicit in Goldthorpe's exposition of the difference between phenomenological orientation and his own position is the question of the purpose of sociology. Specifically in the case of phenomenological sociology there appears to be an implicit moral, humanistic orientation albeit individualist; in the case of the positivist-empiricist stance adopted by Goldthorpe a technical-practical orientation is apparent for which the goal is ' . . . to achieve a perspective on the social world which in relation to the standpoint of the actors involved might be radically corrective or revelatory' (1973, p. 455).

In an important sense the phenomenological stance does of course itself represent a radically revelatory perspective, vis-à-vis the layman's or sociologist's understanding of social reality and everyday life, in that it attempts to display the constitutive nature of the social world which the natural attitude masks. However, it is not itself easily mediated or communicable to the layman and more to the point, unlike the orientation of conventional sociology, it does not lend itself to 'application' or interpretation by intermediaries, social engineers, spokesmen, and policy makers; which brings us to the

93

crux of the matter, the thread running throughout the phenomenological critique of sociology, the nature of the (re-)production of everyday life. For Goldthorpe, following Popper, the existence of a 'third world' of objective ideas, or human products, is indisputable. Furthermore he argues that these objects have their own autonomous domain and cannot therefore be considered merely through interpretive procedures, accounts and interaction. Rather, ' . . . such . . . entities may properly be objects of enquiry in, as it were, their own right – apart that is from their actual interpretation in social action and rather as the conditions of such social action' (ibid., p. 457). This clearly illustrates not only Goldthorpe's assumption of the natural attitude but also his explicit faith in the privileged status of the sociologist. Whilst it may be readily accepted that the perspective of the individual, member, or the actor alone is not the panacea for sociology's problems, that from interaction unintended consequences frequently flow, and finally that in particular contexts sociological constructs and understandings do indeed appear to be corrective and revelatory, no indication is provided by Goldthorpe as to how and in what specific socio-historical circumstances such consequences may follow, or alternatively under what particular socio-political conditions sociology may be both corrective and revelatory. Indeed the implicit conception of the discipline's adequacy being reflected in its revelatory and corrective success is most remarkable and seems far more appropriate (adopting his frame of reference) to a political ideology or theological system than to a science of society. For to argue that, 'In certain contexts, that is, in regard to certain problems, such concepts could be corrective and revelatory in relation to lay members' understandings, and be accepted by members as such on rational grounds' (ibid., pp. 457–8) is to beg the whole question of not only the socio-technical constitution of corrective and revelatory criteria but also the social organization, control and purpose of social science in society.

To agree with Goldthorpe that sociology is more than merely one folk construction among others is not to reject outright the phenomenological sociological critique. For in focusing upon the status of the sociologist's account vis-à-vis that of the layman phenomenological sociologists have indirectly drawn attention to the fact that the perception of sociology as revelatory and corrective depends more upon socio-political factors than methodological differences. Through the sharing of assumptions about the nature of social reality or society as well as the mutual internalization and adoption of concepts of authority, expertise, division of labour and a given social distribution of knowledge by both laymen and sociologists (treating their own everyday assumptions and privileged status unproblematically), sociology becomes revelatory and corrective.

Although Goldthorpe is not unaware of the conditioning of language and associated cognitive processes by social relations of power and control, indeed he specifically refers to the ethnomethodologist's neglect of the question of the effect upon situations of the differential control of political, economic and symbolic resources brought by participants to interaction situations, he fails to reflect upon the ramifications of such an analysis for sociological work in general and the positivist-empiricist approach in particular. The revelation of limitations to the phenomenological position cannot serve as a recommendation for a return to the natural attitude, tolerance of unexamined presuppositions or an acceptance of the sociological reification of social reality. To be critical of the neglect of power relations in the phenomenological approach does not reduce in significance the revelation of the study of interpretive procedures as vital to sociology. What is crucial is that sociologists remain more than superficially receptive to the possibility of paradigm shifts, that the desire to retreat within the shell of an inflexible retention of the initial presuppositions of 'normal' science does not prevent the necessary emergence of alternative paradigms. For without doubt, uncertainty, and critical examination of methodological presuppositions the development of a humane, liberative science of society will not be possible and the progress of manipulative, technocratic pseudo-social science will continue unabashed.

Schutz

In the discussion of the impact or relevance of phenomenology for sociology, in the controversy surrounding the question of the disciplinary status of phenomenological sociology, namely whether philosophical or 'genuinely' sociological, scientific or non-scientific, the work of Schutz has been of central importance. Although it may be argued that Schutz was more concerned with philosophy than sociology it cannot be denied that his work is sociologically relevant especially in so far as he sought to elucidate the a priori structure of the world in which sociological phenomena emerge and are comprehended.[7] Drawing upon accounts and analyses of Sartre's, Husserl's and James's work Schutz's primary orientation was towards the study of the life-world. The fact that he did not recognize the constraints of 'discipline-defined phenomena', seeking instead an explanation of the constitution of social phenomena by both 'laymen' and 'experts' alike, in no way prevented him from addressing issues of specific sociological interest and relevance. In particular his attempt to explicate the structures of the life-world, to show the nature of scientific theorizing's frequent dependence upon common-sense assumptions of everyday life, as well as the arguable reconciliation of differing currents of philosophical and social thought, exemplifies the extent of his contribution to sociological discourse.

In this brief examination of Schutz's work four areas will be considered:
  (i) Social reality
  (ii) Provinces of meaning
  (iii) Social structure, objectification and determinism
  (iv) Science, knowledge and empirical sociology

Social reality

For Schutz analysis must begin with the problem of social reality; it is primary, the self-evident reality of the 'natural attitude' and as such pre-scientific. The 'commonsense world', 'world of daily life' and 'everyday life world', are the expressions which Schutz employs to refer to the social world in his account of the methodology of the social sciences, phenomenology, and social reality. Implicit in each expression is the understanding that the world is not a private place, not 'in the mind' as some theorists have implied in considering Schutz's work, but rather is intersubjective in character, each individual taking for granted that other individuals exist in this, 'their' world. In the natural attitude the individual therefore assumes that the social world is much the same for all other individuals. Schutz argues, however, that not only is social reality intersubjective but furthermore, ' "nature", the province of things in the outer world . . . is inter-subjective' (Schutz and Luckmann, 1973, p. 4). Hence the distinction between the natural and social worlds becomes redundant from this point of view, for objects belonging in the natural world are only 'knowable' through the mediation of the social. Consequently in the natural attitude both social and natural reality are assumed by the individual to be fundamentally the same for all other individuals as for himself. Reality is therefore experienced by the individual as objective, little or no distinction being made between the 'stratified social and cultural world' and the 'natural or physical world'. Indeed in the natural attitude of everyday life it is assumed or taken for granted that the social world is historically pre-given as a frame of reference in a manner as taken for granted as the natural world.

For Schutz therefore the salient issue becomes that of how the natural attitude is possible. Individuals do not merely receive intuitive understanding of the objects of external perception but in order to provide for the possibility of such understanding must have internalized lower-order meaning strata as a result of which natural things are experienced as cultural objects. This is not only necessary but furthermore represents an inevitable part of the social process. The meaning strata actually achieve 'reality' only through being coupled with events, objects, or facts in the world, and the events, objects or facts only 'appear' or become manifest because of their meaningfulness. Agreeing with Santayana's statement that 'the mind never has ideas, much less ideas which it can communicate, without a material means and a material occasion. . . . The hands holding tools or plans must intervene in order to carry out the project' (quoted in Schutz and Luckmann, 1973, p. 6), Schutz proceeds to argue that the individual's actions gear into the life-world, modifying and changing relationships and changing objects. Hence in a manner resembling in some respects Marx's discussion of reproductive labour Schutz asserts that social reality is modified by way of the individual's actions and yet through a dialectical relation social reality modifies the action itself. Implicit here in Schutz's work is a recognition of the existence of an objective order and a limitation on action through the constraints inherent in the natural and social world. The question of objectification, social structure and determinism, left latent in this brief introduction to Schutz's conceptualization of social reality, will be considered below.

Provinces of meaning

Schutz rather than referring to the concept of an homogeneous social reality proffers the term multiple realities. In a discussion of William James's work he proposes that 'there are several, probably an infinite number of various orders of realities, each with its own special and separate style of existence' (1971, p. 207). Schutz refers to these orders of reality as finite provinces of meaning. Examples of finite provinces of meaning include the everyday life-world, the world of dreams, the world of science, and the world of religious experience. Each particular province of meaning is regarded as finite in so far as it manifests a unity of lived experience. In other words, the particular provinces of meaning are not compatible, no one particular finite province of meaning may be reduced to or transformed into another. Any attempt at transition from one to the other needs must be accomplished by a 'leap', the exchange of one style of lived experience for an alternative. As each finite province of meaning results from the specific internal unity of its structure of meaning, transition between provinces gives rise to what Schutz terms a jolt or a 'shock'. For example he states,

> Only when we are motivated by our life plan to accept
> another attitude . . . or when we are disturbed . . . only when
> we experience a specific shock that bursts the limits of that

which is for us a momentarily 'real', finite province of meaning, must we transfer . . . the accent of reality to another province of meaning (1973, pp. 24–5).

Now although it is indeed likely that the everyday life-world will constitute the primary finite province of meaning, from which other finite provinces of meaning may appear only to be quasi-realities, it is also the case that from the perspective of the world of science the everyday life-world at times appears to be only a quasi-reality. In the former province of meaning there is a suspension of belief in every doubt concerning the existence of the world and its objects; for the scientist it is this natural attitude which is to be 'bracketed' or doubted. Consideration of the above, in terms of a comparison of the social world as defined and studied by sociology (the world of sociological science) and the everyday life-world of which the sociologist is a member as two finite provinces of meaning is interesting in that according to Schutz there is no way of reducing or translating from one finite province of meaning to another:

All these worlds – the world of dreams, of imageries and phantasms, especially the world of art, the world of religious experience, the world of scientific contemplation . . . and the world of the insane – are finite provinces of meaning. . . .
This finiteness implies that there is no possibility of referring one of these provinces to the other by introducing a formula of transformation (1971, p. 232).

This proposition does not represent a denial of sociology but rather a re-affirmation of its place as one among many possible accounts of reality, one of many 'coexisting orders'.

Social structure, objectification and determinism

The individual experiences each situation in which he finds himself as only to a small extent his own creation. Frequently his own and others' subjective-meaning contexts and modes of apprehension will seem to be part of an objective order. Schutz recognizes that such situations are limited and predetermined from the beginning, stating that 'Certain elements of the world-structure are irrevocably imposed on the individual. A historical social structure, which has a specific relative-natural world view, is ingredient in the elements of the biographical situation already on hand' (1973, p. 244). Although Schutz recognizes the institutionalization of action in social settings, the objectification of human intentions in sign systems and language, as well as the objectivated results of human acts, he appears to consistently avoid analysing their objective basis, viewing the latter as not a vital part of his investigation. Where he does specifically elaborate on an issue inherent in the process of objectification, for example language, he fails to develop his consideration of the constitution of reality by the individual beyond a mere reference to the filtering and consolidatory role of language. Whilst it is useful to recognize that the reality to which the individual responds is filtered and consolidated by means of language in line with the structure of meaning of the relative natural world-view, no account is offered of the multiplicity of empirical variations which can act as a filter for the appropriation of language and the given natural world-view. Rather Schutz appears to accept the fact that the social structure represents a rigid boundary within which the daily plans and priority structures of the individual take form. In fact in his consideration of social structure Schutz's work appears to be situated quite securely within conventional sociology, stressing for example in one case the division of labour and differentiation of roles as integral in providing for the possibility of differences in typical contexts of experience and action between individuals. In another example Schutz notes

> Every man stands in mutual relations to other men. He is a member of a social structure into which he is born or which he has joined, and which existed before him and will exist after him. Every total social system has structures of familial relationships, age groups, and generations; it has divisions of labour and differentiation according to occupations; it has balances of power and dominion, leaders and those led; and it has these with all the associated hierarchies (1973, p. 18).

However, despite alluding to structural factors, social position, status, role, prestige, social stratification or whatever, Schutz's intention is not a considered appraisal of the reasons why stratification or other social relationships may differ between societies or groups; such problems are merely delegated as being the sphere of interest of an empirical sociology.[8]

Science, knowledge and empirical sociology

No analysis of Schutz's work, no matter how brief, can avoid consideration of his discussion of science and knowledge, for it is in the field of methodology that his work has had the greatest impact upon sociology. He argues that one school approaches the analysis of social reality, interaction, or the actor, in the same way in which the natural sciences analyse their phenomena, that is to say by taking for granted that the methods of the natural sciences are the scientific methods. Alternatively there is a school of thought which argues that there is a basic difference in the structures of the social and natural worlds, the consequence of which is the understanding that the social sciences are in many respects distinctly different from the natural sciences. For Schutz both positions are inadequate. In the case of the former school of thought there is an assumption that by adopting the methods employed by the natural sciences reliable knowledge of social reality will be gained. Such an approach neglects the understandings of men in the reality of daily life and therefore becomes redundant for Schutz. The second school of thought which rejects entirely the natural scientific method may justifiably be seen to be tossing the scientific solution out with the bath water; this view according to Schutz disregards entirely the fact that certain procedural rules relating to valid thought are common to all empirical sciences.

Although Schutz argues that there are multiple realities and that each one represents a finite province of meaning, there being no way of reducing or transforming the one into the other, his methodological contribution appears to be levelled at providing just such a 'translation service' between the everyday life-world and the world of science. For even though Schutz asserts that scientific knowledge is merely one of many provinces of meaning within the total social reality it seems that his methodological postulates and his discussion of phenomenology and the social world are oriented towards sensitizing the social scientist to recognize his own assumption of the natural attitude, and further to then offer guidance as to how the scientist might proceed to the study of social reality. Schutz asserts that

> The main problem of the social sciences (is) to develop a
> method in order to deal in an objective way with the subjective
> meaning of human action and that the thought objects of the
> social sciences have to remain consistent with the thought
> objects of commonsense, formed by men in everyday life in
> order to come to terms with social reality (1971, p. 43).

Now of Schutz's methodological postulates, the postulate of adequacy is most relevant to the question of the possibility or impossibility of translating, transforming or reducing one finite province of meaning to another.[9] The postulate of adequacy asserts that if a scientific account of human action were to be presented to an individual actor as a script it must be understandable to that actor, translatable into action by the actor and furthermore comprehensible to his fellow actors in terms of a common-sense interpretation of everyday life. To achieve this end the constructs of the social scientist must be consistent with the constructs of common-sense experience of the social reality. Hence to be able to meet the postulate of adequacy the scientist must not just be able to 'leap' from one finite province of meaning to another but on the contrary be able to operate simultaneously within both the finite province of meaning of everyday life and the world of science.

It appears therefore that in Schutz's work the postulate of adequacy must founder upon the finite provinces of meaning which the world of science and everyday life represent. In order to save the sociologist from merely offering one account of a social situation among many, Schutz asserts that an attempt must be made to ground the account in the subjective experiences of the individuals constructing the situation. To achieve adequacy the sociologist's constructs must be compatible with the constructs of everyday life, for if

> the social sciences aim indeed at explaining social reality, then the scientific constructs on the second level, too, must include a reference to the subjective meaning an action has for the actor. . . . All scientific explanations of the social world can and, for certain purposes, must, refer to the subjective meaning of the actions of human beings from which social reality originates (ibid., p. 62).

Which brings us back to the central problem of the relationship between two finite provinces of meaning, 'the world of science' and 'the world of everyday life'. Not only is the question of how adequacy may be achieved left unresolved by Schutz but furthermore the relationship between the finite provinces of meaning and the postulate of adequacy is left ambiguous thus hindering the prospect of a re-constituted scientific explanation of the social world.

Knowledge and power

In his consideration of the social distribution of knowledge Schutz glosses over a great many important issues. Whilst recognizing that the social distribution of knowledge is a necessary consequence of the accumulation of differentiated knowledge Schutz considers that it makes little difference whether the learning of knowledge is socially conditioned, imposed, or whether the choice is left to the individual concerned. Such matters are structural problems, the solutions to which differ from one type of society to another. This is typical of Schutz's lack of concern with the content of knowledge and its distribution in society. Again, where he refers to differences between individuals in terms of knowledge, the 'uninitiated' are recognized to need only to turn to those who have been 'initiated'. Although the question of differences in knowledge is addressed Schutz fails to consider the possibility of inequities resulting from, and manifest in, the varying degrees of expertise. Rather, admitting the institutional basis of the differentiation of roles in the division of labour the impression given is one of reciprocity whereby 'for their part the specialists become the uninitiated in other problem areas' (1973, p. 301).

Similarly where writing of the autonomy of theoretical areas of knowledge from the life-world act-contexts Schutz is aware of the social-historical process which has led to the establishment of the theory and self-regulation of the history of ideas but he neglects altogether to examine the preconditions for the division of material and mental labour, issues at the centre of Marx's work on the division of labour and consciousness. In contrast to Schutz, Marx is explicit in asserting that the division of labour was originally nothing but the division of labour in the sexual act, only becoming truly the social division of labour with the separation of mental and manual labour through increased productivity. It is this division which has provided consciousness with the possibility that it can really flatter itself,

> that it is something other than consciousness of existing practice, that it really represents something without representing something real; from now on consciousness is in a position to emancipate itself from the world and to proceed to the formation of 'pure' theory, theology, philosophy, ethics, etc.
> (Marx and Engels, 1970, p. 52).

Schutz controversially rests his case with the proposition that the most obvious and empirically probably the most significant examples of the division of knowledge are those relating to age and sex. No criteria, however, are offered as to how the probable empirical significance or 'obviousness' became known, and further, as if aware of the possibility of an invidious comparison with Marxist accounts he states that 'it must be stressed that a generally valid material determination of the provinces of the social stock of knowledge is not possible' (1973, p. 311).

Further areas for extending the comparison with Marx include alienation, ideology and power. In discussing the nature of the 'we-relation' it is argued by Schutz that in certain circumstances the individual upon meeting his fellow man may hold back from a 'we-relation', replacing it with a 'they-relation'.[10] Now although Schutz correctly regards this orientation as exemplified by institutionalized acts, for example retailer-consumer, and notes that it may possibly indicate the beginning of the reification of the 'other person', the topic is considered to be beyond the scope of his project and so he merely acknowledges by way of a footnote the growing interest in the particular field concerned deriving from the concept of alienation in Marx's work. No attempt is made to analyse the structural pre-conditions which influence the individual's action in holding back from a 'we-relation' and adopting a 'they-relation' and no analysis is provided of the distinction, inherent in Marxian analysis, between objectification and reification.

An additional point of comparison emerges from Schutz's recognition that different versions of knowledge may coexist in particular socio-historical contexts, perhaps eventually being adopted by particular social groups or classes in the form of 'ideologies'. He argues that if the differences between the 'versions' becomes too great (polarization?) communication between the groups becomes difficult and the unity of society comes to depend more upon the distribution of power than upon common knowledge or relevances. Then, in a statement which in substance if not tenor approaches Marcuse's account of the constitution of one-dimensionality, Schutz asserts that industrial societies in order to avert the difficulties following from the different ideologies and their respective versions of the common good, attempt to transmit the essential ingredients and values inherent in a common good equally through highly specialized institutions, the intention being to minimize the effect of the filtering function of the institution of the family, providing thereby for some basic consensus between members of the society.

The final aspect of Schutz's work to be considered here concerns his brief references to the concept of power. In describing the growing gap between members in terms of knowledge he notes that the latter can become more and more of a power factor. However, this admission occurs in the context of further revelations that everyone is at the same time not only a layman but also a specialist, the consequence being an implicit counterveiling theory of power predicated upon knowledge. Although Schutz recognizes the existence of social structure, ideology, stratification, and power, and in addition is sensitive to the growing gap between expertise and the lack of it, as well as the increasing dependence of the layman on the expert, no attempt is made to offer any insight into such issues; rather, each is regarded as of great interest for the empirical sociology of knowledge only. In consequence it appears that although Schutz's work may have considerable critical methodological relevance for sociology it is potentially reconcilable with, even requires, an empirical sociology (cf. Zijderveld, 1972). Certainly he recognizes the existence and indeed necessity of such a domain, where the empirical issues 'outside' the scope of his project may be addressed. The question still remains, however, of the justifiability of deferring or transferring the onus of responsibility for such issues to the empirical sociology of knowledge, for the issues of social structure, ideology, stratification and power have long been central tendencies within sociology largely because of their apparent significance in determining the outcomes of given social interactions. Beginning with the question of how social reality is possible, how intersubjectivity materializes, it is surprising that Schutz postpones consideration of potentially significant issues directly bearing upon the constitution of the social world. Although Schutz's work is rich in insights it is, as Sallach has observed, 'staggering that a social scientist . . . could remain unconcerned with the influence that social and material existence may have upon consciousness' (1973, p. 32). Schutz's work is undoubtedly an important contribution to sociological work; however, the neglect of any consideration of the precategorical foundation of social life restricts its sociological relevance considerably. Whether phenomenology can accommodate issues and topics central to a Marxian analysis is a problem inherent in the development of a phenomenological Marxism in the writings of Paci (1972) and Piccone (1971).

Reflexive sociology

What is reflexive sociology? One view of reflexive sociology provides the impression that it is a neo-sociology of knowledge, a soul-searching sociology of sociology. . . . Alternatively reflexive sociology is presented by other writers to be either implicit and inevitably present in all sociologizing, in that all speech, writing or communication is presentable and comprehensible only through an awareness of a relevant situated context which does not appear explicitly in the communication. Accounts necessarily act back upon and depend upon the social setting being described, providing for its constitution. Or, in other cases reflexive sociology is regarded as a different way of doing sociology, taking the form of a prescription it is asserted that sociologists should be reflexive, that the latter should itself become a topic for sociology.

Perhaps the most obvious example of the 'first' version of reflexive sociology is that found in the work of Gouldner (1971). Basically reflexive sociology is described as having the following tasks:

(a) to be a radical sociology;
(b) to transform the sociologist and transcend sociology as it now exists;
(c) to develop the sociologist's self-awareness and his ability to provide valid and reliable information about the social world of others;
(d) to restore to men what is rightly theirs, namely society and culture;
(e) to construct a sociology of sociology.

As may be observed from the by no means fully comprehensive listing of the purposes and goals of a reflexive sociology, Gouldner's conception is indeed rather broad. The highly motivated desire for a better sociology rests not alone with methodological considerations but rather requires the sociologist to (re)discover himself in order that there might be a possibility for the discipline to 'act humanely in the larger world' (ibid., p. 512).

Gouldner's version of sociology seems to assume that reflexivity will develop spontaneously providing sociologists view their own beliefs as they view those held by laymen. Now although it is by no means uncontroversial that the sociologist's understanding of the laymen's beliefs are beyond reproach, no consideration is given by Gouldner to the necessity to re-think the nature and preconditions for sociological understanding, beyond, that is, a mere assertion that the subject-object distinction is redundant. The absence of a reflexive sociology may well be a consequence of sociologists' inability to be reflexive, to do a reflexive sociology. Certainly Gouldner provides little instruction or demonstration as to how it is to be done. However, what is perhaps most difficult to accept in Gouldner's proposal for a reflexive sociology is the belief that if only the sociologist could see himself as he sees others then not only would he better understand himself but also other men and their social worlds. Whilst this in itself is not especially controversial or indeed novel – one might regard it as elementary – the general tone of Gouldner's exposition is patronizing and oblivious to essential differences between the sociologist and laymen. For example, he asserts that

> We should increasingly recognize the depth of our kinship with those whom we study. They would no longer be viewable as alien others or as mere objects for our superior technique and insight; they could, instead, be seen as brother sociologists, each attempting with his varying degree of skill, energy, and talent to understand social reality (ibid., p. 490).

Now whilst it may be agreed with Gouldner that there are similarities between the sociologist and layman more attention needs to be given to the nature of important differences in their respective interests, relevances, opportunities and constructs. Indeed the very demand that sociologists should set their own beliefs up for scrutiny in much the same way that they investigate the beliefs of laymen in itself denotes the possibility of a significant difference between 'professional' and 'lay' sociologists. It is no less than a demand for a suspension of the natural attitude, of which the possible adoption by the sociologist would lead to a further basic difference between himself and laymen living in their social worlds, worlds viewed unproblematically.

It is not enough to assert that reflexivity depends upon self-awareness, or listening to and confronting ourselves, any more than

105

it is justifiable to assume that 'everything unusual is potentially radical; everything radical is morally good' (Zijderveld, 1974, p. 110). To proffer a reflexive sociology with any degree of credibility the attempt has to be made to show reflexivity. Certainly Gouldner offers many stimulating ideas and criticisms of sociology but the product is not so much an alternative, namely reflexive sociology, as several, at times juxtaposed, alternatives straddling phenomenological, Marxist and empirical terrains. If reflexivity is understood to be the radical searching and inquiring for, and of, the grounds of any position, then its search is never over, and whether such a quest is compatible with what passes for conventional or traditional sociology is controversial. Certainly a reflexive sociology must go beyond the self-awareness Gouldner has pleaded for to become a continual programme of questioning not only of beliefs and conclusions, but methods and the procedures by which the questioning of beliefs is conducted, a questioning of the questions so to speak. Phenomenologically speaking, to be radical means to open up the infinite regression to the roots of the problem, to the very ultimate presuppositions and assumptions, to engage in fact in a process of 'back questioning'. The question of such a sociology's relationship to traditional sociology whether as a philosophical laundry for sociological understandings or as an alternative to the conventional approach is aptly clarified by Filmer. He notes that

. . . to be interested in the essential reflexivity of sociologists' accounts would be to be doing reflexive sociology, and thus not doing the practical sociological inquiries constitutive of sociology (which is not reflexive). That is to say, it would not be doing sociology as it is traditionally understood, precisely because to be doing reflexive sociology is to be rendering problematical, and thus the central topic of inquiry, that very tradition in whose (unexplicated) terms sociology is understood as what it is (Filmer et al., 1973, p. 122).

If sociology can be reflexive, that is if it can be agreed that the doing of reflexivity can be reconciled to an activity which may be regarded as sociological, what form might it take? Will it be anything more than a constant searching for the grounds of reading, writing, and speaking? Will it, in the terms of traditional sociology, ever begin to 'get anywhere'? These questions and the problems which the very idea of a reflexive sociology seem to provoke suggest that it will remain incompatible with traditional sociology either until sociologists recognize the problematical nature of their tradition and the preoccupation with the progressive accumulation of information, data, and 'facts' about the world, or alternatively until reflexive sociology is compromised and transformed in such a way as to become a resource in the creation of a 'more objective, assumption-free', science of society.

Ethnomethodology

The inclusion of ethnomethodology as a type of phenomenological sociology is not uncontroversial, for although many argue that it exemplifies the development of phenomenological premises (Zaner, 1973; Mayrl, 1973; Heap and Roth, 1973) others claim that ethnomethodology is more broadly in agreement with positivistic approaches than with phenomenological principles (Bauman, 1973; Hindess, 1973). Although this disagreement is interesting it cannot be considered as a topic for investigation and description in this project, for to account for the nature of ethnomethodology let alone its fulfilment of the phenomenological promise is a task beyond the confines of the present work. An attempt will be made here to provide a description of the features of a particular type of investigative setting described by the members engaged in the constitution of the particular setting as ethnomethodology.

In Garfinkel's (1967) version of ethnomethodology the features of the social world are inseparable from the interpretative procedures by which the world is constituted, accomplished, or accounted for in ongoing social situations. Critically for conventional sociological approaches it is stated by Garfinkel that the objectivity of accounts is not independent of their uses in socially organized settings. Consequently not only is it being proposed that practical activities, circumstances, and sociological reasoning be considered topics for study, but furthermore, that the nature of accounts emerging from such studies will be tied to the occasions of their use, will be non-generalizable. Hence both the notions of objectivity and generalizability are called into question. Garfinkel thus presents ethnomethodology as a very radical departure from conventional sociological work, emphasis being placed upon the fact that contrary to the latter approach any occasion whatsoever may be a topic for study. Furthermore it is stressed that the distinction between objective and indexical expressions in sociology is based upon a gross misunderstanding of the nature of, and insensivity to, the analysis involved, and finally that attention should instead be given to the way in which members' accounting practices accomplish, or constitute, a social setting as recognizable and familiar. Central to this type of work is a concern with members' accounting practices, communication, language and conversation. It is an approach which not unlike phenomenological sociology focuses upon the common-sense world, in particular upon how members accomplish a sense of objective reality.

Contrary to conventional sociology there is for Garfinkel no correctional or competitive aspect to ethnomethodology. Whereas for the former the layman's account is frequently regarded as inadequate, uninformed and in need of enlightenment, for ethnomethodologists both laymen's and sociologists' accounts are of interest as topics of inquiry. For Garfinkel it is clear that the task is not to remedy members' accounts; rather the topic of interest is that of how an account or sense of world or reality is accomplished or possible. This topic is recognized to have been either assumed, neglected, or considered settled by theoretical representation within sociology. Hence the focus of his work is upon the background features, the hidden aspects of everyday situations. However, before proceeding a brief reference to the question of remedying accounts is required, namely that whilst Garfinkel is not concerned with remedying members' accounts it is clear that his work represents in itself a remedy for sociologists' accounts. That is, one of its purposes is implicitly to remedy sociological accounts by displaying what sociology has not attended to, and showing its importance to sociological work.

As is by now well known Garfinkel's method for revealing the importance of background expectancies involves the staging of a disruption, the possibility and creative knowledge of which is, although interesting, not considered as a topic of study. It is particularly ironic that Garfinkel's demonstrations are 'uninterestingly reflexive' upon his members' knowledge of practical jokes, pranks, conning, etc., and his access to resources, specialist knowledge, and facilities following from his privileged position as an academic. Garfinkel does not address this issue nor the question of his privileged status vis-à-vis his victims.[11] Rather his attention is apparently devoted to modifying the objective structure of the taken-for-granted situation, the intention being to reveal the existence of background expectations through their absence, by way of their disruption. In such circumstances it then becomes possible to note members' procedures for re-storing a sense of what the situation 'really' was (is). The infringement of the individual's stock of 'natural facts of life' relevant to a given setting is then seen to give rise to the individual having to do interpretive work in order to re-construct the 'facts'.

Now although the demonstrations are perhaps initially fascinating and even amusing (providing one is not involved) there is more than a sense in which such work is unsatisfactory. Specifically there is the absolute lack of any recognition of the structural factors which provide for and allow of the possibility of doing, writing, and publishing books about ethnomethodology. To name the most obvious factors there are political, economic, and military circumstances pertaining to the acceptability and toleration of 'unproductive' work and its financing. Can 'Any Man' obtain the necessary finance and resources for projects which apparently serve no other purpose than to offer different scenarios for the display of ethnomethodology? Is 'Any Man' in a position to proceed to reek bewilderment, anxiety, stress and embarrassment on others purely in the interest of displaying or revealing a dependence upon background expectations? If not then the question necessarily arises as to the structural factors and specific distribution of opportunity which gives rise to not merely a sense of the possibility of ethnomethodology but more to the point the actual resources necessary for its conduct. To pose such questions of Garfinkel's work is to draw attention to the question of the nature of the social world in which it is possible to do the work which he finds interesting, it is to emphasize that there is more than a sense in which the social world exists, beyond the interpretive procedures by which a given sense of the social world is described or communicated. While there is justification for being critical of conventional sociological approaches trading in reificatory representations of reality there are also reasonable grounds for rejecting the point of view which reduces social structure purely to interpretive procedures.

Curiously Garfinkel's ethnomethodology focuses entirely upon accounts of everyday situations to the almost total exclusion of any consideration of social action and its material effects. His world communication and hence is one of his sociology neglects the factors which implicitly provide for a given distribution of cultural resources from which members needs must draw in order to provide an account of any given situation. It is a type of sociology which tends to focus on talk, and talk about talk, rather than seeking to get to grips with the nature of what people do, how they account for their actions and the nature of the dialectical relationship between thought and action. The exception in Garfinkel's work occurs in the case of his study of Agnes, a 'genuine' as opposed to a 'manufactured' social situation in the sense that there is no explicit attempt to produce a new situation through a disruption of her background expectancies.

Agnes

Descriptively the situation was as follows. Agnes sought a particular medical service from a specific social group within an institution. In order to be granted the service she had to submit herself to interview over a given period of time. Garfinkel was a member of the interviewing panel, 'passing off' as a genuine member of the medical team concerned with the case. In his account of the case Garfinkel relates Agnes's account of her biography and interestingly it serves for

Garfinkel as an illustration of the way in which sex status is a managed achievement, that is, may be seen as the outcome of a member's knowledge of what is required to pass as 'female'. For Agnes the encounter was eventually successful in that she 'qualified' for the services, successfully passing the interview by convincing those involved that her condition was genuine and that her desire for an operation to 'confirm' her sexual status was warranted. It is important to note at this point that Agnes's success was achieved against, or rather at the expense of, some opposition, in particular from the urological intern. However, Agnes had the operation and proceeded in due course to lead a 'normal' life. Garfinkel's problems occurred some considerable time after the completion of the study, namely through the revelation by Agnes that her condition was induced by hormone tablets. Characteristically Garfinkel with a heads I win, tails you lose manoeuvre turns the revelation to advantage by remarking that 'This news turned the article into a feature of the same circumstances it reported, i.e. into a situated report' (1967, p. 288). However, the problems with this example are deeper than Garfinkel admits and serve to exemplify more general limitations in his overall approach.

First, there is the question of Garfinkel's working with a psychiatrist-psychoanalyst, and a psychologist, passing off as being medically informed, playing the part of a medically qualified member of the panel. The question of his 'success' in passing off as a genuine member of the panel is not addressed, neither does he consider how (if it is the case) he is able to pass off in the appropriate manner. Where the question is approached he is brief and oblique, specifically in an admission that he was aware at times during conversations with Agnes of his own lack of medical knowledge and her 'need' for 'authoritative answers', that is to say answers to medical questions supplied by a physician. The implicit question here of the social distribution of medical knowledge, expertise and the possibility of other types of knowledge and ability being inequitably distributed is not addressed by Garfinkel. Second, there is at no point in his account of the case any discussion of the interview as a structured situation, to which the different parties may bring vastly different resources. Although it is implicit in his account that Agnes presented herself for interview for a specific purpose it is not acknowledged that the goal she was seeking, namely an operation, was a service or resource access to which was controlled by the interviewers, by those who eventually had to arrive at a decision. That Agnes was engaged in persuading, negotiating and appealing for the particular service is recognized but the stratified nature of the social situation is not made explicit.

Additionally the question of the decision-making process itself is not considered at all by Garfinkel. This is an unfortunate and critical omission in that without doubt the distinct decision-making roles played by the psychiatrist-psychoanalyst, psychologist, ethnomethodologist (Garfinkel), and the urological intern (and possible others) who was firmly opposed to the decision to operate, seem to be of direct relevance to an understanding of the case. It appears that one 'sense' of what was the 'right' decision triumphed over another, and the question of how this occurred and what was involved in producing the given outcome is clearly important, although apparently in view of its absence, uninteresting to Garfinkel. In retrospect, the intern's feeling that the operation was neither necessary nor ethical plus Garfinkel's own admission that there were vital areas of Agnes's biography of which the medical team had no knowledge lends credence to the view that the decision-making process is vital to an understanding of what possibly transpired.[12]

In view of the unusual nature of the Agnes case, specifically the necessity for her to 'prove' her sexual status (or rather as it transpired to prevent others from disproving her adopted sexual status), Garfinkel's assertion that Agnes's performance constitutes a resource through which an understanding of a member's methods for accomplishing normal sexuality is gained, must be considered highly problematical. One lesson to be drawn from this study of Garfinkel's is that accounts are not everything. For members' accounts give rise to actions which have consequences and although the understandings and readings of the accounts and even in some cases the consequences of the actions might be 'reversible' the same cannot besaid to hold in every case for the consequences of every action. Sociologists in addition to studying accounts must also study actions and their outcomes.

Ethnomethodology and sociology

The common element uniting the various ethnomethodological projects on for example science, theorizing, peasant talk, making a telephone call, or the art of walking, is the overriding concern with practical reasoning, the preoccupation with the ways in which members render situations intelligible or achieve a sense of 'world'. For the ethnomethodologist it is apparent that 'knowledge' constitutes the world in which we live, it is individuals' subjective meanings which create the reality of the world. As a consequence the focus of attention, the topics of ethnomethodological inquiry are the very issues and themes which conventional sociologists take for granted as resources. Typically ethnomethodologists assert that

The presented texture of the scene, including its appearance

111

as an objective recalcitrant order of affairs, is conceived as the accomplishment of members' methods for displaying and detecting the settings features (Zimmerman and Pollner, 1971, p. 95).

Hence ethnomethodology treats as problematical the established procedures upon which sociologists and laymen alike depend, sociology itself being treated merely as one among many accounts of the social world, as a kind of 'folk discipline'.

Now in so far as ethnomethodologists focus upon the concept of social structure as an 'accomplishment' there need be no disagreement. For the question of how a 'sense' of social structure is accomplished is important in its own right, it is per se interesting and relevant to sociology, but not to the exclusion of an analysis of the characteristics of the social structure itself, its emergence, construction and determination of consciousness. That is to say, the concern with the possible variety of 'senses' of social structure and the nature of their respective accomplishments must not be allowed to displace analysis of the differentiated and stratified character of the sources of common-sense constructs of the social structure. For the latter represent the very preconditions for the emergence of the accounts which appear to be ethnomethodologists' major interest. Of course it is important to examine, as Zimmerman and Pollner argue, the 'fact of the factual properties' of social situations and objects. Clearly the question of how individuals 'provide for the fact that status hierarchies are factual features of the member's world' (ibid., p. 38) is important to sociological work. However, to address such a question without first giving any consideration to the possibility of the differential distribution of resources (e.g. knowledge, awareness, opportunity) available to members, or second, without providing any analysis of the variable resources upon which members might draw for accounts, is to offer little in the way of a comprehensive attempt at an understanding of the many salient issues involved. For example the apparent ethnomethodological predilection to ignore the question of the role of ideology, propaganda, censorship, education, the media, force, power and control, in the constitution of the features of a social setting as it appears to a member is unsatisfactory. Not only is there an absence of analysis of members' senses of ideology, force, power, etc., but more importantly no allowance is made for the possibility that factors such as these, outside or beyond the immediate sense of what members take to be the features of a social setting, might well be central to the constitution of the very sense that is ignorant of them.

As Bauman has noted in his critical discussion of ethnomethodology '. . . the notion of "false consciousness" cannot be sensibly discussed within the confines of ethnomethodology' (1973, p. 17). Not that ethnomethodologists regard this issue as presenting any particular problem. Far from it, in such instances the ethnomethodologist writes and talks of a policy of indifference and appears to be abstaining from all judgments of value, adequacy, importance, or significance. An example of this reaction is McHugh's statement that,

> To say 'false consciousness' is to replace one criterion (common sense) with another (institutions according to sociology).
> All well and good, except that it is unreasonable to ascribe subjectivity to one and objectivity to another, since both are objective in their own terms – it is the relation between the two criterion which is distinctive (1968, p. 10).

Note that McHugh's terms of reference for discussing false consciousness are undifferentiated laymen's accounts and sociologists' accounts. By affirming that both are objective in their own terms McHugh is side-stepping the issue, namely that 'terms' are evaluated and stratified in social communities such that for example scientific accounts are frequently accorded status and authority whereas laymen's accounts are held to be uninformed and in need of revision or correction. Furthermore the issue is not as simple as McHugh suggests, it is not a case of one criterion, common sense, versus another criterion, institutions according to sociology. Sociological accounts are compatible with particular common-sense understandings and accounts and incompatible with others. Hence sociology may be considered to be bourgeois apologetics (Horton, 1971), sociological accounts being treated as scientistic legitimations of 'bourgeois' common-sense understandings and therefore as a form of false consciousness. Alternatively sociology may be treated as a form of social criticism, as a radical and critical science of society, in which case the sociological account may well contradict or conflict with prevailing common-sense understanding whilst nevertheless being compatible with radical or revolutionary common-sense accounts of the social world. The comments McHugh makes are inadequate especially in so far as he does not address the question of the social significance and evaluation of science (social or natural science) or the socio-political procedures by which scientific or other social communities arrive at agreement over the status of an idea, proposition, theory or event. Stating that it is 'unreasonable to ascribe subjectivity to one and objectivity to another' is to neglect entirely the fact that social communities do ascribe, stratify and evaluate. Minds are not only displayed they are weighed or judged. Although 'in their own terms' common-sense accounts and scientific accounts may both be objective, to leave the issue there is to neglect altogether the socio-historical context within which people are consciously creating, communicating, acting upon and judging accounts of the social world. Judgment and evaluation occur in a social context through the employment of specific determinate criteria. To say false consciousness, is not merely to replace one criterion with another but to be critical of the criterion from the standpoint of an alternative social community's intersubjectively constituted criterion.

Ethnomethodologists are concerned only with the practices members employ to accomplish or sustain a sense of an objective structure of social activities, not with the effects of social activities upon the members, or upon their sense of the structure of social situations. Furthermore no consideration is given to the social organization of communication or to the accomplishment of a sense of a specific objective structure of social activities and the differential role played by specific social groups in the constitution of the latter structure. From each of these issues ethnomethodologists seek the shelter of their own particular cloak of neutrality, namely the policy of indifference. Their concern is not with the consequences of actions nor with the relationship between thought, knowledge, talk, action and their respective consequences, but with the question of the methods and procedures adopted by members in the constitution of the features of a social setting. Whether such an activity may be regarded as a type of sociology, let alone *the* sociology, or whether it needs must be recognized as a form of self-indulgent and privatized philosophy will no doubt continue to receive interest and comment from both the converted, the opposed, and the bewildered.

Summary

Phenomenological sociology is regarded within the discipline as either an alternative to, complementary with, or finally completely irrelevant for, sociology. Whilst the phenomenological critique of aspects of conventional sociology has been important, the tendency to regard it as an alternative form of sociology has been counter-productive leading to a preoccupation with accounts, descriptions, conversations, and talk about social settings, to the detriment of any examination of social reality, social structure, or the consequences of action. The development of sociology towards an understanding of the nature of sociological work itself, the (re-)production and transformation of social structures and the procedures by which members accomplish a sense of social structure, require much more than an analysis with a one-sided emphasis upon subjectivity. The two opposing forms of analysis predicated upon subjectivity and objectivity must be replaced by an alternative capable of incorporating, and allowing for, the dual nature of social reality.

4 Phenomenology and Marxism

Phenomenological sociology and Marxian analysis have both been considered as the source of basic criticisms of classical and contemporary sociological approaches, producing a 'new direction' for sociology and yet another re-birth of Marxism as the only science of society, in contra-distinction to 'bourgeois' sociology. The results have so far been generally disappointing for in each instance not only have the initial limitations of sociological thought remained, in some form or other (less generous critics might suggest that they have been enhanced), but in addition an understanding of the nature of the social world, of the relation of man and society, has not been forthcoming. Indeed the continuing inadequacy of social thought as well as the frustration of social practice has produced, as we have seen, a plethora of writing addressed specifically to the question of the failure of both sociology and Marxism to account for the nature of society and social reality in general, and specific social milieu in particular. As a result the attempt to forge a synthesis of, or create a merger between, phenomenology and Marxism may be regarded as a response to the particular inadequacies of social and sociological thought, as well as to the limitations of orthodox Marxist attempts to account for social relations in societies variously described as industrial, post-capitalist or rationalized. It is perhaps true to say that the major impetus for this particular development rests more with the increased recognition of the poverty of traditional Marxist thought, in particular the omission of a theory of consciousness, rather than with any controversy over, or within, sociology and phenomenology. However, both sociology and phenomenology are addressed by phenomenological Marxism, indirectly in the case of the former, directly as far as the latter is concerned. The encounter between Marxism and phenomenology achieves significance for sociology when we examine the relationship between the theoretical base of the phenomenological sociological critique of positivist sociology and that of the Marxian critique of pseudo-scientific approaches to the analysis of social relationships (e.g. political economy). Therefore in examining the idea of a phenomenological Marxism discussion should not be restricted in relevance to Marxist thought alone.

What has been called the crisis of Marxism, in particular the failure of the revolution in its presence (USSR) as well as its absence (the capitalist world), has led many scholars to reject the sterility of orthodoxy and to cultivate the regeneration of what is regarded as the 'genuine' Marxian project. The most relevant example of this tendency is in the work of the 'young' Lukács, in particular the controversial *History and Class Consciousness*, an important root source for many attempts to formulate a phenomenological Marxism.[1] To a lesser extent the work of Merleau-Ponty may also be treated as an important resource for the development of a phenomenological Marxism.[2] However, there is a significant difference between Lukács and Merleau-Ponty in that disillusionment for the latter materialized in terms of a critique of Marxism, eventually leading to a total rejection of Marxian analysis (and hence the abandonment of a phenomenological Marxist analysis), whereas for Lukács the early work manifesting a phenomenological-existential influence was subsequently punished by the party and later disowned and subjected to self-criticism as a necessary prelude to Lukács's return to the fold. Work which therefore lent itself to a phenomenological Marxist orientation was rejected in favour of a relatively 'orthodox' interpretation of Marx. Our interest here clearly cannot be with the particular idiosyncrasies of Lukács's biography; rather his work must be treated as of significance in so far as it addresses the issues of consciousness, reification and subjectivity, topics central to the debate on the possibility of a phenomenological Marxism.

In Lukács's terms the essence of Marxism is method, 'the scientific conviction that dialectical materialism is the road to truth' (Lukács, 1971, p. 1). Upholding the distinction drawn by Marx between the outward appearance and the essence of things he outlines his position on empiricism, science, knowledge and the dialectical method. In considering Lukács's views on these topics it is important to situate the analysis in its explicit political context, namely in terms of his preoccupation with not only defending and reviving Marxism but also elucidating the revolutionary basis of the method inherent in the revelation of the dialectical relation between the subject and object in the historical process. It is therefore not surprising that an interest in promoting the re-unification of theory and practice, dependent upon the emergence of the consciousness of the proletariat (which itself depends upon the revelation of the underlying social relationships hidden beneath the appearance of reality) should be high on Lukács's list of priorities. This concern with the conditions necessary for the emergence of consciousness led Lukács to reconsider the nature of the historical process and social reality. Interestingly several of the issues with which he was indirectly concerned in the course of these investigations, for example the nature of socio-historical facts, as well as empiricism and its relationship to science, are still of considerable relevance in contemporary social science constituting important topics in critical theory, sociology, phenomenology and Marxism. Adopting a critical stance to what he termed the 'blinkered empiricist' approach of the sciences Lukács sought to reveal the 'true' nature of facts, namely that they were not self-evident but rather represented the product of interpretation on the basis of a given albeit frequently implicit theory. Indeed his comments on the relationship between the natural attitude of the social sciences predicated upon the methods of the natural sciences and the social structure of capitalism are close to Husserl's own discussion of the consequences of Galileo's 'mathematization of nature' for European science. For Lukács the dialectical method makes problematical the illusion of self-evident facts and provides the possibility of a recognition of the historical character of social facts. Because in his conception science is an inherently social enterprise, 'pure' facts whether of the natural or social sciences become conceptually problematic. The sciences and scientific method which operates with allegedly 'pure' facts are treated by Lukács as harmonious and compatible with the dominant interests in a capitalist society. In particular the proliferation of separate disciplines with their respectively distinct provinces of meaning, subject matters and 'facts' is representative of and even a catalyst to the reification of human relations and the extension of the division of labour, both of which in turn further transform the nature and perception of social phenomena. To this Lukács proposes an alternative; namely an analysis of the apparently isolated facts of social life as aspects of the historical process, integrated into and treated in terms of the totality which alone can represent reality. The sub-division of reality by the sciences of capitalism is rejected in favour of an approach which recognizes the essential unity of the whole.

If self-evident, culturally located, common-sensical and historically mediated understandings are accepted as scientific 'fact' then according to Lukács the essence of 'facticity' is being neglected, namely its historical constitution. Facts are the products of definite historical epochs and as a result must not be accepted uncritically as unchanging, self-evident, objective and external. Failure to subject such 'facts' to critical analysis can only lead in one direction, namely to sterile description which reifies structures by elevating the given reality to the status of an externally determining objective world in which subjectivity has neither place nor validity. Hence when scientific conceptualization is based upon the self-evident data of the pre-theoretical life-world it must stand condemned of basing itself upon the factual appearance of the historically and culturally specific society within which it exists. For Lukács this is a case of science taking 'its stand simply and dogmatically on the basis of capitalist society' (1971, p. 7). However, through the dialectical method the 'real' existence can be revealed, the essence of reality can emerge from behind the veil of appearance. This involves an analysis of the relationship between the actual phenomenon and the form in which it appears. Such an analysis must treat the particular appearance of the phenomenon, as much as the phenomenon itself, as a product of the historical process, both having 'grown in the soil of capitalist society'. Lukács, following Marx, therefore urges that only by treating social facts as aspects of the historical process, as integrated in a totality producing both the phenomenon and its appearance, can an understanding of reality be achieved. The alternative, exemplified by what Lukács alludes to as bourgeois science, is to treat the various elements in reality as independent and autonomous, that is to accept the extant form of the division of labour in society as a valid basis for scientific conceptualization. The consequence of this tendency and the concomitant adoption of the methodology of the natural sciences as the model for science in general is that science becomes an 'ideological weapon of the bourgeoisie'. Not that all science is ideological; on the contrary it is the attribution of eternal validity and externality to the categories and laws of bourgeois society which produces the critique of 'its' version of science.

In capitalist society there is a dual concealment of reality which serves to obstruct the pursuit of knowledge and understanding. First, the world is regarded as composed of unchanging objects when in reality 'the objective forms of all social phenomena change constantly in the course of their ceaseless dialectical interactions with each other' (1971, p. 13). Only when the object is analysed in terms of its relationship to and function within the totality, only when the conceptualization of the object and its laws are recognized to be the product of 'fetishistic illusions enveloping all phenomena in capitalist society', is it possible to begin to distinguish appearance from reality and hence come to understand the objective forms. The second type of concealment is related to the first in that the categories of, for example, economics or sociology appear to men as objective and external facts rather than abstractions of the relations of men with one another. This form of concealment, reification, is central to Lukács's analysis in that it provides an opportunity to reveal the significance and relevance of subjectivity, not in the idealist sense whereby thoughts on reality are confused with reality itself but in terms of the active participation of subjects in the creation and constitution of their social world. Whereas empiricist social sciences predicated upon the methodology of the natural sciences treat social relations between men as things, reducing men to roles or objects in social encounters, the Marxian method adopted by Lukács allows for the reconciliation of subject and object in the constant historical production of reality. This dualism of subject and object, along with that of theory and practice, as well as their respective 'remedies', occupies a central place not only in Lukács's reading of Marx but also in both phenomenological Marxism and critical theory. In addition both issues have long been at the centre of sociological debate prompting sociologists to re-inquire as to the nature of social science, the relationship between sociological and common-sense understanding as well to consider the actual and most beneficial relationship of sociology to the social world. For Lukács the path to enlightenment, emancipation and 'true' consciousness appears only to be possible through dialectical materialism, the science of society.

The occasion for Lukács writing *History and Class Consciousness* is clearly very different from the interests central to the present work. Lukács was writing in defence of Marxism, seeking to revive and develop Marxist thought, whereas this particular work is directed towards sociology and the significance or relevance of Marxian analysis for sociologists. Necessarily therefore the inflexion is different and the emphasis placed by Lukács upon the revolutionary mission of the proletariat, his retraction and self-criticism, as well as the significance of such changes in his work, will not be addressed here. However, particular aspects of Lukács's work have been considered in so far as they represent a significant resource for phenomenological readings of Marx, explicitly in the case of Kosik (1968, 1969), Piccone (1971) and Miller (1970) and implicitly (that is to say virtually unacknowledged) by Paci (1972). Second, many of the issues discussed in *History and Class Consciousness* are now regarded as important in their own right within sociology, their incorporation as with Marx's own work frequently being through a process of dilution and mediation by sociological authors, one important example being what has come to be known as *The Social Construction of Reality* thesis (Berger and Luckmann, 1967). The major difference between Lukács's work and that of sociologists Berger and Luckmann, besides that is the assumed intended readership, is that whereas the former explicitly attends to the question of the historical process, albeit neglecting to amend Marx's concepts and categories to take account of the change in historical circumstances, the latter (Berger and Luckmann), although seemingly aware of the relevance

119

of the historical process and historical forces for their analysis, generally gloss over the problem. In consequence their analysis of the process of institutionalization is abstract and ahistorical, there being no attempt to relate the work to concrete historical reality. On the other hand Lukács's work itself appears to be rather abstract in that, outpaced by the passage of time, it suffered the irony of appearing 'when it had already become evident that Marxist revolutions in Western Europe had been defeated' (Piccone, 1971, p. 8).

Lukács's work represents an attempt to revive Marxism through an incorporation of the active subject. By recognizing the need to compensate for the lack of an adequate theory of consciousness in Marxism Lukács sets the parameters of his analysis to deal with the emergence of consciousness, the problem of reification and the conceptualization of social reality as a processual and historical totality. One problem does, however, emerge in the dialectical materialist analysis he provides, namely the question of the relationship of social reality to the natural or physical world. Are there any pre-categorical, 'natural' determinants? Can we have a dialectics of nature? Lukács largely avoids a reasoned rejection of the case for a unification of the dialectic of man with that of nature merely asserting that Engels was in error to attempt to formulate a dialectics of nature. The dialectical method is, therefore, restricted by Lukács to history and society and Engels's account is regarded as the product of a misunderstanding of the method. This aspect of Lukács's work has, however, met with a very critical reception; for example Gramsci notes that,

> It seems that Lukács asserts that one can only speak of the dialectic for the history of man but not for nature. . . . If his assertion presupposes a dualism between nature and man, he is wrong, because he falls into a view of nature proper to religion, Greco-Christian philosophy, and also idealism, which in reality does not manage to unite man and nature and relate them together other than verbally (quoted in Piccone, 1971, p. 11).

This question of the relationship of social reality and nature features significantly in Paci's discussion of the pre-categorical economic structure and its relationship to the life-world and will therefore be considered below. Although Lukács's work is clearly controversial within the mainstream of Marxist thought its significance and contribution to the development of a phenomenological Marxism is more certain.

What, however, is phenomenological Marxism? One view has been that it seeks to discover Marxist problems, aims and methods in phenomenology, particularly Husserlian phenomenology, and a transcendental phenomenological grounding in Marx's writings. By regarding Marxism as an outcome of phenomenology and phenomenology as inherent in Marxism it is argued that it becomes possible to achieve a reconciliation mutually beneficial to both. In most cases the rationale for a phenomenological Marxism is the desire to overcome the 'crisis' of Marxism, to move beyond the fossil of orthodoxy held to be characteristic of Marxist thought. Certainly this seems to be the orientation of Piccone (1971) and Rovatti (1970). In the case of Paci's analysis the orientation is broader, his work representing the seminal attempt at a merger (rather than a synthesis) of phenomenology and Marxism through a detailed and concise discussion of the work of both Husserl and Marx. The central orientation of his work is a discussion of their mutual concern with estrangement and reification and an analysis of three important and interdependent crises, namely those of science, capitalism and Marxism. Because of the depth and scope of Paci's analysis, as compared to other works, consideration of phenomenological Marxism needs must commence with an analysis of his *The Function of the Sciences and the Meaning of Man* (1972).

The convergence of phenomenology and Marxism

Paci's work focuses upon the common interests apparent in both Husserl's and Marx's writings on the crisis of existence, the estrangement of man from society, and man from his 'self'. He provides a reading of Husserl which places emphasis upon the analysis of the natural attitude of man's self-knowledge and understanding of society and nature, namely science, and a reading of Marx in terms of the critique of political economy and capitalism. Paci seeks to establish common points of reference in Husserl's and Marx's work concerning the importance of history, the desirability of the unity of the sciences, the alienation of man's subjectivity and the rational society as humanity's telos. The thesis in fact divides into two almost distinct books, indicative perhaps of the difficult problems surrounding the formulation of a phenomenological Marxism. The first section attends to Husserl's work on the *Crisis of European Sciences*, the second offers a reading of Marx prefaced by brief accounts of the work of Labriola, Gramsci, Merleau-Ponty and Sartre, and an even more slender reference to the work of Lukács. The apparent insignificance attached to Lukács's work is surprising in so far as Paci's phenomenologically sensitized reading of Marx appears to 'trade off' Lukács's earlier work *History and Class Consciousness*. However, before proceeding to review and analyse Paci's attempt at a merger of phenomenology and Marxism it is important first to examine his reading of Husserl's *Crisis*. This is necessary not merely because it represents part of the basis for his analysis of phenomenological Marxism but also because Husserl's work has featured both directly and indirectly (through Schutz) in the constitution of a phenomenological sociology and is therefore very relevant to any evaluation of contemporary sociology.

Husserl's *Crisis*

In *Crisis* Husserl is considering the failure of modern science to provide a 'forum for questions central to man' (Husserl, 1970, p. 6). Just as in Marx's critique of political economy and the capitalist mode of production so for Husserl's critique of science, man has become an object, an object not of capital, not a slave to a machine but rather an object in an objectified world, for science. In consequence Husserl's analysis may be read as showing the possibility of retrieving the lost meaning of science, as concentrating upon rediscovering the actual past meaning of the sciences as a possible future remedy for the alienating sciences of the present. In order to reach an understanding of the possibility of science for man Husserl engages in a radical reflection in a 'thorough historical and critical fashion' akin to Marx's own assertion and practice that to be radical it is necessary to delve back to the roots of the problem, to the origins. Indeed in the case both of Husserl's analysis of science in general and Marx's critique of the science of political economy in particular, understanding materializes only by the unconcealing of the reality beneath the appearance, by the revelation that the experience and scientific study of an 'objectively true world' rests upon and indeed is a product of the intersubjective basis of the relationships between the members of the given world.

Husserl asserts that the original meaning of science has been lost, to be replaced by methodic and technicist concerns. The only 'real' world, namely the one given through perception, which is experienced in our everyday life, is replaced in science by 'the mathematically substracted world of idealities' (1970, p. 48). As a consequence the idea of nature as a self-enclosed world emerges, a world in which every occurrence, every event is determined in advance. Accordingly 'the new idea of "nature" as an encapsuled, really and theoretically self-enclosed world of bodies soon brings about a complete transformation of the idea of the world in general' (1970, p. 60). In fact the outcome is seen to be dualism, the splitting of the world into nature and psyche, the construction of the object-subject duality. The effect of this 'event' has been transmitted into sociology not alone by the subsequent ramifications of natural science for the experience of everyday life, the pre-categorical experiential basis upon which science is based, but also by the desire to emulate the theoretical and practical successes of such science. So we find in sociology that the natural sciences guided by mathematics serve as the model of genuine knowledge. To quote one devoted exponent advocating the mathematization of sociology,

> When a discipline achieves scientific maturity, this is almost always correlated with at least a partial mathematization. This is not to take up a positivist position; it is simply an assertion that the two facts are concomitant. . . . It is easy enough to show by a variety of examples that sociology, difficult as it has been . . . to connect it with mathematics, ought on the face of it to expect the same advantages as other sciences (Boudon, 1974, p. 12).

Now perhaps Boudon is correct that 'a discipline comes to be regarded as scientific when it is within reach of speaking a language free of ambiguity' (ibid., p. 11) and that mathematics is just such a language, non-ambiguous by definition. However, we must also consider the possibility that what Boudon might mean by ambiguity, the absence of a one-dimensional mathematical world, is resolved only at the cost of meaningfulness, comprehensibility and appropriateness. In other words that the science of society, a science of the social becomes not a science for men and women, promoting understanding and enlightenment, but rather a science which objectifies man, seeking as its goal the privatization of meaning and engineering through the adoption of a mathematical vocabulary divorced from the pre-categorical life-world, a scientism which constrains and further magnifies estrangement. It is the critique of such a science with which Husserl is preoccupied, revealing that the mathematical logic underpinning all the objective sciences is nothing but naïveté, 'Its self-evidence lacks scientific grounding in the universal life-world a priori, which it always presupposes in the form of things taken for granted, which are never scientifically, universally formulated' (1970, p. 140). Husserl recommends that scientists must reflect upon and systematically inquire into the taken for granted, they must seek to recognize the 'unspoken ground of their cognitive accomplishments', the grounds of science being the pre-categorical life-world. Interestingly in contrast to Husserl's advice for scientists to become aware of the fact that 'knowledge of the objective-scientific world is "grounded" in the self-evidence of the life-world' (1970, p. 130) sociologists have consistently, with the possible exception of phenomenological and ethnomethodological sociologists, shown a predilection to divorce 'objective science' from the world in which the scientist lives, thereby failing to treat science as a human formation related to human actualities and potentialities. Belief in the distinctiveness of sociological science from the self-evidence of the life-world, a topic which has been the source of much debate in sociological circles, may perhaps be explained in so far as it serves to preserve the sociologist's self-esteem and expertise. Certainly in the case of both the 'prophetic' and 'priestly' modes a firm belief in the superiority of the sociologist's judgment is a pre-requisite.[3] Unfortunately the attempt to translate and show the relevance of the Husserlian project and phenomenological analysis in general to sociologists appears to have had little effect. Indeed the consequence seems to be that there has been an assimilation of phenomenological and ethnomethodological approaches into sociology with precautions being taken to ensure that only minimal contact occurs with the hegemonic positivist and empiricist approaches. This is understandable if regrettable in so far as Husserl's project is remote and alien to the positivist-empiricist conception of sociology, for whereas the latter is guided by a 'constructive concept of a world which is true in itself' (1970, p. 173), the former is not at all concerned with what the things in the world actually appear to be. Indeed Husserl rejects the interest in what the world taken as a totality actually is and as such his work must be considered as equally problematical for Marxism as for sociology.

Although Husserl rejects any interest in 'true being' and prediction related to praxis, his work does have an important bearing on the question of validity, knowledge and action. He argues that the world is intersubjectively constituted and further that living within the world therefore literally becomes the source of validity. Validity is brought into being through men living within the world, it is effected by man's being. Hence 'truth' and knowledge necessarily become historical, products of man's historical reflection. Husserl notes that the world is a place existing in man's communal experiencing of it, it exists for the community of men and in consequence the modifications of validity are revealed to be a product of the reciprocal correction of communalized perception.[4] Husserl states that,

> Intersubjective harmony of validity occurs (establishing what is) 'normal' in respect to particular details, and thus an intersubjective unity also comes about in the multiplicity of validities and of what is valid through them. . . . All this takes place in such a way that in the consciousness of each individual, and in the overarching community consciousness which has grown up through social contact, one and the same world achieves and continuously maintains constant validity as the world which is in part already experienced and in part the open horizon of possible experiences for all; it is the world as the universal horizon, common to all men of actually existing things (1970, pp. 163–4).

Unlike the objective sciences Husserl's purpose is not to secure objectivity but to explain it, to account for the experience of objectification, for the appearance of an intersubjectively constituted world. Indeed the empiricist sciences in their 'dogmatic slumbers' seem sublimely unaware of the possible relevance of Husserl's elucidation of the ultimate grounds of science. As he remarks, the empiricist talk of scientists creates the distinct impression that science is predicated upon experience of an objective nature. However,

it is not in this sense true that these sciences are experiential sciences, that they follow experience in principle, that they all begin with experiences, that all their inductions must finally be verified through experiences; rather this is true only in that other sense whereby experience (yields) a self-evidence taking place purely in the life-world and as such is the source of self-evidence for what is objectively established in the sciences, the latter never themselves being experiences of the objective (1970, p. 128).

It is clear therefore that for Husserl the ultimate foundation of all objective knowledge, of science and scientific topics, is the life-world existing prescientifically for all of us purely through experience. Interestingly in view of Paci's comparison, Marx may also be read as inferring the essential significance of the life-world as the basis of scientific knowledge, in particular that 'sense perception (experience) must be the basis of all science' and that 'one basis for life and another basis for science is a priori a lie' (Marx, 1973b, p. 143). The question of the relationship of Marx's, and Husserl's work will be considered below in an analysis of Paci's account of phenomenology and Marxism.

Paci's reading of Husserl's *Crisis*

Paci's interpretation of Husserl is best summarized by his suggestion of the following alternative title for the *Crisis*, namely, 'The Struggle against the Alienated Use of the Sciences in order to regain the Meaning of Man, his Society and his History' (1972, p. 196). The purpose attributed to Husserl is the returning of subjectivity to man, the freeing of man from every fetishism through the revelation of humanity to itself. Husserl's *Crisis* is treated by Paci as a work oriented towards the overcoming of objectification and alienation, the very source in fact of the crisis of the sciences symptomatic of the crisis of existence. As with certain readings of Marx's work the concept of history in Husserl is deemed to imply the progressive self-realization and actualization of what is hidden or latent within man. Man is depicted as being in a kind of 'pre-existence' (prehistory) and as not living according to reason (species-being). Such a condition in which man is objectified, alienated and exploited is regarded as a direct consequence of the mis-use of the sciences. Specifically Paci stresses that Husserl refers to the sciences and technology as having been used for ends extraneous to those for which they were originally intended and that whereas they were meant 'to liberate humanity and to pursue "infinite rational goals" ' they have in fact in the context of an abstract society been employed in the exploitation and domination of man. Hence Husserl's phenomenology is read 'as the science of the whole man, or as radical humanism', and as proving that 'a phenomenology of the living needs of the subject in the first person can constitute the basis of political economy as a science' (1972, p. 182). In this way the seeds of a prospective fruitful reconciliation of phenomenology and Marxism are sown, elements of Husserl's and Marx's writings being woven together by recognition of the presence of the one within the other. Almost inevitably Paci is drawn on to confront the vital question of the relationship between intentionality, consciousness, and psychic life in general and the pre-categorical economic level of 'living needs'. It becomes therefore a process of 'materialising' Husserl, providing a re-constructive interpretation to take into account issues which Husserl failed to consider but which, when incorporated, do not according to Paci, prejudice the essence of his work.

Admitting of his belief in the need to fill in particular silences in Husserl's work, one particular instance being the 'incomplete' discussion of the relationship between psychology and phenomenology, Paci embarks upon a developmental and re-constructive reading relating Husserl's analysis to the material, psychic, biological and spiritual unity of man. The bland adoption of an ostensibly anthropological Marxist position, which Paci quite clearly affirms was never employed by Husserl, serves the purpose of correcting and transforming phenomenology. In particular it provides for greater conceptual breadth, man being treated not merely as a conscious and psychic being but also as a material and living being with particular historical needs. Whether this represents a modification, correction or total transformation of Husserl is a debatable point. However, viewing man and matter as related in terms of a dependency of the former upon the latter (man needing goods to satisfy his needs), intentionality is interpreted by Paci as meaning not only consciousness of something but also dependence on something. He notes,

> In order to live man must begin by satisfying the most
> elementary economic needs. The ego is dependent and
> conditioned by them. . . . Here we are confronted with the
> binding character of the precategorical economic structure

which is lived in the first person (1972, p. 265).

And so the subtle introduction of Marxist concepts of economic structure, materialism and determinism begins to bring a cautious momentum to the concept of a phenomenological Marxism, whilst at the same time not prejudicing a sense of continuity and harmony with Husserl's work. In fact since Paci attributes to Husserl a conception of social reality that is dialectical, intersubjective and historical, compatibility with Marx's work appears superficially to be of no problem. The one crucial point of criticism which Paci makes explicit, however, concerns Husserl's tendency to reduce the significance of nature and indeed the natural sciences for an understanding of human and cultural relations. For Paci the neglect of the natural sciences and nature, material factors and the pre-categorical economic level of living needs in particular, represents a stumbling block to the unification of the sciences, the purpose attributed to Husserl. The criticisms Paci makes of Husserl's work basically revolve around this central issue and may be considered under the following sub-headings:
   (i) Objectification
   (ii) Technology, sedimentation and language
   (iii) Irreversibility and the life-world

(i) Objectification

Paci's basic criticism in this instance is that Husserl fails to distinguish between the positive and negative aspects of objectification. His analysis of the crisis of science and human existence focuses critically upon naturalism and the natural attitude, stressing the importance of retrieving subjectivity, but there is a total absence of any clarification of the concept of objectification, in particular no recognition of its positive and necessary presence. For example in certain passages Husserl's references to objectification imply in Marxist terminology fetishization and yet there are in other passages references to objectification (in terms of estrangement and alienation) where the meaning appears to be merely that 'the ego experiences and lives in the world' (Paci, 1972, p. 105). The circumstances in which the term is employed differ quite considerably in Paci's estimation. In one context the term is used to describe a condition or relationship alien to man's being whereas in another context the concept of objectification describes the essential condition of man. What is apparent is that there is considerable ambiguity surrounding Husserl's use of the term in contrast to Marx for whom objectification was inherent in social life, a direct consequence of man's creative and teleological nature. Whereas therefore in Marx there is a clear distinction between objectification (positive sense) and reification (negative sense of objectification) which produces estrangement and alienation, in Husserl clarity is lacking, although Paci assures us that 'even though Husserl is unaware of it' his understanding of objectification in the negative sense (alienation) is very close to Marx's.

(ii) Technology, sedimentation and language

Husserl's discussion of intersubjectivity, science and language is viewed by Paci to be incomplete in so far as although there is the 'discovery' of the original problem of the 'loss of intentionality' as the problem of the historical foundation of the sciences this is accompanied by an inadequate consideration of the problem of materialism and the positive function of sedimentation and technology. Husserl's work in the *Crisis* and in particular the appendix on the 'Origin of geometry' represents therefore a somewhat unbalanced attempt to account for the existence of an objective structure or world as the historical product of the merely intra-subjective structure. It displays for Paci a preoccupation with the language-world relationship to the detriment of other, at least equally important, relationships. The world for Husserl is the 'horizon of our life' appearing in our consciousness as an horizon of real objects, other men, possibilities and activities. From the start man is conscious of 'civilization as an immediate and mediate linguistic community', as civilization made possible through language and communication. Hence the objective being of the world 'presupposes man, understood as men with a common language' (Husserl, 1970, p. 359). Men, the world, and language are considered by Husserl to be inextricably bound together, but does the answer to the question of the production of the objective structure rest with reciprocal linguistic understanding alone? For Paci as we shall see the answer is clearly negative, for Husserl the issue cannot be answered simply; in principle there appears to be no categorical exclusion of extra-linguistic factors although his analysis neglects to develop, as Paci notes, anything beyond language and consciousness.

In discussing the conditions which give rise to the objectivity of ideal structures Husserl differentiates between an active and a passive understanding of an event or operation. The important characteristic of an objective structure for Husserl is that although its origin might have been in the past it can still be transmitted, mediated or appreciated in the present. It can be retrieved so to speak for the present as a 'complex of signs and techniques in which it (the operation) has been sedimented in order to be repeated ... even if we have forgotten the original operations' (Paci, 1972, p. 206). In the case of an active understanding, for example where a member of a given group produces an innovation which in turn can be understood and re-produced by the other members, there is not yet an objective ideal structure, for the existence of the ideal object still depends upon the member's existence. For an objective structure to exist there must be persisting existence, the possibility of the structure must be independent of the consciousness or well-being of the given producers or the original constitutive linguistic community. Husserl provides one specific condition which provides for the objectivity of the ideal structure, namely the recording in writing, the documenting of verbal comment or linguistic expression. 'The writing down effects a trans-formation of the original mode of being of the evidence. . . . It becomes sedimented so to speak' (1970, p. 361). It provides in fact for the possibility of communication without either immediate or mediate personal address. The communication which follows from such a recording of linguistic expression is referred to by Husserl as providing for a passive understanding.

Husserl notes that a passive understanding of an expression may be reactivated to reveal the self-evidence, the original meaning; in fact his analysis of science and the origin of geometry seeks to establish this very end, namely to reveal the 'lost meaning of science'. However, he states that ' . . . this is by no means necessary or even factually normal. Even without this he (the individual) can understand; he can concur "as a matter of course" in the validity of what is understood' (1970, p. 361n). For in everyday life, ' . . . the originally intuitive life which creates its originally self-evident structures through activities on the basis of sense experience very quickly . . . falls victim to the seduction of language' (1970, p. 362). Husserl notes therefore that more and more spheres of life become dominated by passive understanding, a passive taking-over of meaning and validity; such is the basis of social life and unfortunately much sociology.

Paci's opposition to this aspect of Husserl's analysis is primarily a response to the perceived relative neglect of technology in the *Crisis*. He argues that it is not only in the case of language that man is engaged in appropriating and constituting the world. For just as 'language transforms physical signs into meaningful signs, the trans-mitted language into my own language and into the language of actual intersubjectivity' (1972, p. 207), so it is the case that technology may appropriate and transform nature into an inter-subjectivity whereby the alienation and domination of man is re-placed by the construction of a rational society of subjects. Paci thus develops Husserl's struggle against the misuse of science into a struggle against the misuse of technology, the critical rider being that for Husserl technology is treated as the source of the occlusion of the meaning-structure of life and history whereas in contrast Paci conceives of technology as providing in principle for the very possibility of an intersubjective society. As in the case of his criticism of Husserl's concept of objectification Paci asserts that there is a preoccupation with the negative aspects of technology and a failure to realize the relevance and importance of the beneficial possibilities latent within it. Without technology relations between men and pre-categorical nature are impossible. In addition the very goal of a crisis free existence depends upon technology as indeed does the creation of an intersubjective society, for 'only through matter and sedimentation in matter can all men constitute a unique intersubjectivity' (Paci, 1972, p. 213).

The irony in Paci's critical reading of Husserl is that the very struggle with which Husserl is identified (not uncontroversially), namely against objectification, is diagnosed as a 'struggle to bring technology back to man in order to free technology from alienation and return it to its foundation and intentionality' (1972, p. 191). However, Paci's disagreement with Husserl over the question of technology reveals a more basic difference in orientation. Husserl asserts quite clearly that his is a 'purely' theoretical interest,

> not concerned with whether and what the things, the real
> entities of the world, actually are . . . we are also not
> concerned with what the world taken as a totality, actually is,
> what in general belongs to it in the way of a priori structural
> lawfulness or factual 'natural laws'. We have nothing like this
> as our subject matter. Thus we exclude all knowledge, all
> statements about true being and predicative truths for it, such
> as are required in active life for its praxis (1970, p. 156).

Paci's interest, however, tends to be more concrete, his explicit concern being with the construction of a rational society of subjects and for this project Husserl's phenomenology is accepted as a most significant resource because it provides a science of the pre-categorical foundations thereby freeing the sciences from reification and facilitating their use by man in the constitution of a truly subjective and rational society. However, quite major surgery or rather transplanting is necessary, specifically in terms of the addition of the pre-categorical determining and conditioning material structure to Husserl's analysis. For example Paci notes that the satisfaction of necessity is basic and that although man may emerge from necessity he cannot dispense with it, for his freedom and that of his community is possible only through its preliminary satisfaction. As he categorically states 'human history is not just nature, . . . [however] it must include it' (1972, p. 260). Hence contrary to Husserl a material basis of 'living needs' is classified as pre-categorically determining and conditioning, technology is found to have a positive function and furthermore the natural sciences in general are held to be relevant to an understanding of human and cultural relations.

(iii) Irreversibility and the life-world

Irreversibility is the basic law of the life-world. As with the criticisms of Husserl's account of objectification, technology and sedimentation this represents yet another example of Paci's judgment that there is an over-preoccupation with the questions of language, consciousness and psychic life as compared to matter, 'real things' and the chain of conditioning in the *Crisis*. This particular criticism of Paci's is dependent upon assumptions concerning man's biological conditioning, in particular the fact that although he may satisfy his life-needs and resolve various natural and physical problems in the context of groups, communities and cultures, in the final analysis he is still dominated by ubiquitous irreversibility and entropy. Unfortunately Husserl does not appear to recognize the significance of the principle of irreversibility and in consequence fails to discover the grounds for the temporal structures domination of economic life, culture and history. Elementary needs, even if in a specific culture they are classified as inferior, are urgent and 'their satisfaction places man in a relation of dependence on the natural environment' (1972, p. 266). Clearly we are here firmly on the ground of a conventional Marxist position including even an account of the inevitable consequences of further dependency produced by a situation emerging in which the means of production for satisfying basic needs are privately appropriated by groups or classes or for that matter societies.

Finally Paci takes issue with Husserl's portrayal of the philosopher as having a 'ruling function'. This provides the ideal occasion for Paci to display his Marxist credentials, first through his denial of Husserl's differentiation of philosophers from other men and second by attributing to the proletariat (interestingly considered conceptually unproblematic), the emancipatroy role in humanity's struggle for liberation from estrangement. In the case of the philospher/artisan,/technician,/proletarian relationship Paci argues that all men are philosophers in so far as they become conscious of their own meaning. This position resembles that propounded by certain sociologists of 'everyday life' who deny the significance of any sociologist-layman distinction thereby concealing important aspects of the relationship between sociology and the everyday world. The second point, namely the emancipatory role of the proletariat, is again a predictable stance, sadly lacking any analytical examination or grounding. With philosophy as the 'head' of the emancipation of humanity the proletariat is assumed necessarily to constitute the 'heart', which of course raises all sorts of questions in particular concerning the mediation of awareness and understanding from head to heart. The important problem of the emergence of and pre-requisites for consciousness is in this context pushed into the background. As a result the tenor of Paci's closing comments preaching the liberation and emancipation of humanity through the proletariat seems strangely out of place in the context of Husserl's *Crisis*. Indeed Paci's earlier statement that 'we have attempted to understand the . . . ethical and economic implications of objectifications by analyzing Husserl's hints in a way not developed by Husserl himself' (1972, p. 269) seems to exemplify in retrospect the art of understatement.

Phenomenological Marxism

Paci's attempt to show the possibility of reconciling phenomenology and Marxism, commencing with the identification of Marx's philosophy within Husserl's phenomenology and developed further by an interpretation of their respective works as evidencing common interests, proceeds from particular criticisms of Husserl's *Crisis* to an elaboration of the crucial question of pre-categorical determination. To recapitulate, Paci argues that Husserl fails to provide an adequate analysis in so far as the questions of 'living needs', pre-categorical conditioning of the life-world and temporal irreversibility are largely neglected. His intention therefore is to extend and even in some respects transform Husserl's analysis whilst at the same time trying to preserve its radical essence. By developing Husserl's phenomenology Paci's appears to believe that it is possible to reconstruct Marx's analysis in such a way as to escape the bourgeois readings which attribute a scientistic or positivistic orientation to the Marxian project. Such a view is not uncommon among critical Marxists many of whom might agree with Piccone's assertion that Husserl is as important to contemporary Marxists as Hegel was to Marx. Paci's critical, phenomenological reading of Marx begins with the disclosure that a disoccluding hence phenomenologically oriented analysis already exists in Marx's analysis. As Paci notes, 'to take things at their roots, and to discover man who is his own root, is to discover what ideology hides. This is a disoccluding analysis . . . a phenomenological analysis' (1972, p. 383).

Before proceeding to a discussion of the phenomenological reading of Marx it is necessary to review briefly Paci's distinction between the materialism of his reading of Marx and the naturalism constituting the focus of Husserl's critique of science. Paci stresses that there can be no doubt that man is conditioned by his pre-categorical dependence upon the satisfaction of his 'living needs' but that even though this is the case intentional will and freedom are not obstructed. It is of course necessary to recognize that in certain cases the emphasis upon matter and the economic structure, considered by

Paci to be a reaction on the part of Marxists to the insignificance attached to the economic pre-categorical by bourgeois ideology, has led to a reduction of the subject to the status of a determined object. Indeed this appears to be explicit in the case of scientistic or vulgar Marxism. It may be noted in passing that the economic determinist reading of Marx is quite common within sociology being a product not alone of sociological misinterpretation and misrepresentation but also following as a consequence of certain naturalistic tendencies inherent in Marx and Marxism. Whereas therefore materialism recognizes both the pre-categorical conditioning of man and also the importance and significance of subjectivity, naturalism reduces man to a mere natural object thereby alienating and estranging man from his essential humanity. It is the criticism of naturalism by Husserl, specifically in terms of the crisis of the sciences, which for Paci represents the basis of a critical Marxism able to return to not only the phenomena themselves but also to the whole man. Through phenomenology 'we can speak of materialism without speaking of naturalism', we can take account of the pre-categorical determination and conditioning of man's organic body without denying free and conscious subjectivity.

For Paci the sciences and to some extent Marxism have lost their meaning, falling into objectivism, fetishism and alienation. Rather than functioning to preserve and develop man's subjectivity the sciences have objectified and fragmented the whole man into separate objects each of which constitutes the subject matter of a distinct field. In this way the sciences reduce man to both a technical operator and a victim of technical control. It is interesting to reflect in passing upon Durkheim's thoughts about abnormal forms of the division of labour one of which specifically concerned science. In his account of the anomic division of labour Durkheim stresses the fact that knowledge of the totality, of the whole, seems to have become less and less possible with the advancement of science. One remedy he discusses, apparently inspired by Comte, depends upon the constitution of a new science, a philosophy which must attempt to re-establish the lost unity. However, Durkheim perceives the growing multiplicity of special sciences and their respective complexities to be a major obstacle to a unification through a new philosophy: 'If particular sciences can take cognizance of their mutual dependence only through a philosophy which embraces all of them, the sentiment of unity they will have will always be too vague to be efficacious' (Durkheim, 1964b, p. 364). So for Durkheim there can be no return to philosophy as the collective conscience of science for its role has necessarily diminished with the advancement of the division of labour. The chaotic nature of science is perceived by Durkheim to be a consequence not of the division of labour per se but rather the result of a situation in which the jurist, the psychologist, the anthropologist, the economist, the statistician, the linguist, the historian, proceed with their investigations as if the different orders of fact they study constituted so many independent worlds. In reality, however, they penetrate one another from all sides; consequently, the case must be the same with their corresponding sciences. This is where the anarchical state of science in general comes from. . . . If they form a whole without unity . . . it is because they are not organized (1964b, pp. 367–8).

In Durkheim's terms the anarchical state of science is held to be a consequence of the *anomic* division of labour. With characteristic optimism Durkheim attempts to assure the reader that this condition is a consequence of the immaturity of the social sciences and that with the progressive development of 'researches farther from their points of departure, they [social scientists] will necessarily end by reaching and, consequently, taking conscience of their solidarity' (pp. 370–1). Thus the unity of the sciences is seen to arise or emerge of its own accord through the steady progress of 'normal' science. Interestingly, although Durkheim's work has frequently served as the legitimating classical base for the development of sociological research little attention has been given to his comments on the disorganized nature of social science. Indeed much of the work which has developed in the Durkheimian tradition has not only lacked the quality of that of its mentor but in many cases has tended to advance even further the fragmentation and dispersion of knowledge of the totality. However, Durkheim's optimism as to the unification of the sciences is clearly not shared by Paci and Husserl both of whom place emphasis on the need to act decisively to restore intentionality and unity to the scientific project.

For Paci the crisis of the sciences 'is the crisis of the capitalist use of the sciences, and, therefore, the crisis of human existence in capitalist society' (1972, p. 323). The root of this crisis is the reduction of man both in science and production in capitalist society to the status of an object (or commodity). This crisis has arisen as a result of the objectification of reality, a process in which science lost sight of the fact that what is objectively valid is subjectively constituted, a product of intersubjective activity. To the extent that science forgets 'that it is based upon concrete subjectivity . . . then science will fall into objectification in Husserl's sense, i.e. alienation' (1972, p. 312). We must recognize that science has its foundation in the life-world. Science is not basic; on the contrary the world of pre-categorical life is the foundation of science, and phenomenology is the science of that pre-categorical foundation. By re-discovering science's subjective foundation, by recognizing and hence providing for the possibility of realizing subjectivity, the constitution of a rational society, a human intersubjective society, free from alienation takes form.

Science in this context is not reduced to separate distinct disciplines, for isolated in their separate fields they will be unable as is readily evident from the chaotic nature of our physical, ecological, economic, political and social environment to resolve man's problems. Not that we can unite the sciences as they stand; on the contrary Durkheim's comment on the difficulty of reconciling the multiplicity of complex sciences seems more appropriate than ever. However, given the possibility of a philosophy understood as a new science (phenomenology), 'the becoming-conscious of human and historical goals' should in both Paci's and Husserl's terms provide the occasion for a reunification of the intentionality of the distinct sciences, the point being that although Paci is critical of the separate sciences, the capitalistic sciences, in so far as they deny 'the intentional unity of man and knowledge, of praxis and truth' he admits that it is not possible to eliminate them. On the contrary an understanding of man can only be gained through the socio-historical context which has conditioned him, and the sciences are part of that context. As Paci notes,

Science may study the material or organic body, or the psyche. But since the subject is the whole man, the intentional totality of the sciences or of the ontologies corresponds to this totality of man. We know that the teleological idea of history is the idea of the agreement of all ontologies and well founded sciences. Ultimately, it is this very idea which returns their function to the sciences, and in studying man (e.g. in anthropology) I can very well make use of mathematics, physics, biology, and the other sciences, never forgetting, however, that it is men who found the sciences and give them their meaning of truth (1972, p. 329).

Science, capitalist society and sociology

In Paci's analysis the return to the concrete subject represents a common point of reference both for phenomenology and Marxian analysis. Just as Marx in the *Economic and Philosophic Manuscripts* asserts that 'above all we must avoid postulating "Society" again as an abstraction vis-à-vis the individual' (Marx, 1973b, pp. 137–8) and in fact proceeds to affirm the importance of subjectivity, so Husserl may be interpreted as offering a critique of similar objectifications. In developing his analysis of subjectivity, objectification and the concept of 'society' Paci depends once more upon a free use of the class metaphor, assuming that the concretization of the abstraction 'society', which is set up in opposition to the individual, is the product of a realization on the part of a specific group of individuals that society is a means to their domination of other groups, classes and individuals. Paci states that '. . . disoccluded the contraposition of society and individual turns out to be the class struggle' (1972, p. 335). This poorly explicated aspect of his analysis stems from a specific oversight, namely, that Marx does not 'tend to destroy all objectification'. On the contrary there are positive aspects of objectification which Paci earlier notes in his qualifications of Husserl's undifferentiated critique of objectification. Specifically Marx's work implies that the very essence of man's being presupposes objectification,

> . . . each of his human relations to the world – seeing, hearing, smelling, tasting, feeling, thinking, observing, experiencing, wanting, acting, loving – in short, all the organs of his individual being . . . are in their objective orientation or in their orientation to the object the appropriation of that object (Marx, 1973b, pp. 138–9).

In other words even in a society free from alienation, because of man's essential social being there will be objectification, all objects becoming for man the 'objectification of himself, become objects which confirm and realize his individuality' (Marx, 1973b, p. 140). In addition to the absence of any differentiation between positive and negative aspects of objectification Paci makes several unsubstantiated references to the importance of the proletariat as 'both a real and a typical group'. The problem with this is that his account of the proletariat may be read in much the same way as accounts of the individual-society relationship of which he is critical. In other words the concept of the proletariat may, like the concept 'society', be interpreted as an abstraction which through Marxism has been objectified. Does it not seem to be the case that one of the weakest links in Marxian analysis has been the 'blank cheque' concept of a 'real' proletariat engaged, or more often about to be engaged, in the struggle? Surely this also represents a suitable topic or occasion for a disoccluding phenomenological analysis, for a coming to terms with the changed nature of historical circumstances and the consequent necessity for conceptual revision. The references made by Paci to the proletariat as both a real and a typical group struggling against the bourgeois class and in his earlier analysis of Husserl, as the 'heart' of the emancipatory movement, appear as discordant interruptions in the flow of his development of a critical phenomenological Marxism. Unfortunately no provision is made for an analysis of the nature of either the genesis or persistence of the proletariat or the form(s) of its transformation in the historical process.

Returning to the central theme of Paci's work, namely objectification and the return to subjectivity, the analysis is developed through a critique of the reduction of man to an object-commodity under the capitalist mode of production. Both within the sphere of production and consumption (in what is regarded as the economic system) as well as in science (specifically in the scientific treatment and explanation of the varied aspects of man's life), man, the subject, is reduced to the level of a thing, an object, a commodity. It is asserted by Paci, following Lukács, that the objectification of man and social relations between men is objectively necessary for the capitalist mode of production 'in so far as the commodity form facilitates the equal exchange of qualitatively different objects, [and] . . . can only exist if that formal equality is in fact recognized' (Lukács, 1971, p. 87).

Quantification and exactness are therefore considered by Paci as essential for capitalism and both are seen to owe their origin to a human operation which eventually becomes submerged beneath the principle of rational calculation, in which the mathematization of nature serves as the model for the mathematization of the social (conceptualized as natural, obvious and taken-for-granted). Paci's discussion of objectification and the reduction of man to a commodity is directed not only to the analysis of labour under capital but also to the theorizing of labour-capital relations in the science of political-economy. However, besides being relevant to a consideration of the relationship between man and homo oeconomicus it is also pertinent to the relationship between the man of everyday life and psychological man (a relevant analysis being Husserl's), man and homo politicus and lastly and most significantly for our present purposes man and homo sociologicus.

Homo sociologicus

Within sociology there has long been a debate over the sociological conception of man, man in sociological theory and the relationship between this conception and the real 'flesh and blood' living man. In some cases the development of sociological theory has been seen to produce a conceptual convergence which 'removes subjective and conscious intentionality from the activity of man' (Atkinson, 1971, p. 119). Another view compatible with the above tends to regard sociologists as operating with an over-socialized conception of man, the latter being seen specifically as an unfortunate product of the sociological protest against 'the partial views of man contained in such doctrines as utilitarianism, classical economics, social Darwinism and vulgar Marxism' (Wrong, 1970, p. 128). It is argued by Wrong that sociologists sought to expose the unreality of the abstractions of homo oeconomicus, politicus and religiosus as well

137

reveal the limitations of the Hobbesian, Darwinian and Freudian conceptions of man. But, the sociological idea of man with its narrowly conceived view of the individual-society relation is in its own way as limited as those of economics and psychology. An interesting and important example of the sociological conception of man is Dahrendorf's *Homo Sociologicus* (1973). The crux of his account is the nature of the relationship between sociological man and the 'real' man of everyday experience. Sociology has the reputation for many people of being the science of man. For Dahrendorf this understanding is an example of misrepresentation for he believes sociology is not so much concerned with man as with the reduction of man's actions to rational terms, mathematization rather than understanding. Specifically the sociologists' terms of reference are society, and in consequence social man or 'man in society'. It appears that for Dahrendorf the whole of sociology is oriented to this one fact, namely '[the fact of society] as accessible to our experience as the natural facts of our environment' (1973, p. 4). The focus of the discussion falls therefore upon the area in which 'the individual and society intersect'. This in itself is a confusing way of posing the problem in so far as it may be argued that the individual cannot be conceptualized as being anywhere other than in society and furthermore that the very individual-society distinction is itself based upon an ungrounded ahistorical abstraction. However, for Dahrendorf 'the problem is to find an elementary category in which both the individual and society can be accommodated' (1973, p. 6) and the concept of role provides, in sociological terms, for just such an accommodation. It is important to stress that Dahrendorf is not unaware of the difficulties surrounding sociological conceptualization, in particular the problem of the incompatibility of common sense and scientific understanding. However, such issues do not feature as predominantly in his analysis as one might expect, the discussion tending in fact continually to return to the theme of homo sociologicus and 'real' man without actually getting to grips with the underlying assumptions. In consequence although the question of the relationship between real human beings and sociological abstractions is seen correctly to be more than an epistemological question, the moral significance is left largely undeveloped. Overall the work serves to legitimate unconvincingly the process of sociological abstraction without actually subjecting that process to any critical examination. This remains to be done.

Dahrendorf's analysis deals with two important sociological abstractions, society and homo sociologicus. The account provided, however, of the relationship between society, homo sociologicus, and the man of everyday experience is at times confusing, largely because of Dahrendorf's constant conceptual oscillation between the scientific abstraction and the concrete reality. Indeed this occurs in such a disguised fashion that it is not surprising that he has been accused of reifying homo sociologicus. How else can one interpret statements such as the following?

From the point of view of society and sociology, it is by learning role expectations, by being transformed into *homo sociologicus*, that man becomes a part of society and accessible to sociological analysis. Man devoid of roles is a nonentity for society and sociology. To become a part of society and a subject of sociological analysis, man must be socialized, chained to the fact of society and made its creature (1973, pp. 38–9).

Dahrendorf's discussion is littered with references to society which more than lend themselves to criticisms of reification. Even though he appears to recognize that society is not an acting subject he elsewhere in the essay uses such phrases as 'society says he must', 'he yields to society's demands', or 'society hands him a role to play', each of which serves to confuse his account of the individual-society relationship. Perhaps the nearest Dahrendorf approaches to a reconsideration of the concept of society is his reference to it as 'the alienated persona of the individual, *homo sociologicus*, a shadow that has escaped the man to return as his master' (1973, p. 26). Such a brief insight does not, however, produce a thoroughgoing rejection of the representation of the individual as in opposition to the abstraction 'society', nor does it produce an awareness of the sociohistorically constituted character of the abstraction or appearance, which has become concrete or real. Indeed Dahrendorf's Marxian roots seem to be completely severed from the body of his homo sociologicus essay with the result that although he comes to regard the personification of society as too imprecise for sociological analysis he fails to consider critically the constitution of society as the product of intersubjective relations. Society as an accomplishment is an issue which remains unaddressed even though his analysis at times points in that direction. As a result his analysis offers both qualifications of the use of the term society, for example that it should in certain circumstances be replaced by the more specific term 'reference group', and yet at the same time manifests a continual preoccupation with society as an external social fact, as a reality sui generis: 'every society is faced with the task of bringing together positions and men' (p. 35) or 'the individual must somehow take into himself the prescriptions of society and make them the basis of his behaviour' (p. 38).

Dahrendorf's failure to analyse critically and situate historically the society-individual distinction is responsible for the problems he confronts when attempting to address the question of the homo sociologicus man of everyday experience relationship. The paradox of the 'two human beings' is nothing other than man's construction, for in reality there are only men *and* women, subjects, the creators of science, who have become alienated as a consequence of the loss of science's intentionality (Husserl) and the predominance of the commodity form of production (Paci). Dahrendorf, however, proceeds with an adopted conception of science which in Husserl's and Paci's terms represents the source of the paradox. For Dahrendorf sociology must, in order to make its statements testable and precise, reduce its potential subject matter 'to certain elements from which may be systematically constructed . . . a structure in whose tissue a segment of reality may be caught' (1973, p. 4). Indeed in order to achieve scientific status he acknowledges that it was in fact genuinely necessary that 'sociology lost sight of people as human beings'. Such a development appears to Dahrendorf to have been inevitable as part of the price of scientific status. The loss of intentionality is in consequence greeted as a sign of sociology's coming of age. He states,

> As long as sociologists interpret their task in moral terms they
> must renounce the analysis of social reality; as soon as they
> strive for scientific insight, they must forgo their moral
> concern with the individual and his liberty. What makes the
> paradox of moral and alienated man so urgent is not that
> sociology has strayed from its proper task, but that it has
> become a true science (1973, p. 59).

Dahrendorf ironically therefore confirms Husserl's and Paci's condemnation of the nature of contemporary science, the difference being that whereas for Dahrendorf the rejection of 'moral concern with the individual and his liberty' appears as a sign of 'true science' for Husserl and Paci it is the source of the crisis, of man's estrangement and alienation. It seems then that Dahrendorf's conception of sociology contributes to man's estrangement and objectification; intentionality and the possible constitution of a society of subjects being readily exchanged for the accolade of 'science'.

Although rejecting the idea of a 'moral' sociology, Dahrendorf does recognize the need to be aware of the extent to which sociological propositions and theories are disseminated in a society which eagerly replaces common sense by scientific theory. In particular Dahrendorf seems concerned by the prospect that we may not be far from the time when the basis of 'real' man's self-conception will in fact be homo sociologicus, that we may be approaching a time when social engineering and the general scientization of everyday life will produce confirmation of the sociological conception of man, its validity being achieved or created by men living within the world according to the canons of science.[5] However, the possibility of this particular kind of reification of homo sociologicus is not for Dahrendorf a consequence of the sociologist's action; on the contrary it is considered to be the result of a general misunderstanding by the public at large. This of course is a fairly well known ploy adopted until quite recently by a great many natural scientists. It seems, however, that natural scientists have come to realize the folly of pretending that they are not in part responsible for the 'mis-use' of their work; it surely cannot be long before more sociologists also begin to awaken to the responsibility their work demands. Dahrendorf concludes his essay by keeping both of his options open: on the one hand homo sociologicus is held to be scientifically useful in that it enables the sociologist to 'reach much further . . . than statements that aim at an accurate description of man's nature' (1973, p. 77), on the other hand the potentiality for the acceptance of homo sociologicus as the scientific truth about man leads Dahrendorf on to affirm the need for caution, in particular for the sociologist to 'dissociate his image of man from *homo sociologicus*' (1973, p. 83). All of which might well lead us to ask whether the concept of homo sociologicus is after all really of any use at all. It seems that it does not address the topic of men in everyday life and furthermore its relationship to such 'real' men *and* women remains unexplicated. What therefore can it tell us about social reality or social experience? What can it explain? What is the relationship between the sociological abstraction 'society', homo sociologicus and the social experiences of men and women in everyday life? Unfortunately these issues do not feature significantly in Dahrendorf's analysis for he is guided by a particular conception of science which largely excludes such questions. In his terms, a 'good' sociological theory is one allowing definite, precise and unrestricted predictions with the added advantage of considerable explanatory power. How far this particular conception of Dahrendorf's is consistent with his fear of an alienated '1984 type' world is an interesting question. Even more interesting, however, is the realization that only through the preservation and use of the concept homo sociologicus can a precise, definite and predictive theory be considered a possibility, for once we allow man of everyday experience, with will, intentionality and consciousness, to enter our terms of reference Dahrendorf's conception of sociological science becomes inadequate. In contrast to Dahrendorf it must be emphasized that the science of sociology 'is not like astronomy: it cannot make precise predictions, because precategorical causal determinism includes freedom and will' (Paci, 1972, p. 341). Predictability of social and historical events is possible only, as Husserl and Habermas have both noted in somewhat different contexts, 'when the prophet makes the events himself which he has prophesied' (Habermas, 1974a, p. 246). The apparent contradiction in Dahrendorf's work between an empiricist conception of science and a sense of moral commitment for sociology can be resolved but only by re-opening the question, which he treats somewhat prematurely as closed, of the methodological nature or basis of a science of the social. Sociology's scientificity must not be taken for granted.

Paci's reading of Marx

A common underlying theme of the writings of social theorists and sociologists working in the general area of phenomenology and Marxism has been the necessity for a revision of Marxian analysis.[6] Whether the specific interest has been in the regeneration of Marxist orthodoxy or the liberation of social, sociological or historical thought from scientistic objectification, attention has almost always been drawn to the problems of a deterministic or positivistic reading of Marx. Undoubtedly the long tradition of such positivistic readings rests in part upon genuine ambiguities and inconsistencies within Marx's work, in particular concerning references to the infamous base-superstructure relationship, the unity of the sciences of man and nature, and the specific case of the evaluation of evolution and Darwinism. The consequence of reading Marx in a Comtean positivist fashion is that man, the subject, is reduced to an object, the science of historical materialism becoming a social physics, a naturalistic science. For Paci this is ironic as 'Marx's thought aims precisely in the opposite direction, even if the positivistic interpretation is the easiest and most persistent one' (1972, p. 372). His particular reading of Marx falls into the 'continuity' school, emphasis being placed upon the centrality of the alienation-objectification theme both in the 'young' and the 'mature' Marx. This well-rehearsed debate will not be re-considered here nor will any attempt be made to legislate which of the readings represents the 'true' Marx. However, it is important that such debates occur (for example that between Althusser and Lewis), if only because they provide a forum for a re-examination of the problem of relevance of any theorist's work for a present which itself is always constantly in flux.[7] We cannot avoid reconsidering anew the works of our mentors in so far as they are part of the tradition with which we attempt to come to terms in order to comprehend the changing nature of history, society and social reality in general.

For Paci the positivistic or economic determinist reading of Marx in treating his science like a physical science amounts to a transformation of 'Marxism into an ideology or scientistic utopianism'. Such a conception of Marx's work is in total contradiction with the predominant theme of the Marxian project, namely the proletarian realization of man's humanity, for it has as its consequence the perpetuation of the very objectification, alienation and estrangement of which Marx was so critical. Paci's reading therefore affirms not only the necessity of a return to subjectivity, to the roots, man himself, but also the importance of the general Marxian critique of abstraction and the concomitant emphasis upon the concrete totality. As they stand today the sciences of man, the social sciences, fail to consider man as a totality; on the contrary at best they seem able to recognize their own particular conception of man as merely a part of the whole and at worst they are guilty of elevating their own partial conception to the level of the man of everyday experience, man in toto. In consequence we have in the social sciences, as Dahrendorf has noted, sociological, psychological and economic man, each one an abstraction which is problematically related to men in everyday life. Of course it may with some justification perhaps be argued that man is no longer a 'whole' being, that he has indeed succumbed long ago to the pressures of the social division of labour such that he has become man the role player, the man of many parts some of which may well be in conflict with one another. The extent, however, to which the role metaphor with its derivative conceptualizations of 'set', 'conflict' and 'distance' has become reality is controversial and cannot merely be assumed.

Equally controversial perhaps is the question of the relevance of Marx's critique of political economy for the contemporary social sciences in general and sociology in particular. For Marx the beginning is always the social individual, man a social being living with other men, the consequence of which is that society is condemned as an abstraction made concrete and set up in opposition to man through the function of the sciences and the commodity nature of capitalism. Society only appears to be external to man, in reality it is produced and constructed by him to the same extent that he is in turn conditioned and determined by the historical social structure. Only through a process of reification does the product of man's social existence become concrete, external and appear independent of his praxis. Marx's criticism, echoed by Paci, is that the abstract categories of political economy, or for that matter sociology, are transformed into a false concreteness. Within sociology this particular issue has been at the centre of the debate between two particular constituencies which may be loosely referred to as on the one hand positivistically and empirically oriented and on the other phenomenologically oriented. The focus of their respective considerations has been the question of the subject matter, method and nature of sociology as a discipline or to be more precise what should be the subject matter, method, etc. Following Paci it may be argued that the subject matter of sociology should not be society or social structure conceived independently of man but on the contrary that the appearance of society or social structure as real, independent and external to the individual, should be considered as a topic in so far as it represents an historical accomplishment of men and women in a specific socio-cultural context. The concept of society or social structure only becomes meaningful if considered in terms of human operations, activities and praxis constantly to become conscious of, perpetuate, modify or transform the social structural and societal constructions of other individuals in the past and the present. Paci summarizes this position in terms of Marx's affirmation of the dialectical nature of the social process: 'society is not already constituted: it is in the process of being constituted' (1972, p. 381). Man is here seen as carrying within himself the essence of society in so far as he is the potential creator of the 'real human society', the constitution of the latter being the goal attributed to both Marx's and Husserl's analyses by Paci. Clarification of this issue really hangs on the question of Paci's conceptualization of man. Frequently in social thought man is treated as primarily a rational being, possessing the faculty of abstract thought. This has led in specific cases to the consideration of man as primarily a lingual being. Further examples may of course be drawn from the belief in man as above all a social being or alternatively a creative and working being. In each case, however, the attempt to 'discover the single property that makes man can catch us up in an unpleasant vicious circle' (Petrovic, 1967, p. 116). The conception offered by Paci is that man is a being of praxis, praxis being not only a continuous and renewed process of becoming-conscious but also free, creative and historical activity. Although he recognizes that man is conditioned both by nature and social structure, human relations are not thought to be naturalistic. On the contrary although there is a natural-biological and economic conditioning of man it has to be remembered that despite existing in time and being conditioned by a determinate social structure men can, and do, change both social structure and nature. 'Real' man as distinct from the abstractions produced by idealism (man of spirit) and 'abstract' materialism (naturalist man) is revealed through a disoccluding analysis which removes the mask of ideology. For Paci Marx's work, containing the essence of a phenomenological analysis, exemplifies just such an approach and Marxian analysis becomes therefore the science of human development. Neither abstract empiricism, nor idealism, Marx's work offers a practical materialism.

One of the most significant problems confronting social scientists in their attempts to understand or 'use' Marx's science is the question of disciplinary relevance. The convention appears to be that Marx's analysis represents a fusion of several disciplines, the consequence of which is the reduction of the 'total' Marx to the separate disciplines of for example economics, philosophy, sociology and political science. Rarely is any consideration given to the validity or justification of separate sciences each dealing with an ill-defined and differentiated segment of social reality; rather it seems to be the case that Marx's analysis is deemed less scientific in so far as it does not refer to or employ the distinctions now operative in the scientific study of man. What Paci proposes therefore is nothing less than a reconsideration of the very basis of the sciences of man, implying in particular that the question of the sub-division and categorization of reality by the sciences must be bracketed. Before beginning to plunder Marxian analysis for sociological, economic or philosophic resources the social scientist should reflect upon the contradiction between the notion of distinct social sciences studying separate and arbitrarily delimited segments of social reality and the critical significance in Marx's work of a focus upon the totality, reality conceived as an integrated, indivisible whole. More to the point sociologists might reflect upon the possibility of a special role for their own science in providing the potential for a re-unification of the sciences of man and nature. The design need not be the grandiose regal version proposed by Comte; on the contrary the requirement is for a sociology made sensitive to the importance and significance of a 'return to subjectivity', a sociology reconstituted in terms of a compatibility and reconciliation with the common underlying themes of Marxian and phenomenological analysis. A sociology reconstituted along these lines, clearly requiring an expansion of the parameters of the discipline as it now stands, would be in the position to begin to retrieve and fulfil the lost promise of the development of a more rational and intersubjective society. Just as Marx's analysis may be treated as revealing what lies hidden by political economy in its passive acceptance of the status quo as the natural state, so sociology has the potential to go beyond a mere scientistic translation of common-sense understanding to a revelation and appreciation of the underlying reality. The basic problem with the sciences of man, revealed by both Husserl and Marx, is that the real subject, man, is neglected. Whereas with Marxian analysis the reduction of the worker to an object, to an abstraction, is revealed to be a consequence of the capitalist mode of production and its science of political economy, for sociology the reduction of man to homo sociologicus is treated as an index of scientific status. Paci thus identifies the crisis of science, capitalism and man's existence as inherent in the use of the sciences for the exploitation of man and world domination rather than for the liberation of humanity. Science, or rather the misuse of science, may therefore be credited with having successfully replaced religion with its own mystification of the world in which man is reduced to an object of social, political, economic or scientific processes. It is frequently the case that scientists write as though they are especially immune to such processes, rarely addressing the question of their own reduction to an object implicit in their treatment of other men as objects. Within sociology this issue has received at least minimal attention. Unfortunately such consideration as has been given to the question of 'reflexivity' has normally emerged through one specific conception of man, namely man as primarily a 'lingual animal'. The consequence of this has been that the main body of sociological work has continued virtually unchallenged in so far as sociologists operating with unexplicated conceptions of man, denying the relevance of such conceptions, or alternatively clinging to one of the alternatives to the exclusion of all others, have been able to reject the case for reflexivity through criticism of the narrow preoccupation with lingual man. In so far as the conception of man provided by Paci is not narrowly based on one single property the critique provided by phenomenological Marxism of scientistic objectification has perhaps a greater chance of permeating the positivist, empiricist core of Sociology. It must, however, be remembered that Paci's explicit interests lie not with the reconstitution of sociology, or for that matter the other sciences of man, rather his orientation is towards the fulfilment of the goal of dialectical materialism, namely the material and moral emancipation of humanity.

Reality and appearance

Paci argues that the essence of Marx's project is to unveil or reveal what is hidden behind the 'false appearance, which is presented in society as a factual and insuperable reality' (1972, p. 420). To conduct such an analysis the actual abstraction assuming the form of reality must constitute the point of departure. The concretization of abstractions, their status as fact, must constitute the beginning of the analysis. It is just such an analysis that characterizes Marx's *Capital*. The analysis is by no means simple, as Paci notes: 'We do not have only one appearance and one reality: that would be too simple. We have appearance functioning as if it were not appearance, functioning as an appearance which has become real and which therefore, is real' (1972, p. 423). The underlying basis of a Marxian analysis proposed by Paci is therefore that it must search beyond the ideologies and constructions whose origins have been forgotten to reveal the transformation of social relations into natural relations as a product of bourgeois science. Marxism therefore becomes a critique of badly used science, a critique of the apparently neutral science which in fact 'forces society into fetishization'. Such a transformation of social relations into physical relations, of living labour into dead, is treated in Marx's analysis as typical of the capitalist mode of production. As a consequence Paci asserts that the abstract categories of economics are in a way appropriate, they reflect an objective society in that within capitalist society 'abstract categories function as if they were concrete, i.e. because in bourgeois society the worker really lives as if he were an abstraction, and the relations among workers are conceived as if they were physical relations' (1972, p. 425). The critical qualification is that political economy neglects to consider the possibility that the apparently natural relations are in fact historical, a consequence of the acceptance of seemingly self-evident socio-cultural and historical facts as natural facts. Paci's almost paradoxical comment on this state of affairs is that 'the real is the untrue', in other words that the given present represents merely a step in the process toward the fulfilment of man's unfulfilled potential, a step towards the constitution of a truly rational society. For Paci Marxism represents the 'true defense of the human person, his reality and his truth'. At this juncture in his work speculation begins to supersede analysis, no attempt being made to legitimate or justify the prognosis or for that matter to consider what might appear as unpalatable alternatives. Exhortation and faith replace analysis and there is an assumption that the 'becoming-conscious' of the proletariat, of workers living in the present as abstractions, will merely emerge. That men, or rather some men, can change their social and natural relations is not necessarily in dispute, but Paci's statements imply more than this, at the very least that the majority of all men, irrespective of national, cultural and geographical distinctions, will discover the 'true' reality beneath the 'false' appearance. Ironically such assertions by Paci display a neglect of sociological and historical analyses of societies which show clearly that the majority of men are not capable of philosophical reflection or if so that they do not choose to practise it. Indeed in the industrial and capitalist societies which meet Paci's terms of reference it is patently clear that all men are not philosophers; not only is there in these societies a premium on the scarcity value of knowledge but in addition distribution and communication serve to obstruct and obfuscate rather than stimulate the 'becoming-conscious' of men in general. It is all very well recommending that analysis reveal the 'real' situation by producing an awareness that a 'capitalist' society opposes the 'true direction and end of the historical process'. However, such a recommendation does not by itself insure the fulfilment of the end nor does it guarantee that man can move toward consciousness of his own telos. On the contrary Paci seems to ignore altogether the ideological stranglehold, the power of belief in and significance attached to the self-evident natural 'factualness' of the world. As a result his analysis appears at times to be rather thin, and his exhortations become reminiscent of the very Marxist orthodoxy which he alludes to as being in need of revision. His mere assertion, referred to earlier in criticism of Husserl, that all men are philosophers, not only exemplifies a myopic understanding of the concrete present in which the analysis is situated but in addition by occluding the distinction between philosophy and the common-sense, self-evident understandings of everyday life obscures the problem central to his interests, namely the unaddressed question of the relationship between leaders and led, intellectuals and political movements, the cogniscenti and the 'falsely' aware. Whereas therefore his analysis of Husserlian phenomenology and its convergences with Marxian analysis is both interesting and of relevance to practising social scientists in that it raises critical questions for the debate over the nature of science, objectification and society, the reconfirmation of the inevitability of a particular 'end' for history merely serves to take us back into the provinces of a conventional Marxism with all the attendant problems of inadequate analysis plus reliance upon belief and dogma. An attempt to reconstitute Marxian analysis cannot proceed with an unexplicated concept of the proletariat as a resource; on the contrary it demands a critical re-examination and fundamental disocclusion of the basis of both phenomenological and Marxian analysis.

For Paci Marx's and Husserl's writings manifest a similar concern with the crisis of science, man and society. The emphasis in the case of the writings of Marx is primarily upon the commodity nature of the capitalist mode of production and the alienation of man; in the case of Husserl the focus is upon the objectivist bias in modern science, in particular the substitution of ideal forms (abstractions) for concrete reality and the subsequent objectification of man. Phenomenology and Marxism are recognized therefore to cohere in the production of a dialectical account of how men reproduce themselves and their social institutions. Indeed phenomenological Marxism has been described as

. . . that approach which constantly reduces all theoretical constructs, including Marxism, to their living context in order to guarantee the adequacy of the concept not only to the object it claims to apprehend, but also to the goals it seeks to attain. In fact, its point of departure is precisely the rejection of that theory of reflection so dear to 'orthodox' Marxists which, unfortunately, turns out to be an untenable positivistic left-over (Piccone, 1971, p. 15).

For Paci the work of Husserl, in particular the *Crisis*, constitutes the most appropriate resource for reviving the critical base of Marxian analysis.

In addition to the criticisms outlined above two further criticisms are warranted. Firstly, Paci may be accused of misrepresenting Husserl's work; for example Shmueli (1973) argues that he unreasonably transforms Husserl into a dialectician even though an analysis of any one of his texts can dispel such an attribution.[8] Second, although Paci refers to science and society, the nature of man and other themes central to sociological inquiry, he tends to neglect the science of sociology. Indeed an outstanding weakness of his work, namely its abstract quality manifest in the neglect of any consideration of concrete historical contexts, can be seen as a consequence of the failure to address sociological accounts of contemporary societies and their respective social structures. However, for sociologists Paci's attempt at a reconciliation of Husserlian phenomenology and Marxian analysis is of importance in so far as it provides not only an account of issues at the centre of sociological debate, for example the nature of social reality, the science-society relationship, and the subject-object dist nction, but also displays through the example of a reconstituted critical and non-positivistic reading of Marx the possibility of a genuinely emancipatory scientific theory of society.

5 For a critical science of society

In the course of attempting to develop the case for a thorough re-consideration of the relevance and significance of Marxian analysis for sociology I have drawn attention to the quite considerable dissension and debate within the ranks of both Marxists and sociologists over the validity of their respective projects. Within Marxism this has taken the form of what by now seems like a perpetual controversy over the 'correct' interpretation of Marx's work, including the nature of the relationship of the 'earlier' to the 'later' works, the significance of the alienation theme as well as the question of the work's status as either philosophy, ideology or science. Additionally Marxists have been preoccupied with the possibility that Marxian analysis may no longer be relevant to contemporary societies manifesting an apparent absence of any sign of a revolutionary proletariat. Such symptoms have contributed to a belief that Marxist thought is in a state of crisis. Similarly within sociology a crisis has been diagnosed, a condition apparently manifest in the persisting absence of scientific social laws, the proliferation of new perspectives, opposing schools of thought or divergent positions, and a return to the question of sociology's disciplinary status. Despite the increasing emulation and adoption of the methodological techniques of the ostensibly successful physical and natural sciences sociology remains, by the criteria of these sciences, unsuccessful both in promoting understanding and facilitating control of social situations.

The response by Marxist scholars to the problems of their 'disciplines' has taken various forms including the incorporation of elements of structuralism, existentialism and phenomenology, not to mention a return to specific aspects of Marx's work for the key to a necessary and long overdue revision of the Marxian project. As has been noted by Gouldner (1972) and Worsley (1974) as well as many others the consequence of such responses on the part of Marxists has been a vast proliferation of Marxisms feeding further the fires of controversy over the question of consistency with the 'original' Marxian project. In certain cases the redevelopment or reconsideration of Marxism as the science of society has led to a recognition of the possibility of grounds for a compatibility of Marxian analysis with sociology, even to 'Marxism as a sociology' (Colletti, 1972; Wiatr, 1969; Zivkovic, 1969; Kalab, 1969). Elsewhere the re-birth of a 'truly' critical Marxism has been seen as feasible only by way of a merger or reconciliation with phenomenological philosophy to constitute a phenomenological Marxism (Paci, 1972; Piccone, 1971). Alternatively the reconstitution of a critical theory of society has been seen to depend upon a reformulation and modification of Marxian analysis in conjunction with psychoanalytic theory and an emphasis upon symbolic communication (Brown, 1973; Marcuse, 1969b; Habermas, 1971).

Sociologists for their part have similarly been engaged in a process of attempting to reveal, discuss and resolve the fundamental problems confronting their discipline. In one particular case this has led to a categorical denial of the heterogeneous nature of sociology, the proclamation that sociology is 'not one but many' being viewed as ' . . . one of the most harmful errors of our day . . . doing untold harm to the satisfactory formulation of the subject' (Fletcher, 1974, p. 39). Now there are legitimate grounds for developing a critique of the condition of contemporary sociology, in particular there exist many facile and mythical distinctions between positions within the discipline of which we ought, with Fletcher, to be critical. Nevertheless our discipline is one in which the members (sociologists) operate with, classify, work and communicate in, terms of distinctly different approaches, and even though some of these may be inadequate or subsumable under ostensibly 'alternative' approaches, unity, if it is desirable, cannot merely be assumed or asserted, it has to be shown to exist or shown to be a desirable possibility. The position adopted by Fletcher closely resembles that of a social scientist who has uncritically accepted Kuhn's work and its relevance for sociology (cf. Feyerabend, 1970a). Fletcher apparently believes that our discipline is 'rooted in error', carved up into 'bogus' schools, stuck, because of the absence of a consensus among the sociological community, at a pre-paradigm stage of development. His remedy, involving the affirmation of 'one framework of concepts and principles of theory and method' for sociology, exemplifies Feyerabend's typification of the social scientist who from a Kuhnian standpoint feels he has discovered how to 'improve' his science. Feyerabend states that the solution or recipe, ' . . . according to these people, is to restrict criticism, to reduce the number of comprehensive theories to one, and to create a normal science that has this one theory as its

151

paradigm' (1970a, p. 198). In other words the consequence of the 'unity thesis' is a celebration of a single point of view, the institutionalization of a specific paradigm. Fletcher seems to regard this as necessary for the preservation of sociology's 'substantial centre', the content of its body of knowledge and its status as a body of knowledge. However, not only may we argue that sociology's 'substantial centre' requires re-examination and reformulation rather than uncritical acceptance, but furthermore that the 'unity thesis' itself may be more compatible with dogma than science. In contrast to Fletcher for example, Feyerabend (1972, pp. 165–7) has argued that 'theoretical pluralism is . . . an essential feature of all knowledge' in which case we perhaps ought to be prepared to continue introducing and developing hypotheses which conflict or are inconsistent with predominant theories or accepted 'facts' rather than remain content to 'evolve' our ideas within the existing pre-given framework.

What has become increasingly apparent in sociological debates over the question of scientific status, the definition and characteristics of the subject matter and the dialectical relationship of sociology to society is that the conventional distinctions between the discipline and other areas of inquiry, for example Marxian analysis, philosophy, linguistic analysis and social psychology, have become less and less significant as awareness has increased of the obstructive nature of the scientific division of labour and the vital contribution these ostensibly extra-sociological areas can make to our understanding of the nature of social reality and the socio-historical process in general. As sociologists we clearly cannot begin to assess, debate or reject the merits of topics, approaches and issues which fall outside our respective spheres of competence. We can, however, begin to recognize the possibility that significant contributions are being made to an understanding of the social world from what are all too frequently treated as peripheral areas of inquiry. In particular, important and sociologically relevant contributions to an understanding of the nature of social reality and the relationship between science and society have been emerging from critical theory and phenomenological Marxism. However, among sociologists such developments have largely been neglected, the favoured path still appearing to be that subjected to criticism by phenomenological Marxists and critical theorists, namely the positivist-empiricist search for mathematical models and scientific explanations of social reality predicated upon the methodology of the physical and natural sciences.

Of course there are within sociology alternative conceptions manifest in phenomenological sociology, ethnomethodology and neo-symbolic interactionist works and although these may also have substantial limitations they do at least provide a degree of criticism of the hegemonic positivist approach to sociology. I have tried to show that sociological readings of Marx's work have created a situation in which our understanding of the relevance of Marxian analysis for sociology has been based upon an uncritical acceptance of 'normal' sociology and an at best partial conceptualization of the 'total' Marxian project. Marx's work is rarely read as a critique of the practice of sociology and, when it is, a rejection of the Marxian project as being ideological or anti-sociological (cf. Bottomore, 1968) frequently follows. The alternative of critically examining sociological practice seems not to be considered, apart that is from the works of Marxists who brusquely dismiss sociology as bourgeois ideology (cf. Shaw, 1972; Blackburn, 1969). Typically in sociology Marxian analysis is addressed as a resource for empiricist hypotheses and predictions; hence Marx is treated as a conflict theorist, functionalist or determinist and his writings are examined in the light of their adequacy in correctly picturing the nature of the development of the late nineteenth century capitalist mode of production. We must be careful not to underrate the significance of sociological work which, through an analysis of the nature of contemporary society (e.g. as industrial or capitalist), an assessment of the significance of social class in contemporary stratification systems and an examination of the relationships between social classes or social groups (e.g. consensual, conflictual etc.), has sought to 'test' the relevance of Marx's work for sociology. Sociological work of this kind has not only dismembered Marx's empirical sociological propositions from their methodological, philosophical and political roots, but has also indirectly promoted a specific conception of the nature and practice of a science of society to the exclusion of an unaddressed alternative inherent in the Marxian position.

However, in the case of both Paci's controversial attempt to merge phenomenology and Marxism and in the writings of critical theorists (e.g. Marcuse, Habermas, Wellmer) it is possible to identify the beginnings of an approach to the study of society, drawing upon Marxian analysis and retrieving its critical element, which unlike the positivist-empiricist conception does not reduce man to an object-like victim of externally constraining ahistorical social facts, structures or systems conceived in such a way as to deny the possibility of human emancipation. Further, neither the phenomenological Marxist nor critical theory position suffers the limitations of the phenomenological sociological critique of positivist theorizing in denying the role of conditioning and determining historical social factors and structures. Both phenomenological Marxism and critical theory attend to the question of the nature of social reality as a totality, recognize and address man's subjectivity as a topic, and share an interest in passing beyond the mere appearance of reality, implicit in common-sense understandings and the natural attitude of

positivist-empiricist approaches, to a scientific understanding, awareness and appreciation of the possibilities inherent in the underlying
socio-historical reality. Critical theory and phenomenological
Marxism, in addition to sharing a common interest in retrieving and
restoring the critical element in Marxian analysis, are both oriented
towards the reconstitution of the 'meaning of humanity', the achievement of human emancipation, through a critique of positivist social
science. Whether the precise *political* course implied by their respective critiques is clear or not, is not a directly relevant issue for our
reconsideration of the problems of sociological science. In this work
discussion of the relevance of critical theory and phenomenological
Marxism for sociology is restricted to their respective critiques of
'traditional theory', that is scientific work oriented towards the
perpetuation and legitimation of existing social relationships.[1]
Therefore it is important to re-examine what one sociologist has
described as the 'prevailing orthodoxy of positivism' (Walsh, 1972)
in order to fully appreciate the difference and significance of the
Marxian contribution.

Positivism and empiricism

Despite the recent emergence of phenomenological sociology and
ethnomethodology positivism remains the predominant sociological
approach. Now as many authors have rightly observed positivism is
indeed a much misused word and clearly needs to be defined.[2] Indeed
within sociology positivism appears to have achieved taboo status,
representing in fact the classification most feared and rejected by
self-respecting 'empiricists'. For example Bechhofer (1974) writing on
approaches to empirical research pleads that he is not arguing for a
positivist sociology. However, although he clearly asserts that he
does not regard himself as a positivist he fails to explicate the
distinction which the reader is invited to assume exists between the
positivist and his empiricist approach.[3]

Contemporary positivism should be distinguished from the
Comtean version in that it has tended to relinquish the goal of progress for an apparent moral neutrality. Hence in contrast to Comte's
conception, whereby sociology was subordinated to the moral and
ethical values of man, the contemporary positivist has sheltered
behind the assumed necessity for moral neutrality in doing science,
thereby acquiescing in the values and interests underlying the
empirical-analytical sciences, in particular the interest in technical
control. Contemporary positivism has attempted to

> . . . sever sociology from its philosophical antecedents, and in
> its ideal type its logic is that of nominalism. . . . Its

154

methodology . . . emulates that of the natural sciences; 'social systems' are the favoured basic units of investigation and are studied in a manner comparable to the methods used in the study of 'other' natural systems. . . . Model construction is also esteemed highly, and the really devout executants concentrate on the construction of mathematical formulae (Farmer, 1967, p. 17).

Positivism is then the approach which treats the subject matter of sociology as in principle compatible with the methodological procedures of the physical and natural sciences themselves conceived within the framework of logical empiricism. The goal of such a form of inquiry is the formulation of generalizations and laws with a view to the prediction of social outcomes. Findings are in principle neutral, lending themselves to use by 'Any Man'. As scientific findings (science being conceived as unproblematical) they are held to be free from evaluation and judgment and what is more are regarded as impartial as far as the implementation of particular social policies or forms of social engineering are concerned. Work of this kind tends to adopt the status quo, the given present, as the natural order and in general its orientation is such that the significance of the totality and the socio-historical process is neglected.

One particularly important characteristic of this type of sociological approach is its dependence upon the false assumption that observational categories are independent of theoretical categories. This is manifest in the treatment of the social world as amenable to observation in a pre-theoretical mode, a point of view implicit in the notion that theories may be tested by evidence or data gathered through observations, surveys or manipulations of secondary data. This position is based upon a fallacy, for investigators would be unable to observe, interpret or report anything in a given field of investigation if they were not operating within a theoretical framework or did not possess a 'vocabulary with which to report' (cf. Hindess, 1973, p. 40). In any case to talk of an 'ideal', socially unattached and theory-free observer is unhelpful when we confront a sociological community of social beings with preconceptions, assumptions and expectations. There is no way that observation can occur pre-theoretically. As Morick (1972) has noted, all data, observations and findings are going to arise through a process in which theory is inevitably present, there is 'no such thing as a theoretically neutral description of anything' (ibid., p. 22). In other words our 'facts', concepts and observations must be analysed as the products of a determinate theoretical problematic. Now Bechhofer tries to rescue a particular 'empiricist' sociological approach from such criticisms by drawing upon an unexplicated distinction between

155

positivism and empiricism. We need briefly to consider these terms. Kolakowski (1972) traces the development of positivist philosophy from Hume and Comte down to logical empiricism, which he describes as a 'technocratic ideology in the guise of an anti-ideological, scientific view of the world, purged of value judgments' (ibid., p. 235). The doctrine of logical empiricism has four permanent features:

(1) Rationalism

(2) Nominalism

(3) An anti-metaphysical attitude

(4) Unity of scientific method

As Kolakowski establishes that each of these features is specifically positivist we are left with the problem of the status of the distinction between empiricism and positivism; is it warranted? Clearly there is a difference between Comtean positivism and the contemporary form, sometimes referred to as neo-positivism. The point, however, is that although contemporary sociological research may not be conducted in conscious emulation of Comte, a fact which we may on reflection perhaps regret, it still, as sociologists have noted (e.g. Giddens, Martins, Frisby), is predominantly positivistic.[4] The onus is with Bechhofer and other 'empiricist' sociologists to try to show that their empiricism is not dependent upon positivist assumptions, that it is grounded in the experiences of social reality by men and women in their everyday lives and furthermore that it does represent a desirable, scientific way to proceed. In particular they will have to respond to the criticism of empiricism as a pseudo-science.

On this question of the nature of sociological science Willer and Willer (1973) argue that sociological knowledge is not scientific, its central tendency being characterized as systematic empiricism, a pseudo-science. The authors stress that a scientific sociology can be achieved but not through the market-research repertoire of ' . . . new statistical procedures or scaling methods. Empiricism is not science . . . scientific sociology implies a completely different method' (1973, p. 137). Their conception is in principle that sociology must reconsider the nature of scientificity in order to understand the primary significance of theory and the secondary role of measurement and observation. Theory is an invention, it does not emerge from the collection, gathering, or generalization of experiences. It is not the product of research, operational techniques or the statistical measurement of taken-for-granted socio-historically generated 'facts'. Theory in the scientific sense is a rational system of related concepts produced via abstraction, it is 'a constructed relational statement consisting of non-observable concepts connected to other non-observable concepts' (ibid., p. 24).

In contrast to the position adopted by the Willers there is an argument that sociology by its very nature cannot, or rather should not, indulge in theoretical speculation. Sociology from this standpoint is seen to lack the sort of meaningful relationship between theory and data which exists in the physical and natural sciences. Whereas the latter have 'well-founded and established theoretical frameworks' the former is said to lack an 'overall touchstone theory'. Hence Dixon (1973) argues that if one takes the aim of sociology to be the provision of good explanations of human behaviour the question becomes one of whether or not such explanations need to be formulated in the form of scientific theories. He states that, 'it is better to opt for clarity, plausibility and historical and empirical accuracy in sociological explanations rather than to construct explanations which only parody scientific theorizing or distort history' (1973, p. 118). The conception of scientific theorizing with which Dixon operates is clearly that derived from the physical and natural sciences. It is perhaps strange that he does not consider the adoption of those sciences as the model for theorizing as the root of the problem. For although it may be agreed that our usage 'of the word theory in the twentieth century is inevitably influenced by successful explanations in physical science' (ibid., p. 119) we are free to consider critically alternative uses and meanings. However, even though Dixon places emphasis on the poverty of sociological theorizing he does not entirely advocate the separation of explanatory and observational categories for he argues that all social data are necessarily interpreted (although not theoretically). Interpretation occurs in Dixon's terms within 'a framework of culturally understood meanings which make nonsense of the behaviourists' claim that an uninterpreted observational language is possible' (ibid., p. 13). The crucial difference between Dixon's position and that propounded for example by Hindess is that the former's critique is anti-theoretical, the nature of sociological explanation remaining unexplicited and in consequence uncertain, whereas the latter's position is that observations and concepts are situated within and can only be comprehended in terms of particular determinate theoretical problematics.

Within sociology there is a reasonably broad based critical rejection of positivist-empiricist approaches, ranging on the one hand from the observation that empiricist dominated sociological knowledge fails to achieve scientific status because it does not accurately emulate the natural sciences in their emphasis upon 'concepts which stand for ideas rather than . . . empirical categories which stand for impressions' (Willer and Willer, 1973, p. 12), to an alternative position which states that to equate sociological theorizing with scientific theorizing is not a matter of correctness but in fact exemplifies a degenerate usage of the notion of theorizing (Blum, 1971).

Underlying much of the above work is the theme of failure, that sociology has failed to live up to its own aspirations, that it has not in fact become the 'natural' science of society. Characteristically the positivist-empiricist approach to sociology tends to treat as relevant only 'what is' and in consequence it manifests an inherent conservative bias. Because it treats observation as the criterion of knowledge and as this is based upon the given present its conclusions necessarily tend to affirm that what is, is, and must be. Hence, ' . . . in the social realm this means that empiricism is inherently conservative. Since its procedures of generating new combinations are through the power of control, its necessary social outcome is totalitarianism' (Willer and Willer, 1973, p. 137). In consequence sociological radicalism has been a contradiction in terms, for so-called 'radical sociologists' have tended to be just as preoccupied with a sterile empiricist approach as their political opponents. As a result the work which so far has been produced under the banner of 'radical' or 'critical' sociology has tended to be merely descriptive of the corporate nature of the discipline and of the role of the political-military-economic complex as financiers of social science research. Of course such work is at times both revealing and important and in this context there have been interesting contributions (e.g. Colfax and Roach, 1971). However, if we wish to begin to develop a critical science of society we must pass beyond such works.

As sociology has developed it seems to have passed from critical beginnings to what is now an almost aseptic present. The positivist-empiricist separation and isolation of theory from practice has created a situation in which critique is virtually absent in sociology. As a result the discipline has tended to become 'ahumanistic, ahistorical and aphilosophical'. This development has been primarily a consequence of the pervasiveness of one value, namely that of technical control, the 'interest' which has led to the development of the physical and natural sciences as they now stand. The operational successes of these sciences have served to persuade sociologists of the desirability, efficacy and validity of their methods with the result that the goal of sociological investigation seems to have become the mathematization of the social world and the extension of social control. It may be noted, however, that in the human sciences not only are such methods with their quantification of the qualitative inappropriate but in addition that 'all attempts to provide equivalents of the so-called "exact" sciences have yielded very little in the way of positive results' (Goldmann, 1969, p. 16). The typical reaction to such a criticism of sociology is that the limitations and failings are due entirely to the immaturity of the science.

In one instance the 'youthfulness' or immaturity of sociology is treated as being quantifiable in terms of Nobel prize awards, it being asserted that

. . . the awarding of a Nobel Prize in economics is indicative of
how far that discipline has developed. Physics and chemistry
have better approximations to their limits than do psychology
and economics. Each discipline is at a different stage of
development. The stage of development is influenced by the
number of years in which the discipline has been working with
general variables, the number of individuals who are members
of the discipline, and a number of other factors. Sociology is a
relatively new discipline. Our approximations are quite crude
but they are a start (Hage, 1972, p. 186).

This serves as a good example not only of the well-worn argument
that sociology's inadequacies stem from its infancy but also of the
quantitative assessment of sociology's development. We may note
that Hage gives no attention to the social process underpinning the
award of a Nobel prize; rather the illusion is preserved 'that science
may be treated as something unaffected by and separate from worldly
matters' (Schimanski, 1974, p. 10). It is indeed remarkable that a
sociologist should use such an example to decorate his judgment of
his discipline's status and development, for the very basis of an
award is that it 'shall have conferred the greatest benefit on mankind'
(ibid., p. 11). These words, from Alfred Nobel's will, surely, given a
sociological imagination, invoke decision-making processes, com-
peting value systems, international competition for status and a host
of other sociologically interesting themes and issues. Can the conclusions or results of such unexplicated and uninvestigated decision-
making processes really provide a satisfactory indication of the
development and status or importance of sociology? I trust not.
Indeed even if we wanted to investigate the decision-making process
and the nominations procedure our efforts would be frustrated, for as
Schimanski notes, 'While secret material about nomination discussions would be of interest to sociologists of science, there is little
chance of obtaining it as it is decisions alone, and never anything
else, which are recorded' (ibid., p. 11).

Hage's references to Nobel prize awards as indices of a discipline's
status and maturity, and by implication sociology's lack of status
and immaturity, are grossly inadequate exemplifying a complete
neglect of the interpretive nature of the decision-making process, the
restriction of awards to specific research areas (viz. physics, chemistry, physiology/medicine and economics, instituted only three years
ago) and the domination of the USA among science prizewinners.
Finally and possibly most significant of all for Hage's judgment of
sociology the Nobel prizes date back to an era when scientific
priorities were different. As Schimanski notes, 'Alfred Nobel shared

159

the general belief that science would always be good for people – the typical techno-optimistic philosophy of the 19th century. The Nobel prizes are destined for people who serve human benefit by doing something *for*, and not *against* technological development' (ibid., p. 12). Accepting that awards are given to those 'doing something *for* technological development' it is perhaps not surprising that sociologists with their 'radical' image and doubtful scientific status, not to mention the abstract and intangible quality of their work, have been passed by. Assuming the criteria do not change, it might be more worrying if a sociologist does receive a Nobel prize, especially if we accept Husserl's and Paci's condemnation of contemporary science.

Additional often quoted reasons for the relatively poor performance of sociology, in contrast to the natural and physical sciences, include the nature and complexity of the subject matter and the presence of what has been called a 'sort of sociological uncertainty principle', namely free will. In particular it is argued that social facts are constructed, accomplished or produced by people in the course of their everyday lives and that therefore they are more complex than natural facts which are not seen to be so directly subject to the 'explanation and prediction' destroying powers of man's free will. Phenomenological sociologists have, however, argued that such problems are a consequence of sociologists pursuing a wrong line of inquiry. For example Psathas (1973) states that to the extent that everyday (first-order) conceptualizations are inexact and non-mathematical then scientific sociological (second-order) conceptualizations will themselves be affected. In other words, 'we cannot expect to quantify and mathematize our descriptions of social phenomena if their nature (essence) is qualitative and nonmathematical' (ibid., p. 10). By doing so we may be distorting or falsifying social reality, producing sociological reifications rather than an understanding of social phenomena. Fortunately we do not yet seem to have reached the stage at which the categories of sociology have become 'real', the analogy with political economy is not yet complete, although awareness of that possibility exists (cf. Goldmann, 1969; Horton, 1971; Dahrendorf, 1973; Habermas, 1974a). The point has been reached, however, at which all sorts of constituencies have become aware of the limitations of positivist-empiricist sociology; this is evident in the proliferation of 'alternatives' ranging from phenomenological sociology and ethnomethodology down to the spectrum of Marxian analysis. A common theme running through these works has been a concern over the reduction of subjectivity in contemporary sociology.

In the following sections I will consider the contribution of a critical Marxian analysis to the reconstitution of sociology by examining the work of specific theorists who have either sought to answer the question of the relationship of Marxism or Marxian analysis to sociology or alternatively have addressed themselves directly to themes and issues, for example subjectivity and the question of the subject-object relationship or the theory-praxis relationship, which are central to the problems confronted in the practice of contemporary sociology. Sociology today is divided over the debate between the 'partisans of reified metaphors' and those who deride the role of material factors in determining and conditioning man. The task of Marxian analysis and its relevance to sociology lies in its quest for a viable interpretation and understanding of the role of subjectivity and the nature of social reality as a totality. The idea of an external and objective social world conceived independently of human subjectivity is as untenable as the mythical idea of the autonomous individual at the centre of every social situation. Analysis must come to terms with the nature of social reality as a 'concrete totality' and should recognize the inevitability of praxis as concomitant with sociology's role in the world. To achieve this end a critical analysis of the nature of society is necessary to reveal the inadequacy of the natural attitude of everyday understanding. As one commentator has noted,

> To the ordinary person reared in the tradition of Western empiricism, physical objects usually seem to exist 'by themselves' out there in time and space, appearing as disparate clusters of sense data. So, too, social objects appear to most of us as things: land, labour, capital; the working class and the employing class; the state and the superstructure of ideas, philosophies, religions – all these categories of reality often present themselves to our consciousness as existing by themselves with defined boundaries that set them off from other aspects of the social universe. However abstract, they tend to be conceived as distinctly as if they were objects to be picked up and turned over in one's hand (Heilbroner quoted in Stanley, 1973, p. 418).

It seems to me that sociology should seek as its goal not an extension of technical control, inherent in the positivist-empiricist approach to sociology, but the re-awakening of consciousness so that human beings may realize their role as active agents employing taken-for-granted cultural meanings as resources both in the interpretation of social reality and in the course of their activities which produce a practical transformation or an affirmation of the common-sense world. Clearly this does not mean that the world may be interpreted as we please; meanings are already present in the world, awaiting us, confronting us. Indeed the nature of the Marxian critique of political economy spells out clearly the manner in which specific cultural meanings become transformed from 'appearance' into 'reality'. Sociology, rather than remaining satisfied with attempts to describe the categories and their mutual relations must seek to reveal the role of interpretation and action in reaffirming and modifying the categories in order that human beings may realize the historical relativity of the alienated and estranged world in which they exist. In other words sociology must become a form of social criticism.

Marxism as a sociology

In Colletti's terms sociologists in their preoccupation with society in general, its nature, aims and essence are guilty of substituting an ideal object for the 'real' object, of concentrating upon the abstraction 'society in general' instead of a materially determined real society. The accusation is that sociologists have investigated society exclusively at the level of ideological social relations by substituting a concept for the historical reality which subsequently is reified and thereby confused with the neglected real object. For Colletti, '... the sole way of guaranteeing the possibility of a scientific analysis can only be that of investigating society at its material level, i.e. at the level of the real basis which specifies it and prevents its dissolution into an idea' (1972, p. 5). However, an analysis of this kind unless accompanied by considerable caution can easily lead to a blind return to the most pernicious forms of vulgar materialism or systematic empiricism, the criticisms and limitations of such approaches being conveniently occluded. Certainly Colletti seems aware of the dangers inherent in his position for he asserts that the rejection of idealism does not mean that naturalism or abstract materialism is the answer. On the contrary an exclusive preoccupation with either idealism or abstract materialism will in all likelihood produce a similar outcome, namely the transformation of a given concrete society into 'society in general'. When investigation proceeds at the ideological level alone then consciousness, ideas, language, belief, values and cultural factors in general are taken to be the primary and most specific elements of human society, material relations of production generally being excluded from consideration. Alternatively if attention is devoted to the material level alone there is the danger that the social relationships of human beings to society and nature will be reduced to a 'presocial or asocial fact'. As we have seen in the case of Paci's analysis of phenomenology and Marxism an understanding of social reality cannot be achieved without taking into account its dual nature, both subjective and objective.

The theme of the relationship of subject and object in the totality appears indirectly in Colletti's work in terms of the relationship between structure and superstructure, being and thought or existence and consciousness. His position seems to be that they constitute a unity, a totality within which the structure, being or existence is dominant. For example he states that 'the superstructure is itself an aspect and articulation of the structure; consciousness is itself a mode of being; the knowledge of life is itself a mode and manifestation of life' (ibid., p. 10). Hence art, philosophy and science constitute realities in their own right, have specific and distinct spheres of activity whilst being in turn expressions of society. For Colletti therefore any critical analysis of philosophy, science or consciousness is in turn an investigation of a form of society and in consequence a sociology. In this conception society is treated as an objective object-subject natural and historical process. Colletti's explicit purpose seems to be to rescue a scientific (and yet revolutionary) Marxism from criticism as ideology. This he attempts by drawing upon a distinction between the view that social interactions or relationships constitute social reality, its objective appearance being itself a consequence of the socio-historical process, and the standpoint which affirms that such a statement entails the reduction of human relations to an ideological process. Colletti argues that the relation is between subjects yet these subjects are objective entities. The historical subject is in fact an historical and natural entity.

Within sociology as I have tried to show there has been a tendency to reduce the unity of social reality, the totality, to a dualism. This has taken the form either of the creation of distinctions between supposed 'macro-' and 'micro-' levels of reality or between 'subjective' and 'objective' aspects of reality, the latter (objective) tending to take precedence over the former (subjective) aspect. In fact the failure to recognize man's nature as a conscious and active being, and the corresponding neglect of his ability as an objective natural being with living needs, constantly engaged in the dialectical construction of social reality, has characterized sociological thought from Comte to the present. Sociologists have either treated man as purely an object of investigation (e.g. positivism) or alternatively have focused entirely upon subjectivity, thereby reducing reality to a purely human product. For example Colletti suggests that in the case of Weber the object of study, history, is ultimately reduced to a purely cultural phenomenon, 'man is reduced to a purely cultural being' and the 'economic structure itself is reduced to the mere cultural significance of the economic structure' (ibid., p. 39). Hence reality is reduced until it is exclusively a human product. Colletti argues that Weber's preoccupation with orthodox and vulgar Marxist analysis induced an overreaction which manifests itself in the reduction of reality to 'a product of the conscious or cultural action of man'. In consequence, as with contemporary phenomenological and ethnomethodological sociologies 'it is not what men do that counts but rather the manner in which they conceive what they do' (ibid., p. 39). Weber is therefore portrayed as aiding and abetting the formulation of an aseptic and technicist sociology which is unable to evaluate values or value judgments. All it can offer is a technical critique of the adequacy of means to a given end.

By way of a brief discussion of Weber's work which fails to attend to the problematical character of the Marx-Weber relationship Colletti asserts that the predominant tendency within 'bourgeois' sociology is to identify conceptualizations of the present with an external natural order. Weber began with 'his present' but did not take into account the material organization of the concrete society. Hence Colletti argues that for Weber 'the present' was identified with 'the values present to his own consciousness as a bourgeois intellectual' (ibid., p. 42) and in consequence sociological science rather than being a source of man's emancipation was demoted to a level as arbitrary as any other subjective belief. In Marx's analysis on the other hand Colletti perceives the presence not only of science but also the moral idea – hence its revolutionary character. Additionally, contra Weber, Marx's analysis attends to the social character of apparently natural phenomena and to the significance of subjectivity without at the same time neglecting the importance of the specific socio-historical context manifest, in the case of capitalist society, in terms of the domination of the process of production over exploited and estranged human beings. Although Colletti's analysis is directed towards sociology it does not specifically address the question of the relevance of Marxian analysis for sociological problems; rather it appears to attempt to establish Marxism as a type of sociology coexisting with alternative conceptions. For a more direct consideration of the relationship of Marxism to sociology we have to turn to Wiatr (1969).

Marxian analysis as an alternative to positivist sociology

According to Wiatr sociology and the positivist-empiricist approach in particular is dominated by four basic myths. These are the myths of ethical neutrality, modernity, empiricism and rational engineering. Now although it is probably the case that sociologists have admitted post-Gouldner of the necessity to qualify the 'ethical neutrality doctrine' the consequences have not led to an open awareness and recognition of the social nature of social (and all other) science but on the contrary to a modification of the original doctrine such that values are seen to play a part although their effect may be contained and neutralized through the adoption of more refined technical methods. Wiatr argues that this myth is closely linked to the other three and that all are characteristic of the positivist-empiricist approach. The second myth, that of modernity, implies that science is progressive and progress here of course implies the adoption of new techniques and methods and the severance of the 'umbilical' attachment to the founding fathers. Indeed contemporary sociology seems to be suffering from the tensions which follow from the basic differences in orientation between those who want to proceed with the 'received' interpretation of the founding fathers as a possible resource for technical-empirical research and others who view the 'received' tradition as itself problematical, as the core of the sociological project, requiring continual reflection and revision. It should be mentioned that the perceived need to revise the tradition is not a consequence of the empirical refutation of hypotheses but results from the temporal nature of the socio-cultural and historical formulation of the tradition.

The myth of empiricism refers to the adoption of particular quantitative and mathematical operations and methods. Wiatr argues that little has, however, been achieved through the new techniques and methods beyond the questioning of earlier 'discoveries' because of their alleged technical inferiority. He states, 'It is as if one had to board an atomic submarine for a new discovery of America, a discovery which has to be verified simply because Columbus's "Santa Maria" was technically imperfect' (1969, p. 23).

Finally there is the myth of rational engineering, the product of the other three myths without which it would not exist. Wiatr argues that sociologists have become scientists of the present, 'experts in social life' and that as such the discipline has become embroiled in the legitimation of social relations and in the provision of knowledge for ameliorative social policies. This is a direct consequence not of a conspiracy but rather of the adoption of the natural attitude implicit in positivist-empiricist research. Acceptance of the modified ethical neutrality doctrine plus the belief in the relevance of the methodology of the natural sciences to the progress and advance of sociology has led to the adoption of a particular scientific ethos which Husserl and later Paci have identified as the course of man's estrangement and alienation. Inherent in this scientific ethos, as Wiatr has noted, is a belief that

... the sociologist like the natural scientist studies his subject to diagnose it, but he does not think it possible or appropriate to influence it during the process of the study. The myth of sociology functioning as rational engineering is based on the conviction that the processes of investigation and of theoretical reasoning leave social reality intact, and because of this they can be employed as diagnostic tools in relation to practical actions which, in turn, were undertaken on the basis of a sociological diagnosis and expert evidence (ibid., p. 25).

In consequence we can witness that in sociology theory and practice have long since parted company. For Wiatr this problem is tied up with the discipline's lack of historicism, the inability or failure of sociologists to treat sociology itself as a form of social consciousness situated within specific yet changing socio-cultural and historical parameters. Sociological thinking and social activity are inextricably linked, for

. . . the sociologist's activity consists of changing the image of the world in people's consciousness. This subjective image of social relations is an important component of reality, because it determines the social roles which people accept for themselves and impose on others; and so an intellectual modification of the image constitutes practical activity (ibid., p. 29).

So for that matter does an intellectual mystification or confirmation of the image of social relations. Hence as in the case of Husserl's discussion of the *Crisis of European Sciences*, Paci's critique of the sciences of capitalism or alternatively Habermas's account of the scientization of everyday life, Wiatr establishes that social science, sociology, is necessarily effective in the modification of social reality through human perception and action. This is not a view which can be confined to authors who may be abruptly dismissed as being on the fringes of the discipline; it is also held by authors who direct their work explicitly to a sociological audience (Gouldner, 1971, 1973; Allen, 1974).[5]

For Wiatr the sociological belief in apparently neutral techniques of verification for testing statements about social reality is an illusion, a sociological myth. In reality the process of investigation, the techniques and methods by which social scientists attempt to contrive explanations of their social world, is itself a product of a 'framework of controversial ideologically committed visions of the world'. Social reality in Wiatr's conception, like that of Paci, is both subjective and objective, the distinction between the two being merely an abstraction since there is no distinct sphere of consciousness independent of the socio-economic structure any more than there are socio-economic relations independent of man's conscious activity. The loss of subjectivity, the objectification of men and women, is a product of the separation of awareness from reality itself. This process has received assistance from sociological science which treats the objective world, by means of the processes of abstraction and reification, as independent of subjectivity. In turn this scientifically developed conception of the social world is returned albeit in a vulgarized and sloganized form to individuals as an authorized and legitimate explanation. As Allen has noted,

In a variety of subtle ways conventional theoretical explanations enter the consciousness of individuals and provide them with instant explanations. . . . Conventional social scientists then are, in reality, the producers and purveyors of 'instant explanations for all occasions'. . . . So long as the conventional theories dominate, no serious questions are asked which could embarrass, let alone threaten, the structure of the society. It so happens that the conventional theories do dominate, not solely because they are supported by the apparatus of the State but also because the vast majority of social scientists conform to them in spite of their obvious defects and object to attempts to change them (1974, pp. 10–11).

Sociological theorizing in the 'capitalist' world is here conceptualized as being of a primarily static kind, preoccupied with a conception of the present order as the natural order. Alternative conceptions which treat the present as necessarily dynamic and temporary have achieved within sociology a 'political' status in so far as they are evidenced to manifest a sense of commitment supposedly in direct contradiction with the 'neutral' scientific orientation.

Where then does sociology stand in relation to Marxian analysis in Wiatr's conception? Sociological knowledge itself is seen to constitute a part of social reality in so far as it organizes and changes consciousness and behaviour, thereby modifying the very reality which it seeks to describe. As such, sociology has no need to struggle for practical applicability, for within it theory and practice are already linked, albeit implicitly and unconsciously as far as most sociologists are concerned. This point is made in different ways by Allen (1974), Freire (1972) and Habermas (1974a). For Wiatr the concept of a socially committed sociology is not as he states, ' . . . an artificial invention nor a proposal for a style in sociology. It is rather a reflection of the actual and inescapable commitment of sociology to the social life which it not only studies but also changes' (ibid., p. 36). Marxian analysis is then not just a sub-field of sociology but rather the alternative path along which a science of society, a sociology *consciously* serving social ends or purposes, may develop.

Sociology and the world of pseudo-concreteness

The world of pseudo-concreteness is composed of fixed objects which pass as natural conditions rather than as the result of people's social activity, fetishized praxis and consequent common representations.

167

It is a world which emerges when reality is treated as an object to be intuited, analysed and theoretically comprehended in contrast to and independent from subjectivity. In this way the phenomenal form of reality is not distinguished from real existence and indeed tends to be taken as the natural world. A critique of such a world and the sciences which re-affirm its existence may also be found in the work of Kosik (1968, 1969). His concern is to develop an account of the distinction and relationship between the world of pseudo-concreteness and what he terms the concrete totality. The problem is that the 'thing itself', the reality, is not directly evident to observation or perception, for immediate perception merely grasps the phenomenon of the thing, its appearance. Hence the primary activity in which science and philosophy should be engaged according to Kosik is the continual interrogation of the phenomenon, a recommendation compatible with Paci's proposal of a 'disoccluding analysis' as the basis of a science of society. However, there can be no finality to the process of a disoccluding analysis, for the 'thing in itself' – e.g. social reality, a social relationship or society – is constantly and continuously in a state of becoming, of transformation, and the analysis or examination of the phenomenon itself contributes to the phenomenon's transformation.

Dialectical analysis in Kosik's exposition attends fully to these issues distinguishing between the representation and the concept, revealing that the world which appears to human beings in fetishized practice is not the real world. Such a world, of appearance, of pseudo-concreteness, is 'the projection of determinate historical conditions that have been petrified into the consciousness of the subject' (1969, p. 25). Kosik uses the term 'pseudo-concrete' not because the phenomenal form of reality is unreal but because it fits the nature of the phenomena in so far as they manifest an independence, externality or objective quality which is merely the product of the reification of social praxis. Dialectical thought submits these phenomena which appear as original, natural and independent, to a critical analysis in which 'reified forms of the objective and ideal world are dissolved' and in consequence appear in consciousness as what they really are, namely the products of human praxis.[6] The orientation of Kosik's work is therefore towards the restoration of subjectivity, to the appreciation of the 'real' world not as a world of real fixed objects but rather as a unity of producer and product, subject and object, or genesis and structure. In contrast to approaches which are fixated on the world of pseudo-concreteness Kosik argues that truth does not rest in the world awaiting discovery, it is not given or predetermined, nor is it unreachable or yet finally obtainable. Truth is made, developed and realized in a world which is constantly in the process of becoming, hence truth becomes an horizon. For Kosik this materialistic destruction of pseudo-concrete-ness is concomitant with 'the liberation of the subject (i.e. the concrete vision of reality contraposed to fetishized intuition) . . . [and] coincides with the liberation of the object' (ibid., pp. 28–9). Hence in the dialectical approach social reality represents the union of subject and object.

Within sociology the world of pseudo-concreteness, the pheno-menal reality, has been taken as the real world. As Kosik has ob-served the social world has in consequence been reduced to only one dimension, mathematized and subjected to the natural attitude. He notes, 'Only the world of physicalism, the world of real idealized values, of extension, of quantity, of measure, of geometrical forms, has been declared to be real while the everyday world of man has been condemned as fiction' (ibid., p. 31). In such a conception men and women are portrayed as mere role players, never as full and active subjects. Now although there have been critiques of this type of position implicit in positivist-empiricist sociological approaches, in general the 'alternatives', phenomenological sociology, ethno-methodology, etc., have tended to neglect altogether the material basis of reality. Hence whereas the latter may be seen to retreat into idealism, Marxian analysis has attempted to grasp the subjec-tive and objective basis of social reality. Why one particular image of reality has become dominant is not an easy question to answer particularly if we recognize that there are alternative ways of seeing and that there are 'separate realities' (viz. artistic world, poetic world). The position I have adopted here is derived from theorists who have attributed responsibility for the reduction of the social world to objectified facts to science and the capitalist mode of production (Husserl, 1970; Paci, 1972; Habermas, 1971, 1974a).

What then is Kosik's conception of social reality? It is a dialectical and structured whole, the dialectical unity of base and super-structure and it contrasts starkly with the conception of social reality as a complex of autonomous structures or institutions reciprocally influencing each other, as in sociology. Whereas in sociology the authentic subject is reduced to homo sociologicus, Kosik's concep-tion re-affirms the individual's status as the 'objective socio-historical subject'. Where there has been sociological recognition of the significance of the individual's activity it is restricted to particular aspects, for example the importance of individuals' definitions of situations; the significance of consciousness in the formation of identity; the use of language. Hence although there is a 'viable' symbolic interactionist tradition and a developing phenomenological sociology (as well as ethnomethodology) which accept and focus attention on subjectivity, each neglects altogether the question of pre-categorical conditioning, avoiding to an unwarranted extent any consideration of society and in consequence precipitating the demand that we 'bring society back in' (Worsley, 1974). Although Paci, Kosik and Wiatr attend to the question of subjectivity and consider the relationship of theory and practice in the context of social science they neglect to include any discussion of the process(es) by which awareness may be increased to facilitate the conscious transformation of history. An attempt to pass beyond an expression of the necessity for increased awareness, consciousness and the promotion of sub-jectivity can be discovered in the work of Freire (1972), in particular in his emphasis upon the role of education in liberating or emanci-pating people.

Doing a phenomenological Marxism

Although Freire's work is essentially situated within the exploitative relationship of the 'director society' and the 'culture of silence', that is to say between the societies of the First and Second 'Worlds' and the Third World, it does have salutary relevance within the director society, in particular for those engaged at any level in the scientific and educational processes. Without doing too much violence to Freire's thought it is possible to perceive in particular its relevance for sociology. Education is the central theme in his analysis because it holds the key to the 'conscientization' of the masses, 'the process in which men, not as recipients, but as knowing subjects, achieve a deepening awareness both of the socio-cultural reality which shapes their lives and of their capacity to transform that reality' (1972, p. 51, n. 2). Just as it has been argued that there is no neutral sociology so Freire asserts that there can be no neutral education. A political function is invariably involved, either, in the case of education, through the conditioning of behaviour and perception in line with socio-cultural tradition, norms and values, or alternatively, in the specific case of sociology, through the legitimation or criticism of the existing structure of society and its power relations.

Freire's position is that the Third World is characterized by a culture of silence, 'the metropolis speaks, the dependent society listens'. The dependent, dominated society receives from the director society a pre-processed and pre-digested reality, the major avenue of transmission of the reality-package being the educational system. (In the case of the pre-processing of reality within the director society the communications media in general represent the major source of transmission.) The problem Freire confronts therefore is how to provide for literacy in the Third World without at the same time inflicting upon the 'illiterate' population cultural imperialism implicit in the educational process of the director society. His attempted solution is derived from a phenomenological Marxist orientation and offers as a proposal that the learning context must provide men and women with the possibility of reflecting upon the process by which reality is apprehended in order that they may pass beyond their original erroneous understandings, beyond the apparently natural order.

Now a case can be made for viewing social scientists and sociologists in particular as being engaged in a process of pre-packaging reality. Indeed this issue is at the centre of the debate over the comparative status and relationship of sociological accounts of reality and common-sense accounts of reality. Unfortunately it is all too easy to claim scientific legitimacy for the former whilst at the same time reducing the latter to near irrelevance or fiction. So what is the relationship? I have earlier, in discussing phenomenological sociology, rejected the idea that there is no significant difference between sociologists' and laymen's accounts. Broadly speaking I think there are three major characteristics which distinguish the sociologist and his account from the layman and his account. These are referred to by Phillips (1973) as being

   (i) Membership of a scientific community
  (ii) Greater information
 (iii) A radically different 'form of life'

Phillips argues that 'the major characteristic' distinguishing the sociologist from the layman is in fact the former's membership of a scientific community. However, although he fully recognizes that this provides the sociologist with 'expert' credentials and status, he fails to address the more significant attributes, which follow from the ascriptive process; namely, access to resources and authority. Membership of a scientific community is not only concomitant with an awareness of an 'enormous amount of "information" ', but also provides opportunities for the communication of ideas and points of view. Opportunities to prognosticate publicly or to assist in the formulation of social policy are not so readily available to laymen.

After having expressed 'skepticism that sociologists possess any unique knowledge with regard to understanding society' (ibid., p. 152), Phillips suggests that what is likely to distinguish the sociologist from the layman is a knowledge of 'who said what about this or that' plus an acquaintance with certain 'facts'. This is all very well but it does gloss over an important issue namely that within contemporary society there has been as Wright Mills (1970) observed, 'a decisive shift in the administrative uses . . . of social science' (ibid., p. 113). In other words although Phillips may be sceptical that sociologists possess any unique knowledge it does not necessarily follow that sociological work is similarly devalued by administrators and civil servants. In considering the sociologist-layman distinction we cannot simply, as Phillips does, ignore the social evaluation and stratification of knowledge, for the scientific community to which the sociologist belongs is part of a larger socio-economic and political community with extra-scientific standards, values and goals. Within that wider bureaucratically organized community the sociologist's possession of 'enormous amounts' of information is sufficient to achieve the status of expert on social life, including that of the layman. The final distinguishing characteristic referred to by Phillips concerns the language sociologists use, 'the way he carves up the world' and the manner in which sociologists negotiate agreement within their discipline as to what constitutes knowledge. Phillips proceeds to discuss the relevance of 'correct' sociological methods and *'agreed-upon'* criteria to the sociologist's form of life and their significance for the sociologist-layman distinction. I want to return to an issue which is a source of major *disagreement* within the sociological community, namely the conceptualization of social reality.

Within sociology either preoccupation is with reality as an objective datum or alternatively it is with man's perceptions and reconstructions of reality. Reality however is both, the consequence being, as Freire states, that 'mechanistic objectivism is [as] incapable of explaining men and the world, as is solipsistic idealism' (1972, p. 53). Sociology as it stands may therefore be unable to contribute consciously to the transformation of the world in so far as it either reduces man to the level of an object whose consciousness is a reflection of reality and who therefore would be unable to transcend the given reality (e.g. sociological positivism), or alternatively by the reduction of reality to purely a creation of consciousness (e.g. phenomenological sociology), the concept of transforming reality is reduced to an imaginative project. How therefore can sociology contribute to people's enlightenment? Clearly the topics of language, thought and consciousness are vitally important. However, we must bear in mind that in certain circumstances, under alienated conditions, 'reality as it is thought does not correspond to the reality being lived objectively, but rather to the reality in which the alienated man imagines himself to be' (ibid., p. 14). In consequence a preoccupation with language, thought and consciousness to the neglect of social relationships and human praxis in general can only lead to a de facto reduction of reality to the creation of consciousness. Freire argues from Marx that recognition must be given to man's teleological nature because only through the realization that man's orientation to the world is not merely an association of sense images but involves the possibility of the act of knowing through praxis can there be any beginning to the process of 'conscientization'. Because man is a being not only in the world but with the world, he is able to reflect upon his situation or as Freire states, to 're-admire his former admiration', to perceive and comprehend the process by which he 'objectifies the not-I'. Man's vocation is here portrayed as a 'becoming-more', as a transcending of the given.

Through the process of the division of labour the function of critical reflection has been usurped by the social sciences and sociology in particular. However, their reflections are no longer critical, 'radicalism' having been curbed in order to achieve the mantle of science.[7] Hence a situation has arisen in which discourses, 'performances in which we seek to show the grounds for cognitive utterances' (Habermas, 1974a, p. 18), are generally absent from sociology with the consequence that the critical and emancipatory basis of the discipline is occluded by a technical, descriptive and inherently repressive orientation. This is further compounded by the fact that we too exist amidst a 'culture of silence' in which the structural relation between directors and dominated, communicators and audiences, teachers and students provides an obstacle to the development of awareness (cf. Enzensberger, 1970). We exist in a world in which 'men begin thinking and acting according to the prescriptions they receive daily from the communications media rather than in response to their dialectical relationships with the world' (Freire, 1972, p. 80). Sociology has contributed to this process rather than transcended it for whilst the sociologist can speak with authority and opportunity the object, man, is necessarily silent.[8] The communication of sociological thought is one-way through a process of dilution and mediation by the popular media; as such there is no dialogue. Sociological knowledge is, in a sense, comparable to a form of recipe knowledge for it participates in the construction of a situation in which men

. . . do not have to think about even the smallest things; there is always some manual which says what to do in situation 'A' or 'B'. Rarely do men have to pause at a street corner to think which direction to follow. There's always an arrow which deproblematizes the situation. Though street signs are not evil in themselves, and are necessary in cosmopolitan cities, they are among thousands of directional signals in a technological society which, introjected by men, hinder their capacity for critical thinking (ibid., p. 80).

Contemporary sociology is a science of man and society rather than a science for men and women in society.[9] It lacks both a critical awareness of its own activities and operations as well as an understanding of the nature of social reality. Basically as sociologists we have a choice: should we give theoretical expression to the contradictions in the reality of everyday life or proceed to offer legitimation for the present social order? Here we necessarily enter the province of critical theory.

Critical theory and sociology

The origins of critical theory lie in the critique of appearances, in particular in Marx's critique of political economy and the capitalist mode of production. Necessarily, such a theory of society, oriented towards emancipation from the present, must confront the fact-gathering appeal of positivist-empiricist approaches if it is to avoid the problem of the reification of socially generated objects into naturally independent and external 'facts'. For many sociologists the very idea of a critical sociology may imply a contradiction with a belief in the scientific enterprise. Not that criticism is absent from positivist-empiricist works; on the contrary it constitutes a logical part of the adopted scientific method, representing a necessary feature in the progressive quest for higher and more comprehensive forms of explanation, as well as for greater accuracy in prediction. However, the confinement of criticism to methods and techniques means that its relevance to the topic of study is indirect and purely correctional, either of falsely grounded common-sense understandings or alternatively technically inferior scientific accounts. Because the reference in such instances is always towards the failure of common-sense or prior sociological explanations to apprehend correctly the object reality (conceived uncritically), the relationship between accounts, understandings and beliefs about phenomena and the underlying reality in which they are produced is neglected. Hence sociology has tended to offer élitist re-mystifications of the world, criticizing and replacing common-sense understandings with scientistic descriptions which better serve the purpose of the legitimation and rationalization of the given social order. As Allen has noted,

> The guardians of conventional theory hide behind the twin ramparts of reification and mystification. Theories, it is insisted, are not for the laymen, for they are constructed with scientific precision by specialists; they are as ex cathedra statements handed out and down by the intellectual stars of the community. But in case reification fails them the theories are made incomprehensible to ordinary people. Simple acts such as going to work each day are obscured by jargon; simple acts like subsisting are transformed through mathematical symbols and computers into incomprehensible equations (1974, p. 14).

Sociology has therefore not been critical in the sense implied in critical theory for it has not sought to reveal the historicity of appearance or to transcend the facts through a revelation of the imminent possibilities of society. There is in fact an appalling absence of a critical sociology despite the existence of a long-standing Marxist sociological tradition. The sociological over-simplification of Marx's work, as I have attempted to show, has indirectly served the purpose of facilitating the process of neglect or neutralization of critical elements in his analysis which provide the basis for a critique of sociology. This process of neutralization has occurred not only through the empiricists' 'testing' of propositions but also by way of an implicit institutionalization and dilution of Marxian analysis in syntheses with functionalist approaches. Rare indeed are attempts to draw from Marx's work anything of socio-logical import beyond descriptions and predictions situated within nineteenth century capitalism. In general Marx's analysis has received a positivist-empiricist interpretation in sociology with the result that its inherent challenge to sociological orthodoxy has been minimized.

Marx's work represents both a critique of the ideological distor-tions inherent in the science of political economy and in addition provides a theory which establishes the possibility of transcending the alienating and exploitative class-based society of capitalism. It attempts to provide a scientific orientation to, or critical knowledge for, action. By way of the distinction between use and exchange value, the theory of surplus value and the revelation of the social relationships at the base of the generation and perpetuation of the commodity form, Marx provided an explicit account of the socio-historical basis, in direct contrast to the apparent natural character, of capitalist society. In *Capital* Marx shows that the categories of political economy are the product of a determinate socio-historical mode of production. As therefore in the case of contemporary positivist-empiricist approaches in sociology, the limitations of political economy are revealed to emanate from an unexamined acceptance of the apparently 'natural' social order or, in the case of Marx's work, the socio-cultural 'facts' of capitalism. The conse-quence of such an acceptance is not only a total neglect of the socially constructed and historical nature of social facts but also the transformation of social relationships between subjects into natural relationships between objects or things. Hence 'capital', 'land', 'rent', 'wages', 'labour', 'money' and commodities in general are not treated as social entities, as the historically produced categories of social relationships which have taken on the appearance of things and indeed have become things under an alienating mode of produc-tion; on the contrary they are treated as subjects and in return men and women are reduced to objects. By scientifically sanctioning the reversal of subject and object political economy performs a legitimating function for the capitalist mode of production. The function of Marx's critical science is to restore the historical dimension to the social process thereby providing men and women with the possibility of recognizing the reificatory nature of social life. It is an attempt to stimulate the process of self-reflection, to encourage 'conscientization' so that people may critically re-think and reinterpret the grounds of legitimacy of existing social practices. Marx achieves this through a critical examination of the commodity form, in particular through the revelation that ' . . . capital is not a thing . . . any more than money is a thing. In capital, as in money, determined personal social relations of production are presented as relations of things to persons, or determined social connections appear as social natural properties of things' (quoted in Howard, 1970, p. 226). In other words in the context of our everyday lives, in the process of production, distribution and consumption, social relationships appear in forms of objectivity, appear as 'things'. We take their 'factual', 'objective' status for granted; naïvely we neglect to doubt or question the status or basis of their existence. As a result the underlying relations of men with each other are concealed and understanding or awareness of the transitory, historical nature of phenomena is obstructed.

Now it is not only laymen or those directly 'participating in the production process' who are deceived by the objective forms of social phenomena; social scientists also fall 'victim to the semblance which reality itself produces' (cf. Habermas, 1974a, p. 220). To avoid such a fate we must learn from the inadequacies of positivist sociology, address the significance of phenomenological sociological critiques and recognize that the manner and form in which 'data', 'things' or social relationships present themselves is not an adequate foundation for sociological conceptualization. As Marx advised, science is unnecessary if the outward appearance of things coincides with their 'actual' form. Sociology attempts to achieve a scientific analysis of social life; to begin to do so successfully it must recognize the historical, socially constructed and interpreted character of social facts. The issue will become clearer when we understand that the phenomenal form in which reality appears is a product and consequence of the nature of underlying social relationships and that our sociological analysis must therefore commence by suspending belief in, by doubting, 'bracketing' and critically examining, the given 'facts', social order or society. In such terms sociology becomes a form of social criticism, a form of ideology critique. Now although a critique may provide the basis of a possible transformation of social relationships, in and of itself it is not enough. To transform social relationships a critique must not only distinguish what men and women think about society from how society actually functions, but in addition it must lead to a relevant praxis. These issues, the extent to which Marx's work may be classified as critical as well as the nature of the relationship between theory and practice in his analysis, have been the source of considerable controversy.[10]

Reformulating Marxian analysis

It has been stated by Habermas that the positivistic elements in Marx's analysis undermine its critical content. For Habermas the idea of a science of man is obscured in Marx's writings by the identification of science with natural science. In consequence the development of critical theorizing is seen to depend upon a reformulation of the positivistic Marxian categories, Marx being accused of never having 'explicitly discussed the specific meaning of a science of man elaborated as a critique of ideology and distinct from the instrumentalist meaning of natural science' (Habermas, 1972, p. 45). Hence in contrast to Paci's reading, Habermas portrays Marx as oriented towards the natural sciences, inferring from the statement that 'there will be a single science' that Marx intended the reduction of the science of man to natural science. He exclaims that,

This demand for a natural science of man with its positivist overtones is astonishing. For the natural sciences are subject to the transcendental conditions of the system of social labour, whose structural change is supposed to be what the critique of political economy as the science of man, reflects on. Science in the rigorous sense lacks precisely this element of reflection that characterizes a critique investigating the natural-historical process of the self-generation of the social subject and also making the subject conscious of this process (1972, p. 46).

Hence whereas Paci perceives Marxism to be merely in need of phenomenological stimulation, Habermas conceives the sterility of Marxism to be a consequence of Marx's narrow focus on social labour to the exclusion of the structures of interaction and communication.

Four factors inhibit Habermas's acceptance of Marxian analysis as a critical theory of society. These are, basic changes in the structure of bourgeois society, the decline in significance of economic emancipation, the dissolution of the proletariat and finally the paralysis of Marxism as a consequence of the development of the USSR. The factors to which Habermas attaches most significance in discussing basic structural changes in bourgeois society are the growth of centralized organization and administration and the scientization of everyday life. In his terms these processes have led to a reduction of the 'economic factor' and a concomitant increase in the importance of the polity, politics no longer being dependent upon the economic base. In addition Habermas asserts that the standard of living has risen to such an extent that for large sections of the population an interest in the emancipation of society is no longer articulated in economic terms. He states, 'At most the pauperism of alienated labour finds its remote reflection in a poverty of alienated leisure – scurvy and rickets are preserved today in the form of psychosomatic disturbances, hunger and drudgery in the wasteland of externally manipulated motivation' (1974a, pp. 195–6). Under such conditions, where economic alienation has been superseded by what might be termed cultural alienation, Habermas argues that the proletarian revolutionary class has been dissolved. Hence in a reiteration of a common theme it is asserted that the working class is no longer a revolutionary stratum and that in consequence revolutionary theory lacks an audience.[11] Finally the Russian revolution and the consequent development of the Soviet system is seen to represent the major source of paralysis for Marxist thought, particularly in so far as it is frequently and incorrectly treated as a testing ground for Marxian theory and thereby indirectly contributes to the disintegration of Marxist thought.

Now these reasons for rejecting Marxism are neither novel – they feature regularly in many sociological works – nor are they entirely convincing. The first reason offered by Habermas really raises the question of his reading of Marx. As O'Neill has noted in an excellent essay on Marx, 'Habermas succeeds in cutting off Marx from critical theory by reducing the synthesis of symbolic structures contained in the theory of historical materialism to a crude form of technological and biological determinism' (1972, p. 247). Not only might such an interpretation of Marx's work in itself be considered controversial but equally the nature of the historical changes occurring during this century may be seen to be oversimplified by Habermas. To assert that 'bourgeois society . . . is forced to resort to political mediation of its commerce for many of its branches' (1974a, p. 195) tells us little about the nature of changes. Indeed it may be argued that political mediation of commerce is indicative not only of the growing socialization of productive forces but furthermore is a sign of the continuing, even increasing, significance of the economic factor. As for the second and third reasons advanced by Habermas, the sublime neglect of the possibly temporary nature of the living standards in advanced capitalist societies and the likelihood of relative dissatisfaction should there be any termination of the rise in living standards, not to mention a reduction, provide grounds for concern. If we consider the nature of the relationships between the First, Second and Third Worlds it is apparent that significant changes are already occurring which may drastically modify trading relationships, distributions of wealth and relative standards of living. Given that increasing affluence or the continual rise in living standards may (have) come to an abrupt end for citizens in some industrial societies, and further, given a continuing predilection for 'quantity' rather than 'quality' of life, then the relative deprivations which may ensue could easily render Habermas's dissolution of the proletariat a little premature. Habermas's final reason for casting doubt on the relevance of Marxian analysis (in its orthodox form) for critical theory is addressed to the specific question of the potentially emancipatory nature of science excluded from vulgar Marxism.

Habermas proceeds by attempting to develop Marxian theory from a pure critique of political economy into a critique of positivist science and theorizing in general. This is made necessary in his terms by the presence of technical rationality as the predominant mode of capitalist consciousness. As one observer has noted, 'if technocratic technology is to loose its hold on our consciousness, a critical theory must lay bare the theoretical reifications of this scientistic image of science' (Schroyer, 1971, p. 135). This is what Habermas attempts, a critique of scientism including a refutation of the naïve posturing of positivist-empiricist approaches in social science, not only the so-called conservative positions but also those which attempt to generate a radical image. Such positions are held to be dependent upon a severance of knowledge from interest through an objectivist attitude which correlates propositions with matters of fact. Habermas shows that this objectivist illusion has deluded the social sciences into treating reality as a reality-in-itself composed of facts structured in a law-like manner. Treating reality in this fashion leads to a concealment of the constitution of facts thereby preventing understanding and consciousness of the knowledge-interest relationship.

A specific consequence for sociology of the dominance of the 'empirical analytical' model of science has been that the socioculturally conditioned nature of the sensory experience implicit in the processes of 'testing' or 'validating' has remained neglected. This represents a basic limitation in the positivist-empiricist approach, for as Habermas has noted, ' . . . even the simplest perception is not only performed categorically by physiological apparatus – it is just as determined by previous experience through what has been handed down and through what has been learned as by what is anticipated, through the horizon of expectations' (Habermas, 1974b, p. 199). In consequence it is argued that knowledge is contaminated at source, the procedures and assumptions inherent in scientific inquiry being firmly situated within the pre-scientific processes of everyday life. Developing this theme Habermas categorizes sciences, according to the relationship between cognition and transcendental interest, as follows:

(1) Empirical-analytical sciences
(2) Historical-hermeneutic sciences
(3) Critical sciences

This distinction enables Habermas to differentiate between the positivist sciences placing emphasis upon technical control, hermeneutic sciences stressing interpretation and the extension of intersubjective consensus and understanding and finally critical science, which is oriented towards the liberation of men and women from both natural and historical determination through a process of theoretical and practical enlightenment. Habermas notes that 'in the constitution of scientific object domains we merely extend the everyday procedure of objectifying reality under the viewpoints either of technical control or of intersubjective communication' (1974a, p. 8). In contrast to these two categories of science, a critical social science, a critical sociology, must be oriented towards an understanding of the underlying interest which links a theory's emergence or production to its application. A critical sociology needs must manifest a consciousness of its interest in emancipation whereas the technical and practical interests in knowledge implicit in the other two categories may, and do, remain covert, unexamined and seemingly unproblematical to their exponents.

The development of a theory of society with explicit practical aims must according to Habermas guard itself against behavioural science, hermeneutics, systems theory and what he terms the development of a 'Marxist theory of society in conjunction with Husserl's analysis of the life-world' (1974a, p. 13). In short it must avoid falling into objectivism, idealism, 'the reduction of all social conflicts to unsolved problems in the regulation of self-governing systems' and in addition must not assume a simple transference from individual consciousness to that of the collective. In addition to these difficulties there is the question of the organization of enlightenment, the nature of the distinction between 'action' and 'discourse' and the related topic of the theory-practice relationship. However, before addressing these problems some attention must be given, albeit briefly, to the question of the relationship between critical theory and phenomenological Marxism. Rovatti (1973) has argued that both critical theory and phenomenology are 'on the attack against a model of scientific development and "bad" rationalization' (ibid., p. 25). Both Husserlian phenomenology and critical theory share a concern for human emancipation. Yet in the case of phenomenological Marxism, in particular Paci's work on Marx and Husserl, and critical theory, although there are common elements, for example an interest in regenerating a critical Marxian analysis, there are also important differences as Habermas's veiled comments on the development of a

'Marxist theory of society with Husserl's analysis of the life world' imply. Differences between Paci's and Habermas's work are not confined, however, to dissimilar readings and assessments of Husserl's work. For example whereas Paci argues for the need to compensate for the objectification of reality inherent in the positivistic sciences by returning to the question of subjectivity and proceeds to identify the proletariat as the revolutionary stratum which will usher in the intersubjective and rational society, Habermas specifically denies the existence of a revolutionary proletariat, attends instead to epistemological questions (cf. *Knowledge and Human Interests*, 1972) and provides a more general discussion of the relationship between a disoccluding analysis, the emergence of awareness or consciousness and action (cf. *Theory and Practice*, 1974). However, having said that, it seems to me that the crux of their differences rests with their respective readings of Husserl's and Marx's work, in particular the significance of Husserl's critique of objectivism for restoring the critical element in Marx's analysis. Although this topic represents a 'separate' project requiring a broader more considered appraisal of phenomenological philosophy and Marxism a few observations are possible and necessary at this juncture to underline the differences between Paci and Habermas.

The question of Habermas's interpretation of Husserl and its significance for his development of critical theory is not uncontroversial. For example Hamilton (1974) has argued that there is a similarity between critical theory and the anti-objectivist phenomenological philosophy of Husserl. Now whilst we can, with qualifications, accept that in the case of Horkheimer and Marcuse there are grounds for believing that phenomenological philosophy represented a resource for critical theory, similar observations do not hold for Habermas's work. It is difficult to accept Hamilton's observation (cf. 1974, p. 59) that there has been a convergence of two initially disparate positions, namely Husserlian phenomenology and critical theory, in the work of Habermas, for Habermas is critical of Husserl's work in such a manner as to deny 'the possibility that critical theory could have a positive encounter with phenomenology' (Rovatti, 1973, p. 27). As far as Habermas's and Paci's work is concerned the differences revolve around their respective assessments of Husserl's critique of positivistic science. Paci treats Husserl's *Crisis* as an appropriate resource for retrieving the critical element in Marxian analysis. He offers a materialist reading of Husserl's work perceiving the goal of the latter's analysis to be compatible with that of Marx, namely the creation of a rational intersubjective society. For Paci Husserl's analysis is vital to the regeneration of Marxian analysis because it offers a critique of reificatory and 'objectivist' science. In contrast to Paci, Habermas seems to view Husserl as being trapped within the concepts of 'traditional theory', still operating with an idea or concept of 'pure' theory, theory independent of practical concern. Hence for Habermas (cf. 1970) Husserl's analysis cannot possibly provide the basis of an emancipatory theory of society for although he criticizes 'the uncritical objectivism of the sciences, Husserl succumbs to another objectivism' (ibid., p. 42) namely the idea of 'pure' theory, theory free from 'interest'. In contrast to Paci therefore Habermas rejects the possibility of Husserl's analysis serving as a basis for the development of a critical, Marxian theory of society.

Habermas's work on the theory-practice relationship represents an attempt to come to terms with the problematic relationship between analysis, knowledge or science on the one hand and action or praxis on the other. This is an issue of significance not purely for Marxism and the thorny problem of the intelligentsia-proletariat, theory-political action relationship but also for sociological science, in particular the sociologist-layman relationship and the question of the effect of the practice of sociology on its 'object', society, social structure or social relationships. For Habermas the rise of the positive sciences to the status of productive forces has been concomitant with an expansion of the scientific domain throughout industrial societies. In particular there has been an expansion of technical control not only over nature but also, indirectly through the social sciences in the form of increased bureaucratic administration, over people. Habermas notes that 'in this process the relationship of theory to praxis can now only assert itself as the purposive-rational application of techniques assured by empirical science' (1974a, p. 254). Hence the potential of science as an emancipatory force is transformed into a reality in which emancipation by enlightenment is replaced by science oriented towards control over objectified processes. As such science is in principle directed towards the possible manipulation of human behaviour.

Now if we are to begin to be able to formulate, or think in terms of, a theory of society with conscious and practical aims we must inquire into the distinction drawn by Habermas between two uses of the concept of enlightenment, one referring to the practical change of existing circumstances, the other to the continual 'discursive valida-tion of claims to validity'. In discourses we suspend or bracket the given facts, events, activities and explanations which are taken for granted in everyday communication and action in order that some degree of rational or reasoned analysis of the phenomena may be possible and furthermore so that within the scientific, in our case sociological, community, some degree of agreement as to the 'valid-ity' or character of phenomena may be established (cf. Phillips, 1973, pp. 151–7, 166–7). However, although discourses are considered to be free of experience and unencumbered by action the opinions which form the input of discourses do indeed as Habermas correctly notes, 'have their origin in the diverse inter-relations of experience and action' (1974a, p. 20). Furthermore discourses are of vital and fundamental significance for action itself in so far as the consensus underlying communicative action is predicated upon claims to validity initially established in or by discourse. Hence the two 'forms' of enlightenment are related, discourses providing the awareness, consciousness and knowledge necessary for the emergence of consensus and the establishment of communication. In turn the consensus inherent in communicative action is vital for the possibility of practical action to transform existing circumstances.

I am in danger of oversimplifying Habermas's argument but it seems to me that in his analysis there is a reappearance of the familiar Marxist problem namely that of the relationship of the intelligentsia to the proletariat and in particular the crucial issue of the formation of class consciousness, of how to establish a revolutionary proletariat with a 'valid' understanding of their situation so that existing circumstances might be changed through practical action. However, the focus of Habermas's interest falls not on the question of the nature of the existence or status of a revolutionary proletariat, but rather revolves around the question of the relationship between theory, enlightenment and action.

In the case of contemporary sociology the interest guiding knowledge appears to be primarily technical, oriented towards control, and the achievement of enlightenment is restricted to a minority. By neglecting subjectivity and placing an unwarranted emphasis upon the social world, social reality or social beings as 'objects' sociologists have contributed to, or legitimated, conventional common-sense understandings of the nature of society, or social reality. Hence the given social order is treated as a natural, unproblematically factual social order. As Pelz has noted of contemporary sociology, ' . . . positivism is pervasive. It is the only respectable creed, attitude, myth. . . . Positivism first and foremost intends to look-at-things-as-they-are, not as they ought to be or could be. . . . The status quo is accepted, quite a-historically as an absolute' (1974, pp. 71–2). In contrast the interest underlying critical science provides, through processes of reconstruction and self-reflection, for emancipation. However, although a critical science may make 'possible the enlightenment of social classes as to their own nature' (Habermas, 1974a, p. 27) it cannot authorize or warrant strategic action. The practical consequences therefore of a critical sociology will be, at best, changes in attitude resulting from the analysis and reflection upon events in the past, both 'distant' and 'near' (what we reflectively experience as the present), rather than the provision of strategies for action oriented toward the future. It thus becomes important to distinguish the process of enlightenment, in which a critical sociology may play an important part, from the organization of action. As Habermas has noted, in his *Theory and Practice*,

> While the theory legitimizes the work of enlightenment, as well as providing its own refutation when communication fails . . . it can by no means legitimize a fortiori the risky decisions of strategic action. Decisions for the political struggle cannot at the outset be justified theoretically and then carried out organizationally (1974a, p. 33).

The goal of a critical sociology is not a blueprint for strategic action; on the contrary it should offer the possibility of reflection and reconstruction such that 'subjects come to know themselves and their situation'.[12] To achieve a critical sociology we need to review our methodological practices, re-examine the basis of the subject-object dualism in sociology by attending to the analysis and discussion of the relationship of subject and object in Marxian analysis, and in addition treat not only the sociological preoccupation with society, social structure or reality, conceptualized as an independent 'object', as a topic for analysis but also consider the practical social consequences of reification in sociology.

Concluding remarks

I have attempted to show that contemporary sociology is limited as a science of society by our failure adequately to attend to the question of the subject-object distinction as well as by a neglect of a related problem, namely the relationship of sociology, its practice and consequences, to social reality or everyday social life. I have tried to demonstrate that the sociological 'project' has suffered as a result of a relatively narrow identification of the relevance of Marxian analysis to sociology and a general disinterest in related developments, viz. phenomenological Marxism and critical theory. This is particularly unfortunate for within Marxian analysis the question of the subject-object distinction, the nature of social reality and the problems surrounding a science of society, in particular its relationship to social practice, are basic. It is not so much the case that Marxian analysis 'solves' all the problems confronted within sociology as that it offers a way of understanding better the nature of the problems involved in doing a science of society because it begins by questioning the 'given'. In other words, it provides us with a challenging occasion to re-think what it is to do sociology, to reconsider what a science of society might be and to reassess what purposes or interests a science of the social might serve.

As sociology lays claim to the status of the science of society and in so far as it plays a part in both regenerating and indirectly changing social policy there is a clear responsibility on our part to reconsider the orientation of the theory and practice of the discipline. For this much is clear: sociological work, teaching, research and privatized theoretical speculation take place within the social world. It is both determined by and determining of the social world and inherent in all forms of sociological practice is not only a theoretical stance but also a moral and political interpretation of man, woman and society.

To an increasing extent sociology has become an applied science in the service of administration offering a more concise scientific representation of social demographic profiles, providing data resources for industrial, educational and criminological policy as well as continually furnishing rules, methods and techniques for the study of social problems, situations and behaviour. Sociological awareness of this involvement is neutralized to a considerable extent by reference within the discipline to models, ideal types or homo sociologicus as the focus of interest and by attempts to preserve or reinstate the value-freedom doctrine through the translation or reduction of social phenomena, via unexplicated and superficially interest – and value-free processes of abstraction, to a quantitative expression or numerical relation. However, the sociologist, even though he may hanker after the apparent detached observer status of his peers in the natural sciences, cannot do his science independently of a social context, for even in the very act of insight and perception we are firmly immersed in the social world. 'Facts' are constituted within a theoretical framework and any observation or enumeration of 'facts' necessarily implies an interpretation. For sociology therefore the choice is not one of science or criticism but rather one of enlightenment and emancipation or mystification and technical control. The choice is both a moral and scientific one for exponents of a science of society cannot help being practically interested in society even if they refuse to recognize as much.

I have suggested that we need to return to Marxian analysis, to reconsider its relevance for sociology. In particular I have placed emphasis upon the dialectical nature of social reality and the importance of recognizing subjectivity. Such a reorientation is critical for a sociology oriented towards an acceptance of the 'objective' and 'factual' status of a given social order, society or mode of production. A reification in this manner of the 'objective' form in which a society appears merely represents an ideological distortion or mystification of the socio-historical process. The immediate task for sociology must therefore be a considered appraisal of the interests inherent in the manipulative scientific model derived from the natural and physical sciences with view to the adoption of a critical and emancipatory approach. This is important, for only by way of a radical change in the state of consciousness and understanding will it be possible to ensure that sociologists do not innocently participate in the division of humanity into social engineers and automatons. This requires a rejection of the approach which extends technical manipulation and reification and the adoption of an alternative position with an interest in subjectivity, liberation from dogma and the development of a rational intersubjective society. The crucial question is whether we can retrieve the critical and emancipatory interest for sociology or whether the discipline is already too far along the road to scientism.

Notes

1 Sociology and Marxian analysis

1 Friedrichs unlike Gouldner discusses explicitly the significance of Kuhn's (1962) analysis of the structure of scientific work for an understanding of changes in sociology. Kuhn's initial thesis affirmed that the concepts of 'normal' and 'revolutionary' periods in science could only be applied to the 'mature' sciences, that is to say the natural sciences. However, in a revision (1970) of his earlier work he explained that the terms were also applicable to sciences in the pre-paradigm stage of development, that is to say the social sciences.

2 I am here adopting and developing the terminological distinction proposed by Giddens (1971).

3 Apart from a passing reference to micro-functionalism (1971, p. 380) Gouldner ignores the macro-micro distinction completely.

4 An interesting discussion of the differential availability of 'role distance' techniques according to social class membership is provided by J. Ford, D. Young and S. Box, 'Functional autonomy, role distance and social class', *British Journal of Sociology*, vol. 18, December 1967.

5 The case study of Agnes is discussed briefly in chapter 3.

6 For example, Nicolaus notes that 'The professional eyes of the sociologist are on the down people, and the professional palm of the sociologist is stretched towards the up people . . . ' (quoted in Gouldner, 1971, p. 10).

Giddens in a similar if less polemical vein remarks ' . . . sociologists . . . have given a great deal of attention to studies of the manual working class, and to the "new" middle class, but they have paid much less heed to the upper echelons of the class structure. The dearth is a striking one' (1972b, p. 345). 'The difficulties involved in systematic research upon these matters, of course, are among the most severe . . . Concealment, subterfuge, but above all probably the ubiquity of informal and personalised relationships and procedures create large blank spots which no form of sociological research is likely to penetrate satisfactorily' (ibid., p. 368).

7 T. B. Bottomore and M. Rubel note that 'The sociology of revolution has so far only one major contribution to record, that of Marx himself' (1963, p. 40).

8 Note in particular the essays entitled 'Anti-minotaur: the myth of a value-free sociology' (Gouldner, 1962) and 'The sociologist as partisan: sociology and the welfare state' (Gouldner, 1968).

9 Within sociology there has been a proliferation of terms to delineate a significant change in the nature of society. Each of the following terms is employed by the authors to denote a form of society significantly different from the capitalist society at the focus of Marx's analysis, viz. post-capitalist society (Dahrendorf), industrial society (Aron), multi-dimensional society (Kerr), post-industrial society (Bell), new industrial state (Galbraith), monopoly capitalism (Sweezy), rational society (Habermas).

10 Birnbaum provides three reasons for the reorientation:
    (i) The emergence of a Marxist existentialism
    (ii) The re-emphasis of the dialectic as a method of thought
    (iii) The systematic explication of cultural totalities by dialectical methods

11 Gouldner is not unaware of the heterogeneity of Marxism although he does not address the issue directly. Consequently although he notes that the fusion of 'Saint-Simonism' with 'the infrastructures of German Romanticism and Hegelianism contributed to the development of Marxism, in the work of Marx, Engels, Karl Kautsky, Nicolai Bukharin, Leon Trotsky and V. I. Lenin' and observes that 'where it renewed its contact with Hegelianism, it was expressed in the work of Georg Lukács, Antonio Gramsci and in the contemporary German School of "Critical Sociology" ' (1971, p. 113), he does not draw any conclusions concerning the comparison of Marxism and sociology.

12 I am not implying that the distinction between scientific and critical Marxism is entirely isomorphic with that between positivist-empiricist and phenomenological sociology, merely that there are methodological parallels.

2 Sociological readings of Marx

1 Note for example Lenski's (1966) discussion of conflict and consensus theories of stratification; Dawe's (1970) analysis of the 'two sociologies' of order and control; van den Berghe's (1967) synthesis of dialectical and functionalist approaches; Dahrendorf's (1968) essay attempting a reorientation of sociological analysis away from a preoccupation with 'utopias' towards a recognition of society's 'two faces': stability, harmony consensus, and change, conflict and constraint.

2 Dahrendorf's 'class and class conflict' reading of Marx's work represents a common resource for sociological authors viz. (i) Appelbaum (1970) discussing theories of social change considers conflict theory as 'the legacy of Karl Marx' and draws in particular upon Dahrendorf's interpretation and (ii) van den Berghe (1967) attempts to develop the

case for a synthesis of dialectical and functionalist positions with Dahrendorf's work as the reference for the Marxian dialectic.

3 Note especially Althusser's generally disparaging reference to Garaudy, Lukács and Humanism in general in *Reading Capital*, 1970, pp. 126–37; *For Marx*, 1969, p. 219n; 'Reply to John Lewis', 1972.

4 See for example L. Goldmann, 1969, ch. III, 'The major laws of structure'.

3 Phenomenological sociology – an alternative sociology?

1 Criticisms of Durkheim's work from a phenomenological sociological standpoint may be found in J. Douglas (1967, 1971) and P. Filmer et al. (1972). In both cases the relationship between Durkheim's work and contemporary positivist-empiricist sociology is taken to be one of unproblematic continuity.

2 Wagner's position depends heavily upon the 'latest' of Schutz's works – *The Structures of the Life-World* (see note 7).

3 Wagner states that in both 'structural' and 'genetic' phenomenology there has been a failure to develop analyses of macro issues, the consequences of which 'may include that the phenomenological approach has nothing to offer that could be relevant' (1973, p. 72).

4 The former position appears explicitly in P. Filmer et al. (1972); the latter position, tending to portray phenomenological sociology as in principle compatible or reconcilable with conventional sociology, is exemplified in different ways by Goldthorpe (1973), Shearing (1973), Strasser (1967).

5 Strasser states that:
Empiricism 'is based on a faulty conception of the essence of experience';
Objectivism 'flows from a misconception concerning the partners playing a role in experience';
Scientism 'results from a metaphysical overvaluation of empirical insights' (1967, p. 525).

6 Note the work of Rickert, Dilthey and Weber, in particular and the methodological controversy concerning the Naturwissenschaften and Geisteswissenschaften.

7 There are problems in interpreting Schutz's work, in particular its 'unfinished' quality. It is argued that *The Phenomenology of the Social World* and the volumes of material in *Collected Papers* were merely leading up to his major project namely an analysis of the structure of the world of everyday life. The latter in the form of a work entitled *The Structures of the Life-World* is now in part available, with volume two still to be published. However, because of Schutz's untimely death only notes and outlines were available, indicating the plan of the book, and it has been Luckmann's unenviable task to make available in a coherent and consistent form the most important of Schutz's works. Clearly the question of 'how this is accomplished' is itself of interest as a phenomenological project, but more importantly the mere knowledge that the work is not Schutz's alone must induce caution in interpretations of

the significance of the material made available.

8 E.g. see Schutz, *Collected Papers*, vol. I, p. 350.

9 The other methodological postulates referred to by Schutz are the postulates of logical consistency and subjective interpretation (cf. 1971, vol. I, pp. 43–4) and the postulates of relevance and compatibility (cf. 1964, vol. II, pp. 18–19).

10 A 'we-relation' is a social relation of reciprocity where the attention of each of the two members is oriented to the other. A 'they-relation' is a social relation of anonymity and impersonality. The reference point for the individual in the 'they-relation' is not the immediately experienced alter-ego but rather the knowledge derived from the social world in general, it is inferred from an objective meaning context. It is virtually a stereotypical relation, viz. customer-postman, defendant-judge, patient-doctor, etc.

11 Garfinkel's relationship to his students and their parents in one of his demonstrations is not unlike the privileged position of the producer of the television programme 'Candid Camera' vis-à-vis the actors involved and the unsuspecting members of the public. In both cases there are important structural differences involving not only resources and facilities but also knowledge. The nature of the differential distribution of the latter resources, etc., is primary to the possibility of staging any form of demonstration and hence precipitating the reactions observed.

12 Areas in which Agnes refused to supply answers were:
  (a) Possible use of hormone tablets
  (b) Details of her male feelings and biography
  (c) Use of penis other than for urination
  (d) Nature of sexual satisfaction
  (e) Possible 'collaboration' with others (e.g. mother)
  (f) Feelings about herself as a 'phoney female'

4 Phenomenology and Marxism

1 Lukács's work may be identified as an important resource for the work of Miller (1970), Piccone (1971), Paci (1972) and Dallmayr (1973).

2 Note in particular *Adventures of the Dialectic* (1974); *Humanism and Terror* (1970).

3 For a discussion of the priestly and prophetic modes in sociology see R. W. Friedrichs, *A Sociology of Sociology* (1970), especially chapters 3–6 inclusive.

4 Husserl's (1970, pp. 162–4) comments on the question of validity, world-perceiving and communalization provide an interesting comparison with Kuhn's work on normal and revolutionary periods in science. In particular the Husserlian notion of 'the alteration of validity through reciprocal correction' by the community and the analysis of what is normal resembles closely the Kuhnian analysis in *The Structure of Scientific Revolutions* (1962).

5 What Dahrendorf appears to fear is a variant of the self-fulfilling prophecy, that is to say men and women accepting and believing in the scientific world-view may, in their respective actions, accomplish,

produce or construct validity for science. As Habermas has noted in the context of politics and public opinion the scientization of everyday life 'is not yet a reality, but it is a real tendency for which there is evidence' (1971, p. 62).

6 A case for a revision of Marxian analysis can be found in the works of Rovatti (1970), Piccone (1971), Kosik (1968, 1969), Miller (1970), Marcuse (1969, originally published in Germany in 1928), O'Neill (1972). A review of the work of some of the above members of the 'Telos' group as well as a brief discussion of Paci's and O'Neill's work is provided by Dallmayr (1973).

7 The John Lewis–Louis Althusser debate on the question of the epistemological break or continuity in Marx may be found in *Marxism Today*: January and February 1972 (John Lewis), and October and November 1972 (reply by Louis Althusser).

8 This criticism developed by Shmueli necessarily raises the question of the continuity between the earlier works of Husserl and such later works as the *Crisis*, upon which Paci develops his case for a reconciliation of phenomenological and Marxian analysis. This issue and the parallel problem of the relationship between existential phenomenology and Marxian analysis cannot be considered adequately in the context of my present work on the relationship between sociology and Marxian analysis.

5 For a critical science of society

1 The distinction between traditional theory and critical theory is provided by Horkheimer (1972). Traditional theory treats knowledge as the reproduction, the picturing of society. Furthermore traditional theorists seek to separate and distinguish facts from values. Critical theory not only treats knowledge as a means to transform society but rejects as impossible and undesirable the attempt to separate facts and values.

2 I have provided a working definition of positivism in chapter 3.

3 Bechhofer states,

In particular, I do not wish to be seen as arguing for a positivist sociology. Now, positivism is a much misused word, and seems at times to be all things to all men rather than referring to a set of fairly closely articulated views of scientific activity. I do not regard myself as a positivist. It is nevertheless clear that the methods discussed in this chapter are mainly, though not entirely, applicable from what might be called an 'empiricist' position, and admitting this from the outset may make things clearer (1974, p. 71).

4 (i) Giddens distinguishes positivism as a philosophy from positivism in sociology, stating that 'the introduction of positivistic assumptions into sociology creates a series of quite specific difficulties which cannot be resolved on the level of generalized philosophical inquiry' (1974, p. 3). He later remarks that 'Positivism in sociology may be broadly represented as depending upon the assertion that the concepts and

methods employed in natural sciences can be applied to form a "science of man", or a "natural" science of society' (ibid.).

(ii) Frisby in an article on critical theory and positivism states that 'Sociology has resorted too often to unexamined positivist prescriptions in order to support both its theoretical orientation and its research practice' (1974, p. 208).

(iii) Martins whilst developing his conception of sociology as a historico-philosophical discipline, sceptically remarks that the decline of positivism 'may well be more apparent than real, especially in so far as it remains entrenched in "methodology" and encoded in the common culture . . . ' (1974, p. 286).

5   Because conventional static theorizing tends to reify the existing power relations and to insulate the system from criticism it is projected throughout society as the only valid explanation: theories enter into the ideological process and emerge in an abbreviated, often vulgarized, sloganized form embedded in language and thought processes alike. They form the basis of common-sense attitudes. They are transmitted through the family, enter into folklore, get expression through the educational system and are monotonously repeated through the mass media. In a variety of subtle ways conventional theoretical explanations enter the consciousness of individuals and provide them with instant explanations. In fact the explanations are so 'instant' that they are used without people knowing they are using them. In a flash all the variables are sorted out and fitted together just like a jigsaw puzzle (Allen, 1974 p. 10).

6 Kosik states that an important resource for such an analysis is Husserlian phenomenology:
The authentic sense of the Husserlian phenomenological method and the whole connection of its rational nucleus with the philosophical problem area of the 20th century has been discovered only by a philosopher with a Marxist orientation whose work constitutes the first serious attempt at a confrontation between phenomenology and the materialist philosophy. The author (Tran-Duc-Thao) explicitly outlines the paradoxical and rich character of the phenomenological destruction of pseudo-concreteness (1968, p. 26, n.5).
The question of Tran-Duc-Thao's later rejection of phenomenology is both interesting and important but cannot be dealt with in this context.

7 E.g. Horton (1964) traces the decline in radicalism from classical to contemporary sociology by examining changes in the concepts of alienation and anomie.

8 The question of the sociologist's relationship to, and choice of, 'subjects', has not received sufficient attention. However, in the case of Nicolaus (1971) and Giddens (1972) attention is drawn to the fact that sociological work resembles a 'view from the top' of the lower levels of society. Appropriately Nicolaus's paper is subtitled 'A view from below'.

9 I have not here addressed the growing criticism of the sexist basis of sociology largely because it is in its own right a complex and difficult topic. However, it is important to recognize that work exists in this area and that sooner or later both male and female sociologists will have to take stock of the consequences of the 'feminist critique'. For those even less well informed than myself Smith (1974) provides a short critique of conventional sociological conceptualization and the Schwendingers (1973) offer a radical analysis of the formative years in North American sociology.

10 In particular, controversy has tended to be based upon:
   (i) The incompatibility of a positivist methodology with a critical theory of society in Marxian analysis (Hamilton, 1974; Habermas, 1972; O'Neill, 1972).
   (ii) The lack of a substantive critical theory of society in neo-Marxist sociology (Kruger, 1969).
   (iii) The question of the nature of the form of an 'alternative society' and its absence from critical theory (Mandel, 1971; Lobkowicz, 1967).

11 Wellmer has, however, argued that Marx's work itself lacked a 'revolutionary' proletarian audience. He states that Marx's theory was addressed,

   to impoverished proletarians whom we cannot reproach for being content with something less than the Commonwealth of freedom. Only in a changed historical situation are the potential critics of critical social theory those to whom it is addressed, and those to whom it is addressed – increasingly – its potential critics (1971, pp. 138–9).

12 Habermas states that 'self-reflection leads to insight due to the fact that what has previously been unconscious is made conscious in a manner rich in practical consequences' (1974a, p. 23).

Bibliography

ALBROW, M. (1974), 'Dialectical and categorical paradigms of a science of society', *Sociological Review*, vol. 22, no. 2.

ALLEN, V. (1974), 'The common-sense guide to industrial relations', *University of Leeds Review*, vol. 17, no. 1.

ALTHUSSER, L. (1969), *For Marx*, translated by Ben Brewster, London: Allen Lane, The Penguin Press.

ALTHUSSER, L. (1972), 'Reply to John Lewis (Self Criticism)', *Marxism Today*, October and November.

ALTHUSSER, L. and BALIBAR, E. (1970), *Reading Capital*, translated by Ben Brewster, London: New Left Books.

APPELBAUM, R. A. (1970), *Theories of Social Change*, Chicago: Markham.

ARON, R. (1971), *The Industrial Society*, London: Weidenfeld & Nicolson.

ATKINSON, D. (1971), *Orthodox Consensus and Radical Alternative*, London: Heinemann.

BANKS, J. (1970), *Marxist Sociology in Action*, London: Faber & Faber.

BAUMAN, Z. (1973), 'On the philosophical status of ethnomethodology', *Sociological Review*, vol. 21, no. 1.

BAUMANN, B. (1967), 'G. H. Mead and L. Pirandello: some parallels between the theoretical and artistic presentation of the social role concept', *Social Research*, vol. 34, no. 3.

BECHHOFER, F. (1974), 'Current approaches to empirical research: some central ideas', in REX, J. (ed.), *Approaches to Sociology: an introduction to major trends in British sociology*, London: Routledge & Kegan Paul.

BENDIX, R. (1961), 'The image of man in the social sciences: basic assumptions of present day research', in LIPSET, S. M. and SMELSER, N. (eds), *Sociology the Progress of a Decade*, Englewood Cliffs: Prentice-Hall.

BERGER, P. (1966), *Invitation to Sociology*, Harmondsworth: Penguin.

BERGER, P. and LUCKMANN, T. (1967), *The Social Construction of Reality*, London: Allen Lane, The Penguin Press.

BERGHE, P. VAN DEN (1967), 'Dialectic and functionalism: toward a synthesis', in DEMERATH III, N. J. and PETERSON, R. A. (eds), *System, Change and Conflict*, New York: Free Press.

BIRNBAUM, N. (1968), 'The crisis in Marxist sociology', *Social Research*, vol. 35, no. 2.

BITTNER, E. (1973), 'Objectivity and realism in sociology', in PSATHAS, G. (ed.), *Phenomenological Sociology*, London: Wiley.

BLACKBURN, R. (1969), 'A brief guide to bourgeois ideology', in COCKBURN, A. and BLACKBURN, R. (eds), *Student Power*, Harmondsworth: Penguin.

BLUM, A. (1971), 'On theorizing', in DOUGLAS, J. (ed.), *Understanding Everyday Life*, London: Routledge & Kegan Paul.

BLUMER, H. (1962), 'Society as symbolic interaction', in ROSE, A. (ed.), *Human Behaviour and Social Processes*, London: Routledge & Kegan Paul.

BOTTOMORE, T. B. (1968), 'Marxist sociology', in SILLS, D. (ed.), *International Encyclopaedia of the Social Sciences*, New York: Macmillan.

BOTTOMORE, T. B. and RUBEL, M. (1963), *Karl Marx – Selected Writings in Sociology and Social Philosophy*, Harmondsworth: Penguin.

BOUDON, R. (1974), *The Logic of Sociological Explanation*, Harmondsworth: Penguin.

BROADHEAD, R. (1973), 'Dialectic in sociology: in defense of a conceptual art form', *Insurgent Sociologist*, vol. III, no. IV.

BROWN, B. (1973), *Marx, Freud and the Critique of Everyday Life*, London: Monthly Review Press.

CLEGG, S. (1975), *Power, Rule and Domination: a critical and empirical understanding of sociological theory and organizational life*, London: Routledge & Kegan Paul.

COHEN, P. (1968), *Modern Social Theory*, London: Heinemann.

COLFAX, J. D. and ROACH, J. L. (eds) (1971), *Radical Sociology*, London: Basic Books.

COLLETTI, L. (1972), *From Rousseau to Lenin: studies in ideology and society*, London: New Left Books.

COSER, L. (1956), *The Functions of Social Conflict*, New York: Free Press.

DAHRENDORF, R. (1959), *Class and Class Conflict in an Industrial Society*, London: Routledge & Kegan Paul.

DAHRENDORF, R. (1968), *Essays in the Theory of Society*, London: Routledge & Kegan Paul.

DAHRENDORF, R. (1973), *Homo Sociologicus*, London: Routledge & Kegan Paul.

DALLMAYR, F. (1973), 'Phenomenology and Marxism: A salute to Enzo Paci', in PSATHAS, G. (ed.), *Phenomenological Sociology*, London: Wiley.

DAVIS, K. (1967), 'The myth of functional analysis as a special method in sociology and anthropology', in DEMERATH III, N. J. and PETERSON, R. A. (eds), *System, Change and Conflict*, New York: Free Press.

DAWE, A. (1970), 'The two sociologies', *British Journal of Sociology*, vol. 21, no. 2.

DIXON, K. (1973), *Sociological Theory: Pretence and Possibility*, London: Routledge & Kegan Paul.

DJILAS, M. (1966), *The New Class: An Analysis of the Communist System*, London: Allen & Unwin.

DOUGLAS, J. (1967), *The Social Meaning of Suicide*, Princeton University Press.

DOUGLAS, J. (ed.) (1971), *Understanding Everyday Life*, London: Routledge & Kegan Paul.

DURKHEIM, E. (1964a), *The Rules of Sociological Method*, New York: Free Press.

DURKHEIM, E. (1964b), *The Division of Labour in Society*, New York: Free Press.

ENZENSBERGER, H. (1970), 'Constituents of a theory of the media', *New Left Review*, no. 64.

FALLDING, H. (1972), 'Only one sociology', *British Journal of Sociology*, vol. 23, no. 1.

FARMER, M. E. (1967), 'The positivist movement and the development of English sociology', *Sociological Review*, vol. 15, no. 1.

FEUER, L. (1963), 'What is alienation? The career of a concept', in STEIN, M. and VIDICH, A. (eds), *Sociology on Trial*, Englewood Cliffs: Prentice-Hall.

FEYERABEND, P. (1970a), 'Consolations for the specialist', in LAKATOS I. and MUSGRAVE, A. (eds), *Criticism and the Growth of Knowledge*, CUP.

FEYERABEND, P. (1970b), 'Against method: outline of an anarchistic theory of knowledge', *Minnesota Studies in the Philosophy of Science*, vol. 4.

FEYERABEND, P. (1972), 'Science without experience' and 'How to be a good empiricist – a plea for tolerance in matters epistemological', in MORICK, H. (ed.), *Challenges to Empiricism*, Belmont: Wadsworth.

FILMER, P. et al. (1972), *New Directions in Sociological Theory*, London: Collier-Macmillan.

FILMER, P. et al. (1973), 'Stratifying practices', unpublished manuscript submitted to British Sociological Association Easter Conference.

FISCHER, E. (1973), *Marx in His Own Words*, Harmondsworth: Penguin.

FLETCHER, R. (1974), 'Evolutionary and developmental sociology', in REX, J. (ed.), *Approaches to Sociology: an introduction to major trends in British sociology*, London: Routledge & Kegan Paul.

FREIRE, P. (1972), *Cultural Action for Freedom*, Harmondsworth: Penguin.

FRIEDRICHS, R. W. (1972), *A Sociology of Sociology*, New York: Free Press.

FRISBY, D. (1974), 'The Frankfurt School: critical theory and positivism', in REX, J. (ed.), *Approaches to Sociology: an introduction to major trends in British sociology*, London: Routledge & Kegan Paul.

GARFINKEL, H. (1967), *Studies in Ethnomethodology*, Englewood Cliffs: Prentice-Hall.

GIDDENS, A. (1971), *Capitalism and Modern Social Theory*, London: Cambridge University Press.

GIDDENS, A. (1972a), 'Four myths in the history of social thought', *Economy and Society*, vol. I, no. 4.

GIDDENS, A. (1972b), 'Elites in the British class structure', *Sociological Review*, vol. 20, no. 3.

GIDDENS, A. (ed.) (1972c), *Emile Durkheim – Selected Writings*, London: Cambridge University Press.

GIDDENS, A. (ed.) (1974), *Positivism and Sociology*, London: Heinemann.

GODELIER, M. (1972), *Rationality and Irrationality in Economics*, London: New Left Books.

GOLDMANN, L. (1969), *The Human Sciences and Philosophy*, London: Cape.

GOLDTHORPE, J. (1973), 'A revolution in sociology?', *Sociology*, vol. 7, no. 3.

GOULDNER, A. (1962), 'Anti-minotaur: the myth of a value-free sociology', *Social Problems*, vol. 9, no. 3.

GOULDNER, A. (1960), 'The norm of reciprocity', *American Sociological Review*, vol. 25, no. 2.

GOULDNER, A. (1968), 'The sociologist as partisan: sociology and the welfare state', *American Sociologist*, May.

GOULDNER, A. (1971), *The Coming Crisis of Western Sociology*, London: Heinemann.

GOULDNER, A. (1972), 'Sociology and Marxism', *New Left Review*, no. 71.

GOULDNER, A. (1973), *For Sociology*, London: Allen Lane, The Penguin Press.

GOULDNER, A. (1974), 'Marxism and social theory', *Theory and Society*, vol. 1, no. 1.

HABERMAS, J. (1970), 'Knowledge and interest', in EMMET, D. and MACINTYRE, A. (eds.), *Sociological Theory and Philosophical Analysis*, London: Macmillan.

HABERMAS, J. (1971), *Toward a Rational Society*, London: Heinemann.

HABERMAS, J. (1972), *Knowledge and Human Interests*, London: Heinemann.

HABERMAS, J. (1974a), *Theory and Practice*, London: Heinemann.

HABERMAS, J. (1974b), 'Rationalism divided in two: a reply to Albert', in GIDDENS, A. (ed.), *Positivism and Sociology*, London: Heinemann.

HAGE, J. (1972), *Techniques and Problems of Theory Construction in Sociology*, London: Wiley.

HAMILTON, P. (1974), *Knowledge and Social Structure: an introduction to the classical argument in the sociology of knowledge*, London: Routledge & Kegan Paul.

HARVEY, M. (1972), 'Sociological theory: the production of a bourgeois ideology', in PATEMAN, T. (ed.), *Counter Course*, Harmondsworth: Penguin.

HEAP, J. L. and ROTH, P. A. (1973), 'On phenomenological sociology', *American Sociological Review*, vol. 38, no. 3.

HEARN, F. (1974), 'The implications of critical theory for critical sociology', *Berkeley Journal of Sociology*, vol. 18.

HINDESS, B. (1973), *The Use of Official Statistics in Sociology: A Critique of Positivism and Ethnomethodology*, London: Macmillan.

HORKHEIMER, M. (1972), *Critical Theory*, New York: Herder & Herder.

HORTON, J. (1964), 'The dehumanization of anomie and alienation: a problem in the ideology of sociology', *British Journal of Sociology*, vol. 15, no. 4.

HORTON, J. (1971), 'The fetishism of sociology', in COLFAX, J. and ROACH, J. (eds), *Radical Sociology*, London: Basic Books.

HOWARD, D. (1970), 'On Marx's Critical Theory', *Telos*, no. 6.

HUGHES, S. (1959), *Consciousness and Society*, London: MacGibbon.

HUSSERL, E. (1970), *The Crisis of European Sciences and Transcendental Phenomenology*, Evanston: Northwestern University Press.

JARVIE, I. C. (1972), *Concepts and Society*, London: Routledge & Kegan Paul.

197

BIBLIOGRAPHY

JORDAN, Z. A. (1971), *Karl Marx – Economy, Class and Social Revolution*, London: Michael Joseph.

KALAB, M. (1969), 'The specificity of the Marxist conception of sociology', in BERGER, P. (ed.), *Marxism and Sociology – Views from Eastern Europe*, New York: Appleton-Century-Crofts.

KENISTON, K. (1968), 'The psychology of alienated students', in GERGEN, K. and GORDON, C. (eds), *The Self in Social Interaction*, New York: Wiley.

KOLAKOWSKI, L. (1972), *Positivist Philosophy*, Harmondsworth: Penguin.

KOSIK, K. (1968), 'Dialectic of the concrete totality', *Telos*, no. 2.

KOSIK, K. (1969), 'The concrete totality', *Telos*, no. 4.

KRUGER, M. (1969), 'Sociology of knowledge and social theory', *Berkeley Journal of Sociology*, vol. 14.

KUHN, T. (1962), *The Structure of Scientific Revolutions*, London: University of Chicago Press.

KUHN, T. (1970), 'Postscript-1969', in revised edition of *The Structure of Scientific Revolutions*, London: University of Chicago Press.

LANE, D. (1971), *The End of Inequality?*, Harmondsworth: Penguin.

LEFEBVRE, H. (1972), *The Sociology of Marx*, Harmondsworth: Penguin.

LENSKI, G. (1966), *Power and Privilege*, New York: McGraw-Hill.

LEWIS, J. (1972), 'The Althusser case', *Marxism Today*, January and February.

LICHTHEIM, G. (1971), *From Marx to Hegel and other Essays*, London: Orbach & Chambers.

LICHTMAN, R. (1970), 'Symbolic interactionism and social reality: some Marxist queries', *Berkeley Journal of Sociology*, vol. 15.

LOBKOWICZ, N. (1967), *Theory and Practice: The History of a Concept from Aristotle to Marx*, London: University of Notre Dame Press.

LOCKWOOD, D. (1964), 'Social integration and system integration', in ZOLLSCHAN, G. and HIRSCH, W. (eds), *Explorations in Social Change*, London: Routledge & Kegan Paul.

LUKÁCS, G. (1971), *History and Class Consciousness*, London: Merlin Press.

MACRAE, D. G. (1964), 'The crisis of sociology', in PLUMB, J. H. (ed.), *Crisis in the Humanities*, Harmondsworth: Penguin.

MANDEL, E. (1971), *The Formation of the Economic Thought of Karl Marx*, London: New Left Books.

MARCUSE, H. (1969a), 'Contributions to a phenomenology of historical materialism', *Telos*, no. 4.

MARCUSE, H. (1969b), *One-Dimensional Man*, London: Sphere Books.

MARCUSE, H. (1971), *Soviet Marxism*, Harmondsworth: Penguin.

MARKOVIC, M. (1968), 'Marx and critical scientific thought', *Praxis*, vol. 4, nos 3, 4.

MARTINDALE, D. (1961), *The Nature and Types of Sociological Theory*, London: Routledge & Kegan Paul.

MARTINS, H. (1974), 'Time and theory in sociology', in REX, J. (ed.), *Approaches to Sociology: an introduction to major trends in British sociology*, London: Routledge & Kegan Paul.

MARX, K. (1954–9), *Capital*, vols I, II, III, Moscow: Foreign Language Publishing House.

MARX, K. (1972), *Marx's 'Grundrisse'*, edited and translated by D. McLellan, London: Macmillan.

MARX, K. (1973a), *Grundrisse*, translated with a foreword by Martin Nicolaus, Harmondsworth: Penguin.

MARX, K. (1973b), *Economic and Philosophic Manuscripts of 1844*, London: Lawrence & Wishart.

MARX, K. and ENGELS, F. (1953), *Selected Correspondence*, Moscow: Foreign Language Publishing House.

MARX, K. and ENGELS, F. (1962), *Selected Works*, vols I, II, Moscow: Foreign Language Publishing House.

MARX, K. and ENGELS, F. (1970), *The German Ideology*, London: Lawrence & Wishart.

MAYRL, W. W. (1973), 'Ethnomethodology: sociology without society', *Catalyst*, no. 7.

MCHUGH, P. (1968), *Defining the Situation*, Indianapolis: Bobbs-Merrill.

MERLEAU-PONTY, M. (1970), *Humanism and Terror*, Boston: Beacon Press.

MERLEAU-PONTY, M. (1974), *Adventures of the Dialectic*, London: Heinemann.

MILLER, J. (1970), 'Marxism and subjectivity – remarks on Georg Lukács and existential phenomenology', *Telos*, no. 6.

MITCHELL, J. (1971), *Woman's Estate*, Harmondsworth: Penguin.

MOORE, W. E. (1967), *Order and Change*, New York: Wiley.

MORICK, H. (ed.) (1972), *Challenges to Empiricism*, Belmont: Wadsworth.

NETTLER, G. (1957), 'A measure of alienation', *American Sociological Review*, vol. 22, no. 6.

NICOLAUS, M. (1971), 'The professional organization of sociology: a view from below' 'in COLFAX, J. D. and ROACH, J. L. (eds), *Radical Sociology*, London: Basic Books.

NISBET, R. (1970), *The Social Bond*, New York: Knopf.

O'MALLEY, J. B. (1970), *Sociology of Meaning*, London: Human Context Books.

O'NEILL, J. O. (1972), *Sociology as a Skin Trade*, London: Heinemann.

O'NEILL, J. O. (ed.) (1973), *Modes of Individualism and Collectivism*, London: Heinemann.

PACI, E. (1972), *The Function of the Sciences and the Meaning of Man*, Evanston: Northwestern University Press.

PARKIN, F. (1971), *Class Inequality and Political Order*, London: MacGibbon & Kee.

PARSONS, T. (1937), *The Structure of Social Action*, New York: Free Press.

PARSONS, T. (1951), *The Social System*, New York: Free Press.

PARSONS, T. (1956), 'The social system: a general theory of action', in GRINKER, R. R. (ed.), *Toward a Unified Theory of Human Behaviour*, New York: Basic Books.

PARSONS, T. (1961), 'The point of view of the author', in BLACK, M. (ed.), *The Social Theories of Talcott Parsons*, Englewood Cliffs: Prentice-Hall.

PARSONS, T. (1964), 'Evolutionary universals in society', *American Sociological Review*, vol. 29, no. 3.

BIBLIOGRAPHY

PARSONS, T. (1967), *Sociological Theory and Modern Society*, New York: Free Press.

PELZ, W. (1974), *The Scope of Understanding*, London: Routledge & Kegan Paul.

PETROVIC, G. (1967), *Marx in the Mid-Twentieth Century*, New York: Doubleday Anchor.

PHILLIPS, D. (1973), *Abandoning Method*, London: Jossey Bass.

PHILLIPSON, M. (1972), 'Phenomenological philosophy and sociology', in FILMER, P. et al., *New Direction in Sociology*, London: Collier-Macmillan.

PICCONE, P. (1971), 'Phenomenological Marxism', *Telos*, no. 9.

POGGI, G. (1972), *Images of Society: De Tocqueville, Marx, Durkheim*, London: Oxford University Press.

PSATHAS, G. (1973), *Phenomenological Sociology*, London: Wiley.

REX, J. (1961), *Key Problems in Sociological Theory*, London: Routledge & Kegan Paul.

REX, J. (1973), *Discovering Sociology*, London: Routledge & Kegan Paul.

REX, J. (ed.) (1974), *Approaches to Sociology: an introduction to major trends in British sociology*, London: Routledge & Kegan Paul.

RIEFF, P. (1973), *The Triumph of the Therapeutic*, Harmondsworth: Penguin.

ROVATTI, P. (1970), 'A phenomenological analysis of Marxism: the return to the subject and to the dialectic of the totality', *Telos*, no. 5.

ROVATTI, P. (1973), 'Critical theory and phenomenology', *Telos*, no. 15.

RUDNER, R. (1966), *Philosophy of Social Science*, Englewood Cliffs: Prentice-Hall.

SALLACH, D. (1973), 'Class consciousness and the everyday world in the work of Marx and Schutz', *Insurgent Sociologist*, vol. III, no. IV.

SARTRE, J. (1968), *Search for a Method*, New York: Vintage Books.

SCHIMANSKI, F. (1974), 'The Nobel experience', *New Scientist*, vol. 64, no. 917.

SCHNEIDER, L. (1971), 'Dialectic in sociology', *American Sociological Review*, vol. 36, no. 4.

SCHROYER, T. (1971), 'A reconceptualization of critical theory', in COLFAX, J. D. and ROACH, J. L. (eds), *Radical Sociology*, London: Basic Books.

SCHUMPETER, J. A. (1961), *Capitalism, Socialism and Democracy*, London: Allen & Unwin.

SCHUTZ, A. (1964), *Collected Papers* vol. II, The Hague: Martin Nijhoff.

SCHUTZ, A. (1970), *Collected Papers* vol. III, The Hague: Martin Nijhoff.

SCHUTZ, A. (1971), *Collected Papers* vol. I, The Hague: Martin Nijhoff.

SCHUTZ, A. and LUCKMANN, T. (1973), *The Structures of the Life-World*, Evanston: Northwestern University Press.

SCHWENDINGER, H. and J. (1973), *Sociologists of the Chair: A Radical Analysis of the Formative Years in North American Sociology (1883–1922)*, New York: Basic Books.

SEEMAN, M. (1959), 'On the meaning of alienation', *American Sociological Review*, vol. 24, no. 6.

SHAW, M. (1972), 'The coming crisis of radical sociology', in BLACKBURN, R.

(ed.), *Ideology in Social Science*, London: Fontana-Collins.

SHAW, M. (1974), *Marxism Versus Sociology – A Guide to Reading*, London: Pluto Press.

SHEARING, C. D. (1973), 'Towards a phenomenological sociology', *Catalyst*, no. 7.

SHMUELI, E. (1973), 'Can phenomenology accommodate Marxism?', *Telos*, no. 17.

SMELSER, N. J. (1968), *Essays in Sociological Explanation*, Englewood Cliffs: Prentice-Hall.

SMITH, D. (1974), 'Women's perspective as a radical critique of sociology', *Sociological Inquiry*, vol. 44, no. 1.

SOROKIN, P. (1928), *Contemporary Sociological Theories*, New York: Harper & Brothers.

SOROKIN, P. (1966), *Sociological Theories of Today*, New York: Harper.

STANLEY, M. (1973), 'The structures of doubt: reflections on moral intelligibility as a problem in the sociology of knowledge', in REMMLING, G. W. (ed.), *Towards the Sociology of Knowledge*, London: Routledge & Kegan Paul.

STEIN, M. and VIDICH, A. (eds) (1963), *Sociology on Trial*, Englewood Cliffs: Prentice-Hall.

STRASSER, S. (1967), 'Phenomenology and the human sciences', in KOCKELMAN, J. J. (ed.), *Phenomenology*, New York: Doubleday Anchor.

TIMASHEFF, N. (1961), *Sociological Theory: Its Nature and Growth*, New York: Random House.

WAGNER, H. (1973), 'The scope of phenomenological sociology: considerations and suggestions', in PSATHAS, G. (ed.), *Phenomenological Sociology*, London: Wiley.

WALLACE, W. (1969), *Sociological Theory*, London: Heinemann.

WALSH, D. (1972), 'Varieties of positivism', in FILMER, P. et al., *New Directions in Sociological Theory*, London: Collier-Macmillan.

WELLMER, A. (1971), *Critical Theory of Society*, New York: Herder & Herder.

WIATR, J. L. (1969), 'Sociology–Marxism–Reality', in BERGER, P. (ed.), *Marxism and Sociology – Views From Eastern Europe*, New York: Appleton-Century-Crofts.

WILLER, D. and J. (1973), *Systematic Empiricism – Critique of A Pseudo-science*, Englewood Cliffs: Prentice-Hall.

WILLIAMS, R. (1973), 'Base and superstructure in Marxist cultural theory', *New Left Review*, 82.

WORSLEY, P. (1974), 'The state of theory and the status of theory', *Sociology*, vol. 8, no. 1.

WRIGHT MILLS, C. (1970), *The Sociological Imagination*, Harmondsworth: Penguin.

WRONG, D. (1970), 'The oversocialized conception of man', in COSER, L. and ROSENBERG, B. (eds), *Sociological Theory*, London: Collier-Macmillan.

ZANER, R. (1973), 'Solitude and sociality: the critical foundations of the social sciences', in PSATHAS, G. (ed.), *Phenomenological Sociology*, London: Wiley.

BIBLIOGRAPHY

ZIJDERVELD, A. (1972), 'The problem of adequacy: reflections on Schutz's contribution to the methodology of the social sciences', *European Journal of Sociology*, vol. XIII, no. 1.

ZIJDERVELD, A. (1974), *The Abstract Society*, Harmondsworth: Penguin.

ZIMMERMAN, D. (1974), 'Facts as a practical accomplishment', in TURNER, R. (ed.), *Ethnomethodology*, Harmondsworth: Penguin.

ZIMMERMAN, D. and POLLNER, M. (1971), 'The everyday world as a phenomenon', in DOUGLAS, J. (ed.), *Understanding Everyday Life*, London: Routledge & Kegan Paul.

ZIVKOVIC, L. (1969), 'The structure of Marxist sociology', in BERGER, P. (ed.), *Marxism and Sociology – Views From Eastern Europe*, New York: Appleton-Century-Crofts.

Index

Alienation, 21, 22, 23, 35, 102–3, 125, 127–8; and objectification, 127–8
Althusser, Louis, 45, 61–3

Base-superstructure relationship, 32–3, 61–4, 69
Bauman, Zygmunt, 112–13
Bechhofer, Frank, 154, 155–6
Becker, Howard, 15, 16
Berger, Peter, 24, 58
Berger, Peter and Luckmann, Thomas, 80, 89, 119–20
Berghe, Pierre L. van den, 28, 55–6
Birnbaum, Norman, 28–36; and structural changes in capitalism, 29–30
Bittner, Egon, 84–5
Blackburn, Robin, 21–5
Blumer, Herbert, 59
Bottomore, Tom, 6, 7–8, 9, 23, 41
Boudon, Raymond, 123
Broadhead, Robert, 23

Capitalism, x, 21, 25, 29, 50, 117–18, 134, 135f; and role of the state, 29–30
Class, 21, 30, 66, 135–6, 153, 183; conflict, 46–8, 51, 56; structure, 29, 50
Cohen, Percy, 6, 68–70

Colletti, Lucio, 162–4
Comte, Auguste, x, 1, 37, 65, 154, 156
Conflict and consensus, 23, 52, 54–5, 57
Conflict theory, 22–3, 26, 45f
Consciousness, 54, 69–70, 104, 115–17, 119–20, 126, 163, 167–70
Coser, Lewis A., 8, 23
Crisis: in Marxism, 9; in Marxist sociology, 28–36; of science, 13, 122f, 134; of sociology, ix, 5, 10–21, 36, 73
Crisis of European Sciences and Transcendental Phenomenology, 121f
Critical theory, 151, 174f; and phenomenological Marxism, 180–2
Culture of silence, 170, 173

Dahrendorf, Ralf, 8, 22, 28, 46–53, 55–6; and *Homo Sociologicus*, 138–42; and structural changes in capitalism, 50
Davis, Kingsley, 8, 52
De-reification, xii, 5
Determination, 61
Determinism, 57–60
Dialectic, 55–7
Dialectical analysis, 168–9

203

Routledge Social Science Series

Routledge & Kegan Paul   London and Boston

68–74 Carter Lane   London EC4V 5EL

9 Park Street   Boston   Mass 02108

Contents

*Authors wishing to submit manuscripts for any series in
this catalogue should send them to the Social Science Editor,
Routledge & Kegan Paul Ltd, 68–74 Carter Lane,
London EC4V 5EL*

● *Books so marked are available in paperback
All books are in Metric Demy 8vo format (216 × 138mm approx.)*

International Library of Sociology

General Editor John Rex

GENERAL SOCIOLOGY

Barnsley, J. H. The Social Reality of Ethics. *464 pp.*
Belshaw, Cyril. The Conditions of Social Performance. *An Exploratory Theory. 144 pp.*
Brown, Robert. Explanation in Social Science. *208 pp.*
● Rules and Laws in Sociology. *192 pp.*
Bruford, W. H. Chekhov and His Russia. *A Sociological Study. 244 pp.*
Cain, Maureen E. Society and the Policeman's Role. *326 pp.*
●**Fletcher, Colin.** Beneath the Surface. *An Account of Three Styles of Sociological Research. 221 pp.*
Gibson, Quentin. The Logic of Social Enquiry. *240 pp.*
Glucksmann, M. Structuralist Analysis in Contemporary Social Thought. *212 pp.*
Gurvitch, Georges. Sociology of Law. *Preface by Roscoe Pound. 264 pp.*
Hodge, H. A. Wilhelm Dilthey. *An Introduction. 184 pp.*
Homans, George C. Sentiments and Activities. *336 pp.*
Johnson, Harry M. Sociology: *a Systematic Introduction. Foreword by Robert K. Merton. 710 pp.*
●**Keat, Russell, and Urry, John.** Social Theory as Science. *278 pp.*
Mannheim, Karl. Essays on Sociology and Social Psychology. *Edited by Paul Keckskemeti. With Editorial Note by Adolph Lowe. 344 pp.*
Systematic Sociology: *An Introduction to the Study of Society. Edited by J. S. Erös and Professor W. A. C. Stewart. 220 pp.*
Martindale, Don. The Nature and Types of Sociological Theory. *292 pp.*
●**Maus, Heinz.** A Short History of Sociology. *234 pp.*
Mey, Harald. Field-Theory. *A Study of its Application in the Social Sciences. 352 pp.*
Myrdal, Gunnar. Value in Social Theory: *A Collection of Essays on Methodology. Edited by Paul Streeten. 332 pp.*
Ogburn, William F., and Nimkoff, Meyer F. A Handbook of Sociology. *Preface by Karl Mannheim. 656 pp. 46 figures. 35 tables.*
Parsons, Talcott, and Smelser, Neil J. Economy and Society: *A Study in the Integration of Economic and Social Theory. 362 pp.*
Podgórecki, Adam. Practical Social Sciences. *About 200 pp.*
●**Rex, John.** Key Problems of Sociological Theory. *220 pp.*
Discovering Sociology. *278 pp.*
Sociology and the Demystification of the Modern World. *282 pp.*
●**Rex, John** (Ed.) Approaches to Sociology. *Contributions by Peter Abell, Frank Bechhofer, Basil Bernstein, Ronald Fletcher, David Frisby, Miriam Glucksmann, Peter Lassman, Herminio Martins, John Rex, Roland Robertson, John Westergaard and Jock Young. 302 pp.*
Rigby, A. Alternative Realities. *352 pp.*

Roche, M. Phenomenology, Language and the Social Sciences. *374 pp.*
Sahay, A. Sociological Analysis. *220 pp.*
Strasser, Hermann. The Normative Structure of Sociology. *Conservative and Emancipatory Themes in Social Thought. About 340 pp.*
Urry, John. Reference Groups and the Theory of Revolution. *244 pp.*
Weinberg, E. Development of Sociology in the Soviet Union. *173 pp.*

FOREIGN CLASSICS OF SOCIOLOGY

● **Durkheim, Emile.** Suicide. *A Study in Sociology. Edited and with an Introduction by George Simpson. 404 pp.*
   Professional Ethics and Civic Morals. *Translated by Cornelia Brookfield. 288 pp.*
● **Gerth, H. H.,** and **Mills, C. Wright.** From Max Weber: *Essays in Sociology. 502 pp.*
● **Tönnies, Ferdinand.** Community and Association. *(Gemeinschaft und Gesellschaft.) Translated and Supplemented by Charles P. Loomis. Foreword by Pitirim A. Sorokin. 334 pp.*

SOCIAL STRUCTURE

Andreski, Stanislav. Military Organization and Society. *Foreword by Professor A. R. Radcliffe-Brown. 226 pp. 1 folder.*
Coontz, Sydney H. Population Theories and the Economic Interpretation. *202 pp.*
Coser, Lewis. The Functions of Social Conflict. *204 pp.*
Dickie-Clark, H. F. Marginal Situation: *A Sociological Study of a Coloured Group. 240 pp. 11 tables.*
Glaser, Barney, and **Strauss, Anselm L.** Status Passage. *A Formal Theory. 208 pp.*
Glass, D. V. (Ed.) Social Mobility in Britain. *Contributions by J. Berent, T. Bottomore, R. C. Chambers, J. Floud, D. V. Glass, J. R. Hall, H. T. Himmelweit, R. K. Kelsall, F. M. Martin, C. A. Moser, R. Mukherjee, and W. Ziegel. 420 pp.*
Jones, Garth N. Planned Organizational Change: *An Exploratory Study Using an Empirical Approach. 268 pp.*
Kelsall, R. K. Higher Civil Servants in Britain: *From 1870 to the Present Day. 268 pp. 31 tables.*
König, René. The Community. *232 pp. Illustrated.*
● **Lawton, Denis.** Social Class, Language and Education. *192 pp.*
McLeish, John. The Theory of Social Change: *Four Views Considered. 128 pp.*
Marsh, David C. The Changing Social Structure of England and Wales, 1871-1961. *288 pp.*
● **Mouzelis, Nicos.** Organization and Bureaucracy. *An Analysis of Modern Theories. 240 pp.*
Mulkay, M. J. Functionalism, Exchange and Theoretical Strategy. *272 pp.*
Ossowski, Stanislaw. Class Structure in the Social Consciousness. *210 pp.*
● **Podgórecki, Adam.** Law and Society. *302 pp.*

SOCIOLOGY AND POLITICS

Acton, T. A. Gypsy Politics and Social Change. *316 pp.*

Clegg, Stuart. Power, Rule and Domination. *A Critical and Empirical Understanding of Power in Sociological Theory and Organisational Life. About 300 pp.*

Hechter, Michael. Internal Colonialism. *The Celtic Fringe in British National Development, 1536–1966. 361 pp.*

Hertz, Frederick. Nationality in History and Politics: *A Psychology and Sociology of National Sentiment and Nationalism. 432 pp.*

Kornhauser, William. The Politics of Mass Society. *272 pp. 20 tables.*

●**Kroes, R.** Soldiers and Students. *A Study of Right- and Left-wing Students. 174 pp.*

Laidler, Harry W. History of Socialism. *Social-Economic Movements: An Historical and Comparative Survey of Socialism, Communism, Co-operation, Utopianism; and other Systems of Reform and Reconstruction. 992 pp.*

Lasswell, H. D. Analysis of Political Behaviour. *324 pp.*

Mannheim, Karl. Freedom, Power and Democratic Planning. *Edited by Hans Gerth and Ernest K. Bramstedt. 424 pp.*

Mansur, Fatma. Process of Independence. *Foreword by A. H. Hanson. 208 pp.*

Martin, David A. Pacifism: *an Historical and Sociological Study. 262 pp.*

Myrdal, Gunnar. The Political Element in the Development of Economic Theory. *Translated from the German by Paul Streeten. 282 pp.*

Wootton, Graham. Workers, Unions and the State. *188 pp.*

FOREIGN AFFAIRS: THEIR SOCIAL, POLITICAL AND ECONOMIC FOUNDATIONS

Mayer, J. P. Political Thought in France from the Revolution to the Fifth Republic. *164 pp.*

CRIMINOLOGY

Ancel, Marc. Social Defence: *A Modern Approach to Criminal Problems. Foreword by Leon Radzinowicz. 240 pp.*

Cain, Maureen E. Society and the Policeman's Role. *326 pp.*

Cloward, Richard A., and **Ohlin, Lloyd E.** Delinquency and Opportunity: *A Theory of Delinquent Gangs. 248 pp.*

Downes, David M. The Delinquent Solution. *A Study in Subcultural Theory. 296 pp.*

Dunlop, A. B., and **McCabe, S.** Young Men in Detention Centres. *192 pp.*

Friedlander, Kate. The Psycho-Analytical Approach to Juvenile Delinquency: *Theory, Case Studies, Treatment. 320 pp.*

Glueck, Sheldon, and **Eleanor.** Family Environment and Delinquency. *With the statistical assistance of Rose W. Kneznek. 340 pp.*

Lopez-Rey, Manuel. Crime. *An Analytical Appraisal. 288 pp.*

Mannheim, Hermann. Comparative Criminology: *a Text Book. Two volumes. 442 pp. and 380 pp.*

5

Morris, Terence. The Criminal Area: *A Study in Social Ecology. Foreword by Hermann Mannheim. 232 pp. 25 tables. 4 maps.*

Rock, Paul. Making People Pay. *338 pp.*

●**Taylor, Ian, Walton, Paul,** and **Young, Jock.** The New Criminology. *For a Social Theory of Deviance. 325 pp.*

●**Taylor, Ian, Walton, Paul,** and **Young, Jock** (Eds). Critical Criminology. *268 pp.*

SOCIAL PSYCHOLOGY

Bagley, Christopher. The Social Psychology of the Epileptic Child. *320 pp.*

Barbu, Zevedei. Problems of Historical Psychology. *248 pp.*

Blackburn, Julian. Psychology and the Social Pattern. *184 pp.*

●**Brittan, Arthur.** Meanings and Situations. *224 pp.*

Carroll, J. Break-Out from the Crystal Palace. *200 pp.*

●**Fleming, C. M.** Adolescence: Its Social Psychology. *With an Introduction to recent findings from the fields of Anthropology, Physiology, Medicine, Psychometrics and Sociometry. 288 pp.*

● The Social Psychology of Education: *An Introduction and Guide to Its Study. 136 pp.*

●**Homans, George C.** The Human Group. *Foreword by Bernard DeVoto. Introduction by Robert K. Merton. 526 pp.*

● Social Behaviour: *its Elementary Forms. 416 pp.*

●**Klein, Josephine.** The Study of Groups. *226 pp. 31 figures. 5 tables.*

Linton, Ralph. The Cultural Background of Personality. *132 pp.*

●**Mayo, Elton.** The Social Problems of an Industrial Civilization. *With an appendix on the Political Problem. 180 pp.*

Ottaway, A. K. C. Learning Through Group Experience. *176 pp.*

Plummer, Ken. Sexual Stigma. *An Interactionist Account. 254 pp.*

Ridder, J. C. de. The Personality of the Urban African in South Africa. *A Thermatic Apperception Test Study. 196 pp. 12 plates.*

●**Rose, Arnold M.** (Ed.) Human Behaviour and Social Processes: *an Interactionist Approach. Contributions by Arnold M. Rose, Ralph H. Turner, Anselm Strauss, Everett C. Hughes, E. Franklin Frazier, Howard S. Becker, et al. 696 pp.*

Smelser, Neil J. Theory of Collective Behaviour. *448 pp.*

Stephenson, Geoffrey M. The Development of Conscience. *128 pp.*

Young, Kimball. Handbook of Social Psychology. *658 pp. 16 figures. 10 tables.*

SOCIOLOGY OF THE FAMILY

Banks, J. A. Prosperity and Parenthood: *A Study of Family Planning among The Victorian Middle Classes. 262 pp.*

Bell, Colin R. Middle Class Families: *Social and Geographical Mobility. 224 pp.*

Burton, Lindy. Vulnerable Children. *272 pp.*

Gavron, Hannah. The Captive Wife: *Conflicts of Household Mothers. 190 pp.*

George, Victor, and Wilding, Paul. Motherless Families. *248 pp.*
Klein, Josephine. Samples from English Cultures.
  1. Three Preliminary Studies and Aspects of Adult Life in England. *447 pp.*
  2. Child-Rearing Practices and Index. *247 pp.*
Klein, Viola. Britain's Married Women Workers. *180 pp.*
  The Feminine Character. *History of an Ideology. 244 pp.*
McWhinnie, Alexina M. Adopted Children. *How They Grow Up. 304 pp.*
● Morgan, D. H. J. Social Theory and the Family. *About 320 pp.*
● Myrdal, Alva, and Klein, Viola. Women's Two Roles: *Home and Work. 238 pp. 27 tables.*
Parsons, Talcott, and Bales, Robert F. Family: Socialization and Inter-action Process. *In collaboration with James Olds, Morris Zelditch and Philip E. Slater. 456 pp. 50 figures and tables.*

SOCIAL SERVICES

Bastide, Roger. The Sociology of Mental Disorder. *Translated from the French by Jean McNeil. 260 pp.*
Carlebach, Julius. Caring For Children in Trouble. *266 pp.*
George, Victor. Foster Care. *Theory and Practice. 234 pp.*
  Social Security: *Beveridge and After. 258 pp.*
George, V., and Wilding, P. Motherless Families. *248 pp.*
● Goetschius, George W. Working with Community Groups. *256 pp.*
Goetschius, George W., and Tash, Joan. Working with Unattached Youth. *416 pp.*
Hall, M. P., and Howes, I. V. The Church in Social Work. *A Study of Moral Welfare Work undertaken by the Church of England. 320 pp.*
Heywood, Jean S. Children in Care: *the Development of the Service for the Deprived Child. 264 pp.*
Hoenig, J., and Hamilton, Marian W. The De-Segregation of the Mentally Ill. *284 pp.*
Jones, Kathleen. Mental Health and Social Policy, 1845-1959. *264 pp.*
King, Roy D., Raynes, Norma V., and Tizard, Jack. Patterns of Residential Care. *356 pp.*
Leigh, John. Young People and Leisure. *256 pp.*
● Mays, John. (Ed.) Penelope Hall's Social Services of England and Wales. *About 324 pp.*
Morris, Mary. Voluntary Work and the Welfare State. *300 pp.*
Morris, Pauline. Put Away: *A Sociological Study of Institutions for the Mentally Retarded. 364 pp.*
Nokes, P. L. The Professional Task in Welfare Practice. *152 pp.*
Timms, Noel. Psychiatric Social Work in Great Britain (1939-1962). *280 pp.*
● Social Casework: *Principles and Practice. 256 pp.*
Young, A. F. Social Services in British Industry. *272 pp.*
Young, A. F., and Ashton, E. T. British Social Work in the Nineteenth Century. *288 pp.*

SOCIOLOGY OF EDUCATION

Banks, Olive. Parity and Prestige in English Secondary Education: a Study in Educational Sociology. *272 pp.*

Bentwich, Joseph. Education in Israel. *224 pp. 8 pp. plates.*

●**Blyth, W. A. L.** English Primary Education. *A Sociological Description.*
1. Schools. *232 pp.*
2. Background. *168 pp.*

Collier, K. G. The Social Purposes of Education: *Personal and Social Values in Education. 268 pp.*

Dale, R. R., and **Griffith, S.** Down Stream: *Failure in the Grammar School. 108 pp.*

Dore, R. P. Education in Tokugawa Japan. *356 pp. 9 pp. plates.*

Evans, K. M. Sociometry and Education. *158 pp.*

●**Ford, Julienne.** Social Class and the Comprehensive School. *192 pp.*

Foster, P. J. Education and Social Change in Ghana. *336 pp. 3 maps.*

Fraser, W. R. Education and Society in Modern France. *150 pp.*

Grace, Gerald R. Role Conflict and the Teacher. *150 pp.*

Hans, Nicholas. New Trends in Education in the Eighteenth Century. *278 pp. 19 tables.*

● Comparative Education: *A Study of Educational Factors and Traditions. 360 pp.*

●**Hargreaves, David.** Interpersonal Relations and Education. *432 pp.*

● Social Relations in a Secondary School. *240 pp.*

Holmes, Brian. Problems in Education. *A Comparative Approach. 336 pp.*

King, Ronald. Values and Involvement in a Grammar School. *164 pp.*
School Organization and Pupil Involvement. *A Study of Secondary Schools.*

●**Mannheim, Karl,** and **Stewart, W. A. C.** An Introduction to the Sociology of Education. *206 pp.*

Morris, Raymond N. The Sixth Form and College Entrance. *231 pp.*

●**Musgrove, F.** Youth and the Social Order. *176 pp.*

●**Ottaway, A. K. C.** Education and Society: An Introduction to the Sociology of Education. *With an Introduction by W. O. Lester Smith. 212 pp.*

Peers, Robert. Adult Education: *A Comparative Study. 398 pp.*

Pritchard, D. G. Education and the Handicapped: *1760 to 1960. 258 pp.*

Richardson, Helen. Adolescent Girls in Approved Schools. *308 pp.*

Stratta, Erica. The Education of Borstal Boys. *A Study of their Educational Experiences prior to, and during, Borstal Training. 256 pp.*

Taylor, P. H., Reid, W. A., and **Holley, B. J.** The English Sixth Form. *A Case Study in Curriculum Research. 200 pp.*

SOCIOLOGY OF CULTURE

Eppel, E. M., and **M.** Adolescents and Morality: *A Study of some Moral Values and Dilemmas of Working Adolescents in the Context of a changing Climate of Opinion. Foreword by W. J. H. Sprott. 268 pp. 39 tables.*

●**Fromm, Erich.** The Fear of Freedom. *286 pp.*

● The Sane Society. *400 pp.*

Mannheim, Karl. Essays on the Sociology of Culture. *Edited by Ernst Mannheim in co-operation with Paul Kecskemeti. Editorial Note by Adolph Lowe. 280 pp.*

Weber, Alfred. Farewell to European History: *or The Conquest of Nihilism. Translated from the German by R. F. C. Hull. 224 pp.*

SOCIOLOGY OF RELIGION

Argyle, Michael and **Beit-Hallahmi, Benjamin.** The Social Psychology of Religion. *About 256 pp.*

Nelson, G. K. Spiritualism and Society. *313 pp.*

Stark, Werner. The Sociology of Religion. *A Study of Christendom.*
Volume I. *Established Religion. 248 pp.*
Volume II. *Sectarian Religion. 368 pp.*
Volume III. *The Universal Church. 464 pp.*
Volume IV. *Types of Religious Man. 352 pp.*
Volume V. *Types of Religious Culture. 464 pp.*

Turner, B. S. Weber and Islam. *216 pp.*

Watt, W. Montgomery. Islam and the Integration of Society. *320 pp.*

SOCIOLOGY OF ART AND LITERATURE

Jarvie, Ian C. Towards a Sociology of the Cinema. *A Comparative Essay on the Structure and Functioning of a Major Entertainment Industry. 405 pp.*

Rust, Frances S. Dance in Society. *An Analysis of the Relationships between the Social Dance and Society in England from the Middle Ages to the Present Day. 256 pp. 8 pp. of plates.*

Schücking, L. L. The Sociology of Literary Taste. *112 pp.*

Wolff, Janet. Hermeneutic Philosophy and the Sociology of Art. *150 pp.*

SOCIOLOGY OF KNOWLEDGE

Diesing, P. Patterns of Discovery in the Social Sciences. *262 pp.*

●**Douglas, J. D.** (Ed.) Understanding Everyday Life. *370 pp.*

●**Hamilton, P.** Knowledge and Social Structure. *174 pp.*

Jarvie, I. C. Concepts and Society. *232 pp.*

Mannheim, Karl. Essays on the Sociology of Knowledge. *Edited by Paul Kecskemeti. Editorial Note by Adolph Lowe. 353 pp.*

Remmling, Gunter W. The Sociology of Karl Mannheim. *With a Bibliographical Guide to the Sociology of Knowledge, Ideological Analysis, and Social Planning. 255 pp.*

9

Remmling, Gunter W. (Ed.) Towards the Sociology of Knowledge. *Origin and Development of a Sociological Thought Style. 463 pp.*

Stark, Werner. The Sociology of Knowledge: *An Essay in Aid of a Deeper Understanding of the History of Ideas. 384 pp.*

URBAN SOCIOLOGY

Ashworth, William. The Genesis of Modern British Town Planning: *A Study in Economic and Social History of the Nineteenth and Twentieth Centuries. 288 pp.*

Cullingworth, J. B. Housing Needs and Planning Policy: *A Restatement of the Problems of Housing Need and 'Overspill' in England and Wales. 232 pp. 44 tables. 8 maps.*

Dickinson, Robert E. City and Region: *A Geographical Interpretation 608 pp. 125 figures.*

The West European City: *A Geographical Interpretation. 600 pp. 129 maps. 29 plates.*

● The City Region in Western Europe. *320 pp. Maps.*

Humphreys, Alexander J. New Dubliners: *Urbanization and the Irish Family. Foreword by George C. Homans. 304 pp.*

Jackson, Brian. Working Class Community: *Some General Notions raised by a Series of Studies in Northern England. 192 pp.*

Jennings, Hilda. Societies in the Making: *a Study of Development and Redevelopment within a County Borough. Foreword by D. A. Clark. 286 pp.*

●**Mann, P. H.** An Approach to Urban Sociology. *240 pp.*

Morris, R. N., and **Mogey, J.** The Sociology of Housing. *Studies at Berinsfield. 232 pp. 4 pp. plates.*

Rosser, C., and **Harris, C.** The Family and Social Change. *A Study of Family and Kinship in a South Wales Town. 352 pp. 8 maps.*

●**Stacey, Margaret, Batsone, Eric, Bell, Colin,** and **Thurcott, Anne.** Power, Persistence and Change. *A Second Study of Banbury. 196 pp.*

RURAL SOCIOLOGY

Chambers, R. J. H. Settlement Schemes in Tropical Africa: *A Selective Study. 268 pp.*

Haswell, M. R. The Economics of Development in Village India. *120 pp.*

Littlejohn, James. Westrigg: *the Sociology of a Cheviot Parish. 172 pp. 5 figures.*

Mayer, Adrian C. Peasants in the Pacific. *A Study of Fiji Indian Rural Society. 248 pp. 20 plates.*

Williams, W. M. The Sociology of an English Village: *Gosforth. 272 pp. 12 figures. 13 tables.*

SOCIOLOGY OF INDUSTRY AND DISTRIBUTION

Anderson, Nels. Work and Leisure. *280 pp.*
●**Blau, Peter M.,** and **Scott, W. Richard.** Formal Organizations: *a Comparative approach. Introduction and Additional Bibliography by J. H. Smith. 326 pp.*
Dunkerley, David. The Foreman. *Aspects of Task and Structure. 192 pp.*
Eldridge, J. E. T. Industrial Disputes. *Essays in the Sociology of Industrial Relations. 288 pp.*
Hetzler, Stanley. Applied Measures for Promoting Technological Growth. *352 pp.*
Technological Growth and Social Change. *Achieving Modernization. 269 pp.*
Hollowell, Peter G. The Lorry Driver. *272 pp.*
Jefferys, Margot, *with the assistance of Winifred Moss.* Mobility in the Labour Market: *Employment Changes in Battersea and Dagenham. Preface by Barbara Wootton. 186 pp. 51 tables.*
Millerson, Geoffrey. The Qualifying Associations: *a Study in Professionalization. 320 pp.*
●**Oxaal, I., Barnett, T.,** and **Booth, D.** (Eds). Beyond the Sociology of Development. *Economy and Society in Latin America and Africa. 295 pp.*
Smelser, Neil J. Social Change in the Industrial Revolution: *An Application of Theory to the Lancashire Cotton Industry, 1770–1840. 468 pp. 12 figures. 14 tables.*
Williams, Gertrude. Recruitment to Skilled Trades. *240 pp.*
Young, A. F. Industrial Injuries Insurance: *an Examination of British Policy. 192 pp.*

DOCUMENTARY

Schlesinger, Rudolf (Ed.) Changing Attitudes in Soviet Russia.
2. The Nationalities Problem and Soviet Administration. *Selected Readings on the Development of Soviet Nationalities Policies. Introduced by the editor. Translated by W. W. Gottlieb. 324 pp.*

ANTHROPOLOGY

Ammar, Hamed. Growing up in an Egyptian Village: *Silwa, Province of Aswan. 336 pp.*
Brandel-Syrier, Mia. Reeftown Elite. *A Study of Social Mobility in a Modern African Community on the Reef. 376 pp.*
Crook, David, and **Isabel.** Revolution in a Chinese Village: *Ten Mile Inn. 230 pp. 8 plates. 1 map.*
Dickie-Clark, H. F. The Marginal Situation. *A Sociological Study of a Coloured Group. 236 pp.*
Dube, S. C. Indian Village. *Foreword by Morris Edward Opler. 276 pp. 4 plates.*

India's Changing Villages: *Human Factors in Community Development. 260 pp. 8 plates. 1 map.*

Firth, Raymond. Malay Fishermen. *Their Peasant Economy. 420 pp. 17 pp. plates.*

Firth, R., Hubert, J., and Forge, A. Families and their Relatives. *Kinship in a Middle-Class Sector of London: An Anthropological Study. 456 pp.*

Gulliver, P. H. Social Control in an African Society: a Study of the Arusha, Agricultural Masai of Northern Tanganyika. *320 pp. 8 plates. 10 figures.*

Family Herds. *288 pp.*

Ishwaran, K. Shivapur. *A South Indian Village. 216 pp.*

Tradition and Economy in Village India: *An Interactionist Approach. Foreword by Conrad Arensburg. 176 pp.*

Jarvie, Ian C. The Revolution in Anthropology. *268 pp.*

Little, Kenneth L. Mende of Sierra Leone. *308 pp. and folder.*

Negroes in Britain. *With a New Introduction and Contemporary Study by Leonard Bloom. 320 pp.*

Lowie, Robert H. Social Organization. *494 pp.*

Peasants in the Pacific. *A Study of Fiji Indian Rural Society. 248 pp.*

Smith, Raymond T. The Negro Family in British Guiana: *Family Structure and Social Status in the Villages. With a Foreword by Meyer Fortes. 314 pp. 8 plates. 1 figure. 4 maps.*

SOCIOLOGY AND PHILOSOPHY

Barnsley, John H. The Social Reality of Ethics. *A Comparative Analysis of Moral Codes. 448 pp.*

Diesing, Paul. Patterns of Discovery in the Social Sciences. *362 pp.*

●**Douglas, Jack D.** (Ed.) Understanding Everyday Life. *Toward the Reconstruction of Sociological Knowledge. Contributions by Alan F. Blum. Aaron W. Cicourel, Norman K. Denzin, Jack D. Douglas, John Heeren, Peter McHugh, Peter K. Manning, Melvin Power, Matthew Speier, Roy Turner, D. Lawrence Wieder, Thomas P. Wilson and Don H. Zimmerman. 370 pp.*

Jarvie, Ian C. Concepts and Society. *216 pp.*

●**Pelz, Werner.** The Scope of Understanding in Sociology. *Towards a more radical reorientation in the social humanistic sciences. 283 pp.*

Roche, Maurice. Phenomenology, Language and the Social Sciences. *371 pp.*

Sahay, Arun. Sociological Analysis. *212 pp.*

Sklair, Leslie. The Sociology of Progress. *320 pp.*

International Library of Anthropology

General Editor Adam Kuper

Brown, Paula. The Chimbu. *A Study of Change in the New Guinea Highlands. 151 pp.*

Hamnett, Ian. Chieftainship and Legitimacy. *An Anthropological Study of Executive Law in Lesotho. 163 pp.*

Hanson, F. Allan. Meaning in Culture. *127 pp.*

Lloyd, P. C. Power and Independence. *Urban Africans' Perception of Social Inequality. 264 pp.*

Pettigrew, Joyce. Robber Noblemen. *A Study of the Political System of the Sikh Jats. 284 pp.*

Street, Brian V. The Savage in Literature. *Representations of 'Primitive' Society in English Fiction, 1858–1920. 207 pp.*

Van Den Berghe, Pierre L. Power and Privilege at an African University. *278 pp.*

International Library of Social Policy

General Editor Kathleen Jones

Bayley, M. Mental Handicap and Community Care. *426 pp.*

Butler, J. R. Family Doctors and Public Policy. *208 pp.*

Davies, Martin. Prisoners of Society. *Attitudes and Aftercare. 204 pp.*

Holman, Robert. Trading in Children. *A Study of Private Fostering. 355 pp.*

Jones, Kathleen. History of the Mental Health Service. *428 pp.*

Opening the Door. *A Study of New Policies for the Mentally Handicapped. 260 pp.*

Thomas, J. E. The English Prison Officer since 1850: *A Study in Conflict. 258 pp.*

Walton, R. G. Women in Social Work. *303 pp.*

Woodward, J. To Do the Sick No Harm. *A Study of the British Voluntary Hospital System to 1875. 221 pp.*

International Library of Welfare and Philosophy

General Editors Noel Timms and David Watson

● **Plant, Raymond.** Community and Ideology. *104 pp.*

Primary Socialization, Language and Education

General Editor Basil Bernstein

Bernstein, Basil. Class, Codes and Control. *3 volumes.*
  1. *Theoretical Studies Towards a Sociology of Language. 254 pp.*
  2. *Applied Studies Towards a Sociology of Language. 377 pp.*
  3. *Towards a Theory of Educational Transmission. 167 pp.*

Brandis, W., and **Bernstein, B.** Selection and Control. *176 pp.*

Brandis, Walter, and **Henderson, Dorothy.** Social Class, Language and Communication. *288 pp.*

Cook-Gumperz, Jenny. Social Control and Socialization. *A Study of Class Differences in the Language of Maternal Control. 290 pp.*

● **Gahagan, D. M.,** and **G. A.** Talk Reform. *Exploration in Language for Infant School Children. 160 pp.*

Robinson, W. P., and **Rackstraw, Susan D. A.** A Question of Answers. *2 volumes. 192 pp. and 180 pp.*

Turner, Geoffrey J., and **Mohan, Bernard A.** A Linguistic Description and Computer Programme for Children's Speech. *208 pp.*

Reports of the Institute of Community Studies

Cartwright, Ann. Human Relations and Hospital Care. *272 pp.*

● Parents and Family Planning Services. *306 pp.*

Patients and their Doctors. *A Study of General Practice. 304 pp.*

Dench, Geoff. Maltese in London. *A Case-study in the Erosion of Ethnic Consciousness. 302 pp.*

● **Jackson, Brian.** Streaming: *an Education System in Miniature. 168 pp.*

Jackson, Brian, and **Marsden, Dennis.** Education and the Working Class: *Some General Themes raised by a Study of 88 Working-class Children in a Northern Industrial City. 268 pp. 2 folders.*

Marris, Peter. The Experience of Higher Education. *232 pp. 27 tables.*

Loss and Change. *192 pp.*

Marris, Peter, and **Rein, Martin.** Dilemmas of Social Reform. *Poverty and Community Action in the United States. 256 pp.*

Marris, Peter, and **Somerset, Anthony.** African Businessmen. *A Study of Entrepreneurship and Development in Kenya. 256 pp.*

Mills, Richard. Young Outsiders: *a Study in Alternative Communities. 216 pp.*

Runciman, W. G. Relative Deprivation and Social Justice. *A Study of Attitudes to Social Inequality in Twentieth-Century England. 352 pp.*

Willmott, Peter. Adolescent Boys in East London. *230 pp.*

Willmott, Peter, and **Young, Michael.** Family and Class in a London Suburb. *202 pp. 47 tables.*

Young, Michael. Innovation and Research in Education. *192 pp.*

● **Young, Michael,** and **McGeeney, Patrick.** Learning Begins at Home. *A Study of a Junior School and its Parents. 128 pp.*

Young, Michael, and **Willmott, Peter.** Family and Kinship in East London. *Foreword by Richard M. Titmuss. 252 pp. 39 tables.*

The Symmetrical Family. *410 pp.*

Reports of the Institute for Social Studies in Medical Care

Cartwright, Ann, Hockey, Lisbeth, and **Anderson, John L.** Life Before Death. *310 pp.*

Dunnell, Karen, and **Cartwright, Ann.** Medicine Takers, Prescribers and Hoarders. *190 pp.*

Medicine, Illness and Society
General Editor W. M. Williams

Robinson, David. The Process of Becoming Ill. *142 pp.*
Stacey, Margaret, *et al.* Hospitals, Children and Their Families. *The Report of a Pilot Study. 202 pp.*
Stimson, G. V., and **Webb, B.** Going to See the Doctor. *The Consultation Process in General Practice. 155 pp.*

Monographs in Social Theory
General Editor Arthur Brittan

●**Barnes, B.** Scientific Knowledge and Sociological Theory. *192 pp.*
Bauman, Zygmunt. Culture as Praxis. *204 pp.*
●**Dixon, Keith.** Sociological Theory. *Pretence and Possibility. 142 pp.*
Meltzer, B. N., Petras, J. W., and **Reynolds, L. T.** Symbolic Interactionism. *Genesis, Varieties and Criticisms. 144 pp.*
●**Smith, Anthony D.** The Concept of Social Change. *A Critique of the Functionalist Theory of Social Change. 208 pp.*

Routledge Social Science Journals

The British Journal of Sociology. *Managing Editor – Angus Stewart; Associate Editor – Michael Hill. Vol. 1, No. 1 – March 1950 and Quarterly. Roy. 8vo. All back issues available. An international journal publishing original papers in the field of sociology and related areas.*
Community Work. *Edited by David Jones and Marjorie Mayo. 1973. Published annually.*
Economy and Society. *Vol. 1, No. 1. February 1972 and Quarterly. Metric Roy. 8vo. A journal for all social scientists covering sociology, philosophy, anthropology, economics and history. Back numbers available.*
Religion. Journal of Religion and Religions. *Chairman of Editorial Board, Ninian Smart. Vol. 1, No. 1, Spring 1971. A journal with an interdisciplinary approach to the study of the phenomena of religion.*
Year Book of Social Policy in Britain, The. *Edited by Kathleen Jones. 1971. Published annually.*

Printed in Great Britain by Unwin Brothers Limited
The Gresham Press Old Woking Surrey
A member of the Staples Printing Group   June 1975